Good Enough

The Myth of Success and How to Celebrate the Joy in Average

Eleanor Ross

First published in Great Britain in 2020 by Hodder & Stoughton
An Hachette UK company

This paperback edition published in 2021

1

A CIP catalogue record for this title is available from the British Library

Paperback ISBN 9781529336146
Hardback ISBN 9781529336122
eBook ISBN 9781529336139

Typeset in Bembo by Hewer Text UK Ltd, EdinburghPrinted
and bound in Great Britain by Clays Ltd, Elcograf S.p.A.

Hodder & Stoughton policy is to use papers that are natural, renewable
and recyclable products and made from wood grown in sustainable
forests. The logging and manufacturing processes are expected to
conform to the environmental regulations of the country of origin.

Hodder & Stoughton Ltd
Carmelite House
50 Victoria Embankment
London EC4Y 0DZ

www.hodder.co.uk

To Mum, Dad and Dave – for all the canalside walks
and curiosity

Contents

Contents

Preface

I was having breakfast on the go the other morning, pastry in one hand, tepid coffee in the other, when I saw an older woman sitting on a bench.

It was down by Victoria Embankment in London, and the bench looked out over the River Thames. She was sitting with her eyes closed, the roar of rush hour traffic on one side and the slosh slosh slosh of the river on the other.

She was a buoy in a stormy ocean, choosing to spend her morning sitting in one of the most polluted places in the city. I'd say she was pushing sixty-five – I only glanced at her through the flakiness of my croissant collapsing all over my wool jumper – and she was wearing uncomfortable-looking office shoes.

People have epiphanies climbing Everest or seeing a beautiful sunset.

They emerge, exhilarated, determined to do more with their lives and 'live in the moment'.

My epiphany came at 7.56 a.m. in February in London, by a bus stop. That this was her future. She was living it.

I just knew I didn't want my future to be hers – trying to catch a breath of peace by a polluted road before attacking another workday. For all I knew she could have been the CEO of a human rights charity or a Nobel Peace Prize winner, but at that moment all reason broke down. I don't want to be doing this forever, I thought, croissant disintegrating in my hand.

With Covid, I think we're all starting to reach our forks in the road. Working out what we're happy to put up with and what changes we want to make. Well, this was my fork.

One path, it's more of the same.

It's staying at work late, it's trying to get to the gym every morning, it's scrolling through social media and wondering why we're not in Tahiti. It's cramming a hastily cooked ready meal into our bodies and immediately feeling guilty about it, but knowing we have no choice if we want to see our friends after work. It's reading about the lives of celebrities and setting our alarms to 3 a.m. to see if getting up early and taking cold showers has any effect on our productivity. It's taking a vacation but spending it learning how to ski or speak Japanese instead of reading a book. It's about an exhausting, fulfilling, but ultimately busy life, that's so intense we just want to scream 'STOP!'

In Jia Tolentino's book *Trick Mirror*, she says that being alive seems to be about 'organising your life around practices you find ridiculous and possibly indefensible'. So, maybe we should think about stopping that.

The other path? There are fewer people yelling at you on social media platforms. Your boss isn't always messaging you on your personal phone. You have time for yourself, doing the things you actually want to do. It's a little brighter. Perhaps, it could be the new normal.

After my last breakdown, when I stood on a bridge in London wondering if this was the last thing I'd see, I knew there wasn't much of a choice left. That first path would be short, at least for me: a cul-de-sac. And nobody wants to stand at a fork in the road and take the cul-de-sac, because it would be a shit adventure. The second one is harder, especially when we've all been primed from a young age to study, graft and be present all the time.

This isn't a self-help book. I wouldn't take advice from me, and I certainly wouldn't try to offer it. But I want to understand why so many of us feel like this – wrung out. I set out to chat to other people, find out if they feel like I do, and why.

What happened to our generation that made it feel fine to say yes to everything? Can we blame everything on the 2008 recession and social media, or is there more at play? It goes without saying that this is a book written from a privileged position. I'm white and I was lucky enough to have a stable childhood, brought up by two parents who still love each other. Not everyone can walk away from their stressful job, and not everyone has the immense privilege of being able to actively choose to reduce their workload or lifeload. But some of us do, and some of us definitely should.

I'm pretty sure there's no one 'right' way to live or wrong direction. But I'm also confident that burnout is just around the corner for so many people I know and love if we don't stop and check our habits. Maybe we should all just pause and go and buy an ice cream. Have a walk in the sun. Read a poem. Whatever makes you happy. Be Good Enough.

Introduction

Did you know when you go to A&E and tell them you
want to kill yourself, they hand you an orange form? Not a
bright, neon orange, but a soft one so it doesn't startle you.
The nurses tuck it under other papers to give you privacy
as they pass the clipboard from colleague to colleague.

A&E.

Where, usually, the staff are overworked, abrupt,
rushed.

But now they stop and hand you tissues and their voices
soften and suddenly you feel cocooned in this bright white
hospital where the tiles smell of Listerine and voices are
dampened by polystyrene and the clinical beds and the
sounds of people screaming for their mothers.

Two paramedics wearing forest green drop off their
latest patient. She is wheeled past, choking on air, her
body fighting to live while you, in triage, fight to die.
Numbness envelopes you and there is a fleeting moment
when you know that the right thing to do would be to
take that pen, the one on the desk, the one lying by the
keyboard, and stab it into your wrist and try to end it.

You keep staring at the green curtain that separates you from the real injuries. Those with broken toes and laughing, limping children. The people who have fallen off ladders or been hit in the face with balls.

These are the people the NHS should be treating, not you. You, who are burdening the staff and wasting a room and feeling like you're in the wrong, alien place.

In case you were wondering, this is my breakdown. Every person's breakdown is different, but mine felt like this. It feels like there is nothing left inside you. That the only thing holding your body together is skin that doesn't belong to you any more.

All of a sudden you feel hot tears and the nurse pops her head around the door and says:

'Did you see . . .'

She nods towards the empty seat where your nurse was sitting.

She's at the printer, you say. Even in death, trying to be helpful. 'She was trying to get it to work.'

But your cracking voice belies your pain and you have to stop, and the nurse, who's wearing her watch upside down and a face that's thinking of chicken and chips for tea, pauses a moment and asks:

'Would you like a cuppa?'

And then, in this hospital, I feel the love and the tenderness and the care.

I am here and I want to die, I say. I don't want tea.

She should say she's heard it all before. She should tut and spin full circle and condemn this teenage response for what it is, especially coming from a woman who's nearly thirty – 'THIRTY! I had two kids when I was your age and I wasn't in here moping about' – she should say all of this. Instead this new nurse, with an Irish name, Aoife, sits and hands me some milky tea and tells me she'll walk me over to another unit.

I let her. I let my fraudulent illness check itself in to the hospital. Another woman on a gurney cruises past, yellow face, closed eyes. And surrounded by death, it makes me feel – still nothing.

I have no epiphany. No sudden drive to live.

I take two sleeping tablets and sleep for seven hours.

This is my first and hopefully last night on suicide watch.

It's funny really, because I imagine being on suicide watch is like having a butler, but for sick people. He, or she – in my case, it mostly seemed to be he – sat at a desk on the other side of a window watching me sleep. Drop anything and the handle on the door would turn.

I'd count the six seconds it took him to leave his desk and walk to the door.

'You OK in there?'

I wouldn't answer, not because I'd tried to strap myself up to the ceiling or strangle myself with shoelaces. Instead I'd dropped my phone and now I was plugged back in, listening to a playlist a boy across the sea had shared with me.

I was too far gone in whatever part of his life he'd committed to Spotify. Strange synth, Morrissey, misery. It suited my heavy mood.

The door clicks open.

'Tell me about a time when you were happy.'

'What do you see for yourself in the future?'

'How will you make your future yours?'

'Do you feel like you have the love of your parents?'

A large man with an East African accent arrives to ask questions. He wears sensible shoes and looks like he's never smiled. He takes a very long time to speak, and when he finally gets going, he scratches long marks across the paper.

'Don't you get cramp?' I asked.

'It's my method, the way I work.'

I don't make small talk with him again, but stare at my shoes, my feet, which hang off the too-tall bed, making me feel small and vulnerable, and I tap my heels together. Still he scratches his pencil against his lined paper.

I should have seen the breakdown coming. The tone change. The way it suddenly took me an hour to do something that used to take me ten minutes.

I should have stopped.

Instead, everything I did kept coming back to me. Rejection. Too rushed. Too hurried. Not up to standard.

I would look at the email from an editor, burning with shame, too shocked and afraid that the work I'd submitted, and I'd thought was good, just simply wasn't.

I could hear the tension in my voice when I spoke to people.

Strained.

Everything was a fight.

Everything was me fighting not to fight.

Every fight was caused by me holding on to the elastic inside my head and stopping it from falling slack, and letting every single ounce of my fear, my anxiety, my terror slam against the salesperson, or the caretaker or the colleague, smack in the chops.

This is what a breakdown feels like.

Take a step back.

How?

I go for a walk and the people rushing past me wearing London-only frowns, bought on Oxford Street during an August bank-holiday crush three years ago, allow me to slip into my disease. The burning sun highlights the brick of London Bridge.

The unanswered emails on my phone weigh so heavily that I want to throw it in the river.

Just answer them.

I can't.

So instead, I press pause, and look back at what got me here. At whether life would be easier, more fun, more enjoyable if I'd said to myself, 'Just take your foot off the pedal. Aspire to be mediocre. Be happy. Stop striving. Embrace that.'

So, let's give that a go.

*

I want to look back at where it all started. Why we're told we're special from the moment we're born. It's not that unusual – you might say it to a weeping kid or a child who needs a pick-me-up after getting knocked back over some homework.

The word comes from the Old French, *especial*, which means 'better than ordinary'.

Extraordinary.

My generation, 'millennials', and now Generation Z, are adults. And many of us will have been told how special, how extraordinary, how able we are from the time we first set foot in school.

In this way, we're lucky – to have been loved and supported rather than kicked down and crushed. Yet, both millennials and Generation Z are experiencing some of the highest rates of mental health disorders that have been recorded. Perhaps some of that can be traced back to standing in our primary school lines, all chipped teeth and scuffed knees, moulding plasticine with our clammy little hands.

The blue-streaked-with-yellow bulb of modelling

clay looks like an engorged bogie, but the teacher, in this era of positivity and support, told him it looked fantastic. Then she said how brilliant he was, and told his mother what a special, clever little boy he was.

But it's time we realised that we are not special, and that this notion of 'being special' is killing us. And actually, by the time we realise this, perhaps the damage is done.

We are not extraordinary.

And we need to let these impossible demands on ourselves go.

We are a noisy, chaotic mash of cells created by two people desperately feeling their own way through the madness of the universe. We are imperfect specimens striving to be perfect, and I think life could be better, or at least more *fun*, if we just admitted that we have no idea what we're doing.

Yet twenty-five years later, after standing in that milk-scented, stained reception classroom, gluey fingers covered in sand from the pit, the world incomprehensibly larger than me, I know now that I was lied to.

Rain.

Cuddles.

Dreams were cultivated in that classroom.

It was where we learned that we wanted to be fire-fighters, actors. It was where we said we wanted to drive trains, and the confidence imbued in us at a young age helped to spark a fresh generation filled with positivity.

It created the activists who march and speak out against climate crisis, and the young people who fight against gun laws and rent control and fair working-practices.

We are amazing, able people, but would it hurt to accept that we don't have to push ourselves to breaking point to prove ourselves? To accept that we *are* great, marvellous, interesting people without having to hike to Antarctica or get 10,000 likes on an Instagram post?

Ambition is excellent, but our constant self-criticism, panic and pain as we compare ourselves to each other is killing us. Almost five times as many people suffer from a mental health disorder today compared to ten years ago, while there's been a 28 per cent rise in counselling.

Much of this is to do with factors outside of our control. There is abject uncertainty as Brexit looms on the horizon, bringing with it the threat of an economic recession. We date online, quickly and through apps. We have fewer friends than any other generation, and 22 per cent of millennials say they don't even have a single person in their lives to have a cup of tea with. Our parents are more likely to live in a different city to us. And we face wage stagnation and a housing crisis where it's almost impossible to buy a home of one's own in our major cities.

When I was a child, I was told I could be anything. If I read widely enough, studied hard enough, and did enough extracurricular sporting activities then I could surmount the world.

Now, I'm finding the energy to say: enough is enough. Like a corny meme shared by a friend when you're having a down day: you are enough. We all need to stop beating ourselves up about being extraordinary.

We are all doing our best; striving to be a little more average, and a little less special, is what we, riddled with our insecurities and fears, maybe need to be in order to survive this crazy ride.

Understanding just how ordinary we are, and how special we are not, is important. It gives us permission to close our work emails before midnight and to not hit the gym for the second time in one day. It lets us open and heat up a tin of baked beans when we're on a tight budget, rather than having anxiety about all the ways we should be eating more healthily, even when perhaps calories are more crucial than calcium. You can be 'enough', but on your own terms.

However brutal it sounds, being told that I was unlikely to ever be prime minister, or the director general of the BBC, or the head of the civil service might have been helpful. Statistically knowing how much the odds were stacked against me – comprehensive school, northern and female – could actually have helped me manage my own insecurities and expectations.

Armed with statistics, it's crucial we're aware of the

obstacles every single one of us faces; the discrimination we will experience throughout life because of our religion, our race, our gender or our sexuality.

Being told we can be anything is damaging. Accepting we are ordinary, just one part of a whole, is the future, whether we're trying to collaboratively save the planet or obeying the rules as we drive along the motorway. Enough with being told how special we are, and instead let's start celebrating just how average we all are.

And how we are all enough, just how we are right now.

*

Fear of mediocrity has a name – koinophobia. I like to turn it over, roll my tongue around it. It sounds impressive. Greek. It actually means the fear of having lived a normal life, but what's so wrong with being normal?

Adventurer Ross Edgley made his triumphant return to dry land in Margate, United Kingdom on 5 November 2018. He had circumnavigated the 1,780 miles around Britain in record-breaking time and had endured jellyfish stings and salt-water erosion so severe he woke up with chunks of his tongue having fallen off on the pillow next to him.

The thirty-three-year-old from Lincolnshire had braved grey stormy seas and hadn't set foot on the mainland for five months, sleeping in a support boat at night and swimming through Britain's freezing waters for twelve hours a day. On that November day, as Ross dragged his tired, broken but elated body ashore, I'd just decided I wanted to change gyms. Nothing too major, but a big enough decision that would see me paying £20 more each month, but with a shorter journey.

On the same Monday Ross collapsed into bed and slept, I checked into my new gym, got yelled at by instructors and then took the Tube to work.

Busy, stressed and having issues with my relationship, I spent the journey listening to The Jam and trying to write a few pages of my new novel, laptop precariously balanced on my knees. Whenever anyone sat next to me, they'd crane their necks to see what I'd written, like when you're walking around a beautiful harbour somewhere hot and there's a man painting a little watercolour of the ocean. Everyone stops. Everyone stops to peer over this man's shoulder to ensure his arrogance matches his talent: that him standing there is justified.

I minimised the font size so people couldn't read it. Size 8. Size 6. Even I can't read that. Once, on the Bakerloo line, the man next to me actually leaned forward, looked at my screen and said: 'That's very small.'

This morning I was thinking a lot about Ross Edgley. About what drives a man to do something so ferociously

improbable like that, and thinking, extremely judg-
mentally, that there must be a hell of a thing driving you
to swim around the coast of Britain.

While I was on the Tube, and Ross Edgley was
contemplating media interviews, another story was
unfolding a few hundred miles south of the Bakerloo
line station my Tube was about to pull in at.

Seventeen-year-old Ameena was sitting in Calais,
planning her trip across the Channel to England. She'd
left Afghanistan months before and was alone. Her
mother was in a dirty and 'frightening' refugee camp in
Athens. In a few months' time, Ameena would make the
journey to Kent in a twelve-foot inflatable dinghy with
an outboard motor attached. When she arrived, she told
the British newspaper the *Observer* that she could not
stop vomiting, and that she had no idea where she was.[1]

'I called the police,' she said. Her boat set off on
Christmas Day because there were fewer ships than
normal. When you're trying to cross the Channel, one
of the world's busiest shipping routes, in a twelve-foot
inflatable dinghy, these are things human traffickers need
to consider.

Despite the calm-for-the-time-of-year weather conditions, Ameena suffered extreme seasickness.

Her crossing was 'very, very dangerous. I was scared,'
she said. Before this, she had been living in the Iranian
capital Tehran, but this was by no means as scary as the

crossing she made in pitch black as she sailed across to England.

Just a few months later, Ameena has improved her English and lives in Kent. She has friends and is about to start studying for A levels at college in Canterbury.

The world is full of heroes, some louder than others.

What does success actually mean?

Our notions of success may be different. Success for someone from a less wealthy background, whose parents didn't go to university and might be fighting through the high levels of unemployment in their region, may be retraining and working as a bar manager against all odds. If you take the three people described at the beginning of this chapter: If you take these three people – Ross, Ameena and Me – it's straightforward to rank those people in terms of mediocrity to success, isn't it?

Ross has broken actual, literal records. He is a winner. He is the most successful, surely? Then Ameena, who has pushed past adversity after adversity to start a new life, alone, in England, thousands of miles away from home. Or me, trundling along on the Bakerloo line to get to a meeting with a new client, desperately typing with sweaty fingers, trying to finish a chapter to give my life more meaning than it currently feels like it has.

Obviously, I would rank myself at the bottom of the pile of we three individuals, no matter what. I am hundreds of metres underground, I have a gross sweat patch on my back, and the most I can hope to make from a new client I've just negotiated with wouldn't even buy a new microwave.

But depending on who you are, and what success means to you, you'd rank us differently. To somebody who has wanted to live in London their whole lives – Ameena, perhaps – maybe I'm the most successful person on this. To somebody who values drive and resilience above all else, then Ross takes the prize. And for someone struggling in the face of adversity, then the award has to go to Ameena.

Everyone who grew up in an outer suburb will have experienced koinophobia at some point.

The gravel-kicking walk down the main street while the lace curtains are drawn across the bay windows, illuminated by the flickering light of the Sunday sports on television. The feeling of isolation, as everyone in the neighbourhood gets into their cars at the same time each morning, slams the doors, and then drives away, leaving the neighbourhood empty.

When you're young, being normal doesn't look too good. Must life be like this? Must life be full of empty drives, neat hedges and sensible pathways? And then as you get older you realise this is what success looks like, and actually being able to afford a house with a neat square of turf and having a fence to creosote is a marker of that.

Maybe it's not *your* marker of success. Maybe you're still suffering from koinophobia, the fear of being normal, of arriving one day in the white removal van, with its loud roll-up door and it opening on the rest of your life. A quiet cul-de-sac, detached brick house with water feature and a bird house.

What's so terrifying about this neat little house?

There's a growing belief that we can do better, that there's a veneer of social mobility. When you try, however, your head bumps hard against the class ceiling. So we work at being the best we can be instead. Tied into this is how the concept of perfectionism has changed. While it has become a more positive trait, says expert Tom Curran from the University of Bath, we need to be mindful that perfectionism actually has roots in sociopathic tendencies.

Seeking success isn't a new thing, but this culture of perfectionism is, he says. His specialism focuses on how perfectionism develops in humans, and he points out within the first minute of our conversation that perfectionism is not a positive trait.

'It's truly, definitely a negative trait,' he says. 'And it's one that I think is becoming more pronounced. I notice people holding their hands up and admitting to it more and more. "Yeah, I'm a perfectionist," they say, but it's not a good thing.'

In an academic sense of the term, being a perfectionist doesn't mean you strive for perfection. It isn't about diligence or doing the best work, says Curran. 'At its very root, perfectionism is about trying to perfect what we perceive to be our imperfect self. It is a belief that no matter what we do, we're inherently deficient, and there's a real determination to show and prove to others that we're worth something. I see it a lot among friends. It's about a need for other people's approval.'

Curran says it speaks volumes for our culture that people admit to it, that they're almost proud of their perfectionism. However, he adds that 'there are no upsides to [it].'

Perfectionists, in the true sense of the word, don't work harder or achieve more. Studies show that there are zero benefits to being a perfectionist, and they actually end up overworking and burning out more because they don't know when to switch off. 'If you're a perfectionist, you work to a point where it becomes uncomfortable. It's a law of diminishing returns – in pursuit of ever-increasing outcomes, you lose out in other ways. You actually make it harder to reach the goals you set yourself.'

Curran says it's not worth the mental stress. 'True perfectionists suffer from tremendous psychological turmoil.'

However, being a perfectionist isn't necessarily a choice. Studies have found that around 40 per cent of our drive for perfectionism comes from our genes. The rest is from nurture and from societies that value the individual pushing their boundaries, and the World Health Organization and the Harvard Business Review claim that it's on the rise.[2] High rates of perfectionism can be found across Asia, says Curran.[3] It's unsurprising that among millenials there's a real fear of not doing well. A study conducted by Curran and Andrew P. Hill tested for generational changes in college students' responses to the Multidimensional Perfectionism Scale between 1989 to 2016. It found that in the later years, young people put significantly more pressure on themselves than previous generations. Curran found that the fear of failure has been exacerbated thanks in part to changing social dialogue and culture, and young people do everything they can to avoid it – this leads to greater anxiety and an attempt to evade it by working too hard.[4]

If you're in your late twenties, thirties or even forties, you probably feel like this is just the way it is. There's a genuine concern among my friends and colleagues that if you choose to take your foot off the pedal, you'll be fired.

But it's not all doom. Curran says it feels like there's reason to be optimistic.

'People are starting to wake up to the fact this perfectionism isn't always possible,' Curran tells me. As an early-years academic, he has developed an 'eager awareness' of what's going on among his nineteen-to-twenty-year-old students. 'They see that the social contract they signed doesn't exist any more. They feel they're being screwed over and that social media is bullshit. The perfect lifestyle doesn't exist, that's clear, and I see a counterculture emerging. Although things need to get worse before they get better, I think young people might be rejecting the status quo.'

Perfectionism, or what many of us in our twenties and thirties feel now – the need to work and do more – was probably exacerbated by market reforms in the 1970s, he says. Today, putting in work and expecting to get something back is a cultural norm based on the principle that the very best will always rise to the top. It assumes that our society is a meritocracy which is fair and gives equal weight to all.

When we took a turn towards market-based reforms in the late seventies, we made an assumption, at least in the West, that market-based principles were the only way to form society. Curran explains that by this, he means that education became obsessed by league tables, everything became ranked, children were set according to ability, and even local and national governments were judged in this way. 'If there was an opportunity to embed market-based principles into a civic institution,' he says, 'they took it.'

As a result, he charts this as the birth of the perfectionism epidemic. People began to internalise the sense that they need to work hard and skill-up to make themselves worth more in the current market. People became goods. We began to understand that in order to succeed, we must polish our CVs and skills until we shined on the job-market shelf.

Is the drive to be successful actually destructive?

It goes without saying that we can't all be the best. We can't all succeed, so I started to wonder whether we should all just tone it down, try to take it easy.

I had a hunch I wasn't alone in feeling so strung-out all of the time. Cities across the world are full of people studying at night classes while working flat-out during the day. The first London Tube that runs each morning is packed with tired people who have spent all night working to provide for their families, joined by sharp-suited under-thirties on their way out to Canary Wharf to sit in on a 6 a.m. call.

What I do know is that it's an absolute privilege to have this dilemma. The dilemma of needing to press pause, but not knowing how to do so. So few of us have the opportunity to decide whether we want to reduce the amount we work or have the opportunity to strive for promotions. According to the Office for National Statistics, around 5 million workers in the UK are casual or work zero-hour contracts. That's a lot of people in insecure work, and around 40 per cent of that 5 million are in low-skilled jobs. Uber drivers, serving staff on zero-hour contracts, cleaners.[5]

Not everyone can 'enjoy' such First World problems as anxiety over whether we go to the gym too much. Being aware of the luxury that I can choose whether or not I want to strive to be successful is a marker of privilege, of being white, of being middle class. And although this privilege doesn't make these anxieties or this stress any less real or important, it's still a better one to have than being fearful of the police or unconscious bias. Many of us, rich or poor, regardless of skin colour or religion, live in a world driven by capitalism, expectation and unrealistic standards. And this is what I hope this book calls to account and challenges.

As humans we strive, and it's in our nature to do so. But at what cost? I'm going to try to figure this out by speaking with friends, experts and strangers about the pressures they face every day to keep pushing forward. How our need to achieve has penetrated our hobbies, our workplace, our friendships, and even our sleep.

I think about this when I'm sitting on that bed back in A&E. What I don't know is if it's all going to be OK.

The 1%: Hitting the Glass Ceiling

'Shoot for the moon. Even if you miss, you'll land among the stars.'
– Norman Vincent Peale

This mantra can be found on tea towels, fridge magnets and posters, probably within a ten-mile radius of your current location. At the risk of pissing on motivational statements, I reckon they can do a lot more harm than good. I've tried to live my life by statements such as this one, because they feel affirming, and like you're doing the right thing by working hard.

And yet, they assume we are all equal. That we live in a meritocratic world where, if you work hard and try, then you will succeed. There's an element of truth to this, but I've found the converse in some cases: that at least in the UK, meritocracy is a myth.

So nepotism is still alive and kicking?

The word nepotism comes from the Latin word *nepos*, meaning nephew or grandchild. It means power being handed out to family members, regardless of talent. Countless sons and daughters who have gained status of office due to their family connections would argue that they also worked hard to get to where they are – but this is where we have to press pause.

Nepotism and its existence in society can be frustrating for people who don't have those connections. It can make striving feel pointless, when you know the boss's son will get the gig you want, or the headline slot at a community festival will go to the organiser's friend.

Does it make the long days we put in studying or staying late in the office worthless? Does it motivate you to fight more, or does it make you take pause and think – will I ever break through?

Here's a helpful technique. Every time I don't get a job that I know I'm perfect for, or miss out on a contract because I failed to network with the right person, I just think about Zac Goldsmith. Zac Goldsmith would appear to be a very good example of what happens when you're rich, white and well connected in Britain, and is a perfect privilege case study. Sorry in advance, Zac.

Perhaps this reads as envy, but in reality, it's more exhaustion. Even if Zac Goldsmith was a budding David Attenborough in his youth, and a remarkable politician, there are many others who are probably just as good, just as passionate, just as talented. And they never get a chance to show what they can do because they don't have the access to wealth and familial privilege that Zac appears to have.

Currently a member of the Conservative Party and Minister of State for Pacific and the Environment, Zac Goldsmith, born in 1975, is high up the political food chain.

For starters, his upbringing was posh. Like, really posh.

His father is Sir James Goldsmith and his mother Lady Annabel Vane-Tempest-Stewart.

That's three hyphens. A triple-barrelled name. He grew up in a house called Ormeley Lodge, which sounds a little like a modest gatekeeper's cottage, but then I noticed it has its own Wikipedia page.

I mean guys, come on. Why aren't we having revolutions in the streets about this shit? How is this even a thing any more?

I'm not wildly advocating we destroy royalty, but I am urging us all to take a step back and look at who you're breaking your back at work for. Is it worth it?

Back to Zac. Let's whizz past all the privilege that comes with living in London – having access to great museums, a place to live while doing work placements (if you don't get directly parachuted into a job) – and go straight to education. Educated at (guess where) Eton College, where he was expelled for having cannabis in his room, he went to Cambridge Centre for Sixth-form Studies to do his A levels. Getting expelled didn't harm his prospects, and Mr Goldsmith skipped university completely, travelled the world courtesy of his uncle Edward Goldsmith for a few years, lived in the US working for a think-tank, and was then appointed reviews editor of the *Ecologist* magazine (owned by his uncle).

Goldsmith had enormous interest in ecology as a boy, and according to an interview with the *Daily Telegraph*, was once given *Ancient Futures* by Helena Norberg-Hodge, a book about ecology, as a gift from his father.

No one can deny he showed interest and probably skill in ecological issues, but can you imagine having worked at the *Ecologist* magazine for decades, and watching the owner's twenty-three-year-old nephew start at a desk, however talented he might be.

Despite losing to Sadiq Khan in the London mayoral elections in 2016 and his Richmond seat in the 2019 elections, Goldsmith still remains deep within Boris's inner circle. It's a position seemingly borne of privilege and shared background.

The reason we've just done a shallow dive into Zac Goldsmith's immense world of privilege is that it can be both exhausting but also helpful to know what you might be up against, although of course we'll never know where Zac might be today if he wasn't a Goldsmith.

Nepotism and connections thread society together everywhere, no matter where you are. It's not just London remaining in awe of Oxbridge; there are global issues with nepotism. It's certainly not confined to Europe.

Even in bastions of what look like progressiveness and inequality, like Canada, have you ever wondered why Justin Trudeau already has an airport named after him in Montreal? Oh right, that was named after his dad, who was president from 1968 to 1979. Justin Trudeau got to where he is now based off years of experience and skill, but there's no doubt that having a famous politician dad can help with image control. South Korea, too, has a decades-long issue with nepotism. Their economy is dominated by chaebols, or family-run businesses. There are about two dozen, and include Samsung, Hyundai and LG Group. Those belonging to chaebol families seem to get free reign in a society dominated by hierarchy. They'll get into the best universities, walk into any job they want, and dominate industry.

In fact, nepotism is so bad in South Korea that when Moon Jae-In, South Korea's president, arrived in office in 2017, he made it his responsibility to stamp out engrained cronyism and nepotism. The issue is so widespread it's not even limited to the private sector. Police have looked into examples of nepotistic hiring in state schools, state-run hospitals and a defence and science research institute and found it is rampant.[1]

Throw charities, journalism, publishing, theatre and art into the worldwide mix and you have a tantalizing assortment of people who slipped their way up ladders, were grabbed and pulled up (hey, Boris Johnson) and those who put the work in but were also helped out by virtue of living in London or having savings to fall back on when the going got tough.

Didn't go to Oxbridge? Problem!

In 2020, there was a problem with an algorithm. Around 40 per cent of A Levels (UK final-year school exams), were downgraded after the exams were cancelled in the wake of the Covid pandemic. Ofqual, which was in charge of deciding what grades students would receive, came under fire after it transpired that the majority of students whose grades were downgraded went to state schools. Private schools saw an increase in the number of students receiving As and A*s, while state schools saw grades plummet. Those in poorer areas, where more children received free school meals, had their grades downgraded regardless of whether they were predicted high grades or not. It showed the government's total disregard for the poor and the clear belief that no one can possibly be intelligent and come from a deprived background. Some students who attended inner-city state schools and were predicted A*s even found their grades shunted to Ds and Es, missing their places at top unversities, purely based on the algorithm.

The Sutton Trust, a charity that explores social

mobility, found that there's a 'pipeline' from independent schools through Oxbridge and into top jobs.

In 2019 the Trust conducted research, known as the Elitist Britain report, that found Britain's most powerful people are five times more likely than the general public to have gone to an independent school. Politics, the media and public service all show high proportions of privately educated people in their numbers, including 65 per cent of senior judges, 59 per cent of civil service permanent secretaries and 57 per cent of the House of Lords, compared to around 7 per cent of the population.

The report adds that 'newspaper columnists, who play a significant role in shaping the national conversation, draw from a particularly small pool, with 44% attending independent school and 33% coming through the independent school to Oxbridge "pipeline" alone.'[2]

The Elitist Britain report shows a starkly divided country. Britain is at a critical juncture, it states, divided by class, gender, race and wealth more than ever. Social mobility is stagnant.

James Turner, Chief Executive of the Sutton Trust, told me that if society wants to change the way people from the most privileged backgrounds end up in most leadership roles, we need to make the most of talent from all sections of society. 'It is vital that young people are able to see people like them across a range of leading roles. We'd also like to see employers adopt contextual recruitment practices for entry-level roles, so that they take account of the opportunities a young person has had in terms of the successes they have achieved.'

The Sutton Trust found that an increase in the UK's social mobility to the average level across western Europe could be associated with an increase in annual GDP of approximately 2 per cent, equivalent to £39bn for the UK economy as a whole (in 2016 prices). The issue is that those who occupy the most influential roles at the top of our society make decisions that affect everyone. 'People are shaped by their background and life experiences when making these decisions, and so for a healthy society it is vital that these roles reflect all geographical areas and social backgrounds,' the report added.

There's nothing we can do about who we were born to or how we were educated. We can't stop our uncles from saying: 'Please, take this job at a magazine I own.' But one thing we can do is become aware of our privilege and aware of other people's privilege, and we can step aside if we don't think we're right for the job.

If we start thinking about all the people who have got ahead because of who they're related to, life takes on a depressing hue. It's why I'm always disappointed when I learn that an actor had famous parents. Or a journalist who is smashing it and whose columns are a joy to read is related to the editor of a big Sunday paper. A little slice of my northern optimistic soul dies because I feel crushed. I can't help it.

I spend my life fervently hoping that everyone who is achieving and succeeding is doing so because they're excellent and have worked their way up.

Learning about how broken social mobility is, was an important lesson for me: stop self-flagellating for not getting that dream job or winning a 30 Under 30 award or . . . anything else that someone ambitious might subscribe to. It's not about giving up. It's about being realistic and setting my own timeline.

But rather than channelling all that anger at the people who get these opportunities, like Zac Goldsmith, it helps to get angry at the system, and then decide to either ride the wave or fight it.

In this muddled up world, it helps to remember that Kylie Jenner was named the world's youngest 'self-made' billionaire by Forbes, with her make-up business Kylie Cosmetics. It's not you, it's the system. Take a deep breath and remember this the next time you're staying late at work, trying to make your own dreams come true (while also transcribing your boss's latest motivational speech).

Jenner initially fought back against criticism that she wasn't self-made, saying she made all her own money and started out financially with nothing. The press hysterically endorsed that.[3] This was a woman who was born into extreme wealth and started out with more than most would ever earn in their lifetimes. Recently, Jenner seems to have backed away from this description of herself, caveating in an interview with the *New York Times* that she 'has had a lot of help and [was given] a huge platform'.[4]

The current order doesn't feel like it works for everyone, which makes it even more important that we try to change it if we're inside the system.

Will it be like this forever?

Thankfully, change, in some sectors at least, is brewing. Companies are already making a start with 'blind recruitment', where pertinent information is blurred out on all job applications. For example, universities and surnames are left blank, so nobody is influenced by their own known or unknown prejudices.[5] The initiative is a way of 'giving under-represented groups confidence that their application will be fairly considered', the CBI states.[6]

We need blind recruitment because humans have subconscious biases. Disabled candidates must apply for 60 per cent more jobs than able-bodied people to have an equal chance of landing a role, while the Women and Equalities Committee found that a Muslim woman is three times more likely to be rejected for a job than women in general.[7]

Large institutions like the British Civil Service are implementing this policy while, in my own experience, the private sector continues to employ 'mates of mates', as one person I used to work with would put it each time he led another white, middle-aged man into the interviewing room.

But what does the current structure look like? Is social mobility really as important as we make out? Surely anyone can be born, work hard and absolutely smash life? Well, according to the government's Social Mobility Commission's latest report, that's absolutely, unfortunately, not the case.

The report, described as 'damning' by the *Guardian*,[8] revealed inequality is 'entrenched from birth to work'. This means that those who are born privileged will likely remain so. The new report shows that social mobility has almost completely stagnated at every single life-stage over the last four years. This means if you're born into a working-class family, chances are you'll remain working class.

It's getting a lot harder to smash the glass ceiling of privilege.

If your mum or dad is a professional, there's an 80 per cent chance you'll also join the professional, white-collar class. This is for a number of reasons: they know what you need to do to achieve; they understand the education system, how student loans work and what sort of connections you need to make. This is knowledge that can't necessarily be taught, just assimilated through constant, multi-generational exposure.

But what if you're from a working-class background and want to make it into the professional classes? Don't rest on your laurels. The report found that 'even when those from working-class backgrounds are successful in entering professional occupations, they earn on average 17% less than their more privileged colleagues.'

Social mobility is falling. Research from the Sutton Trust shows that the probability of men in professional and managerial jobs having come from the lowest occupational classes has declined substantially, from 20 per cent for those born between 1955 and 1961 down to 12 per cent for those born between 1975 and 1981. Not being born in London has a knock-on effect, too. 'Geographical divides in opportunity are a key contributor to inequality. Our research has highlighted that while those born in London have a great chance to fulfil their potential, this has not been the case elsewhere across the country,' a Sutton Trust spokesperson says.

The 'elite' hold the keys to everything, from (almost) every bank and every law firm to every GP surgery and every theatre. And this matters because they're the institutions making decisions for you, from the shows you'll be seeing to the medications you'll be taking.

And if you think that sounds benevolent, just imagine for a second that you've never seen someone who looks like you on screen. You start to imagine this world isn't for you.

And yet, perhaps there's cause for optimism. The 2017 election saw the highest number of comprehensive-school-educated MPs enter parliament, and the report acknowledges that the over-representation of privately educated people in positions of authority is decreasing. The number of 'minority ethnic' MPs in the Conservative Party has increased from eleven to twenty-two people. This is important and positive, but it's too slow if we want to see real change at the top anytime soon.

So, what does this have to do with trying to stop pushing so hard?

Growing up, all I wanted to be was a full-time foreign correspondent. You know the type – the ones who hang around in clubs in the East occasionally leaving their cocktail to file a story about corruption. Essentially, a profession that has been dominated by male, white Hemingways. There's a reason why so few women are able to follow this path. It's riskier and, in so many societies, women are less accepted. The chances of getting a meeting with a local warlord are slimmer. Walking alone as a woman in a warzone is significantly more dangerous than for a man. In addition to being shot, you can also be raped, a recognised weapon of war. So gender is already a barrier. And, like many, being able to afford to take risks is also a barrier. But I have never been able to afford to take a risk that would catapult me into the lofty (and very poorly paid) heights of foreign-affairs journalism, because I just don't have the support network. Say I spent £2,000 on flights to Tahiti because a contact had given me a heads up that a story was about to break. I'd file a story or two and maybe get £400 payment from newspapers. Like most journalists, I've been tipped off multiple times about stories breaking abroad, but been unable to do anything about them.

I've watched wealthier friends drop money on same-day flights to make sure they got their scoop first, and because their mum had once lunched with a general in former Rhodesia, their scoops were drop-dead brilliant. Instead, I tried to funnel that envy into productivity, but it can be hard to grin and bear it. The way I got around it was to think how privileged I was in turn, and how lucky I've been in life too. I wasn't born into conflict, I have shelter, I have food – but sometimes when you're all competing on the same playing field, but the starting blocks aren't level, it can be a bitter pill to swallow. Mostly because I am, by nature, a risk-taker. And I found that I couldn't take so many risks because I didn't have a strong cushion to fall back on.

That said, I also know foreign-affairs journalists who have grafted despite not coming from a wealthy background. They have lived on friends' couches, worked as bicycle couriers to pay the rent and moved to cheaper countries to lower their cost of living. And these guys are the truly impressive ones. Yet, they're also screweed by the system.

As a no-name journalist, I'm paid £330 for 1,000 words at big national newspapers. More often than not, that's £280 for 800 words. Perhaps to a non-journalist that sounds like a good deal, but if I tell you that as a foreign-affairs journalist who would need to cover a flight, about five days' worth of research and then write-up time, that £280 is starting to look very bad.

We keep doing it because we know the world needs to hear about a certain story and also, bluntly, because we're trained journalists and this is literally our job.

I belong to several Facebook groups for journalists, and it's astounding how many people openly admit to being supported by their husbands or partners so they can write.

This is a luxury that harks back to a sort of nineteenth-century 'kept' notion: a husband magnanimously giving his partner an allowance so she can do her little hobby. I'm currently awake at 4 a.m. and have to set my alarm early so I can write and work around my day job. It's a normal state of affairs for most people who want to do something outside their nine-to-five, but many people whose books line your shelves or whose art you enjoy looking at almost certainly have savings to fall back on so they could take time out, or at the very least a supportive home life.

I hit thirty this year and realised with a pang that not only had I not won any significant awards as a journalist (bar a few travel-writing things), I hadn't even bothered to enter anything. I knew that if I'd had the luxury, but also the drive, to solely focus on reporting from China, focusing on crucial coverage, then I might have been listed as a journalist high-achiever. However, realistically I couldn't afford to, and, if I'm being honest, wasn't sure I wanted to live on the breadline for a decade before 'making it'. I beat myself up for that. For not having adequate drive to make it. And the guilt kept me awake for many nights.

Being a journalist, especially a young journalist, means earning a poor salary, no matter whether you live in New York or Paris. It hasn't always been like this. It often means living in a houseshare (if you live in London) and, if not, being in a relationship, to keep costs low. I certainly found myself staying in relationships I should have left, just so I could keep writing.

When I was twenty-eight, I had an epiphany. I'd rather earn a living wage by writing for bigger companies and do journalism on the side. I was frustrated with the bubble-mentality of the journalism industry, and the sort of scathing looks you received (often from people who lived rent-free in London with their parents) when you mentioned you were writing a piece of sponsored content for a brand rather than a hard-hitting report about social injustice.

Although I hate to admit it, giving myself permission to

understand why I wasn't able to break a front page as easily as I might have been had I been born into a different family, for example, helped. If I'd stayed working as a journalist, forever chasing stories and commissions, my breakdown might have been tougher and come a lot sooner.

I made mistakes at times. Sometimes the copy I filed wasn't the cleanest, or I rushed to file too quickly because I needed to get onto the next piece of work so I could pay my rent and made errors. We all have bad days, right? But it was the gigantic schlep of never catching a break and never being able to take time off because there was no safety net which finally made me throw in the towel. These sorts of jobs just aren't sustainable without that gift, and the incredible, fabulous working-class journalists who have managed to make it work are heroes.

Do you need to be privileged to follow your dream?

Olivia Crellin founded PressPad, an organisation that helps young journalists from working-class backgrounds get a foot in the door. This came about from her own personal experience not growing up in London and not knowing anyone in media. 'I have a privileged background and education but not when it came to understanding how the media worked.

'I got a staff job in the UK and saw things from the other side. There's lots of desire to improve diversity and change these workplaces because of the role media plays in society, examining closely who is behind the production of content and the work, and how that affects the way stories are told and debated.'

Individuals began to understand the problem and wanted to do something to help, she explains. People who have signed up to support PressPad might have a spare room, or they might be able to help out people with less privileged backgrounds. She says: 'The journalism community is important and wants to help others out, so I'm leveraging goodwill and resources to support new journalists.

'We're trying to help those – in a very concrete way – who can't get their foot in the door because of geography.'

It's crucial to have a diverse media, she explains. 'It's the mirror that society holds up to itself. If we're not representing everyone in the media or having lots of conversations about the society we live in, you get Brexit! There's a lot of mistrust, a lot of misunderstanding in the world of media, and really, it's a visible representation of society, so it must be diverse.'

That's where UK-based PressPad comes in. The Media is meant to hold the people in power to account. 'You have issues like Windrush, Grenfell, and if you don't have reporters or people from these communities who can reach them, then they can't shed light on aspects that would go unreported,' Crellin says.

She agrees that there's an issue with nepotism in the media. Whether you went to a private school or a state school is a recurring topic. As someone who belonged to the club – 'I went to Oxford, private school and Columbia University: that's where the connections are to be made.'

There are clearly ways to work hard and succeed. But I always find it helpful to think about the myth of having 'inherited natural talents'. The idea that you simply need to work hard and you will be rewarded with success. This notion relies on so much more. It relies on us being in a well-paid job already. It relies on us having the sort of platform where people can see and appreciate our hard work. It relies on the absence of conscious or subconscious racial biases. And it relies on us having the education and knowledge of how to get started. The nouse to network. The ability to move in circles where we might meet the right people.

Not everyone can achieve everything in the first twelve years of their adult life, especially if there are no family connections or helpful trust fund. Not being based in London held me back for the first few years of my professional life, but I think things equalise as careers and life progress.

We're all different, our circumstances are different, and remembering this should be helpful. Moving at a slower pace, being good enough is OK, even if we dream of

44

success. Taking our time, doing it in a way that doesn't involve hurting others or ourselves, and telling ourselves it's fine to move at our own pace, works.

But isn't not pushing hard enough just giving in? Don't we need to challenge the status quo? When you have a stratum of old money at the top, not pushing against that can feel like giving up. Working to be good enough feels like a surrender rather than a positive life choice.

The people who have made change in our society – the Martin Luther Kings, the Ruth Bader Ginsburgs – they have pushed. They have shaken the tree's roots and the bad fruit has (eventually) fallen.

If we don't work hard, then how will we ever elicit change? How will the 'oppressed masses' overthrow the shackles of capitalism? Or the disenfranchised ever achieve parity? It's always been so easy to argue that we must work our asses off to be the change that we want to see. And this is a good mantra, but we have to work smart, not hard. Working the way we are right now will cause burnout for a whole generation.

We also have to keep reminding ourselves that we're working and pushing in a power structure that does not necessarily support who we are or where we're coming from. Understanding the game you're playing is a start.

Keep going. Choose your battles wisely. And assume every opportunity is yours to take.

Social Media

I'm on holiday, detoxing.

Since touching down, data roaming has racked up £32 of charges because I checked my work emails. I just wanted to reassure my boss that I had read his message, but instead found a semi-threatening note warning me to take a vacation and not check office communications.

I'm in a rental car in the passenger seat with my laptop on my knees, trying to finish a piece of work. Ergo, my social detox is not going well.

My one concession is that I've pulled the plug on social media, which I realised I'd become re-addicted to, and have reduced the number of times I check emails to just once a day. I do that on my laptop so there's no temptation to flick the phone open and scroll. Anyone who has a phone understands this sensation. Yesterday I watched two men wearing brown overalls hack ice out of a freezer for twenty minutes, scraping it out to pack into plastic bags for the store, and then sit down on the kerb to scroll through Facebook.

Social media offers these two men the exact same release it offers me when I'm trying to meet a deadline. I read stranger's thoughts on Twitter, hearing that they're reporting from Guadeloupe or acting in a new West End show. Mostly, my Twitter community are actors, directors, journalists and writers. There are a few crazy people who I've picked up as I've written about North Korea throughout my career, who post the latest conspiracy theories or, one of my favourites, a man who reports a weather forecast in Pyongyang and speculates whether famine is going to hit. But otherwise, I'm in a very traditional media bubble.

I'm not alone in experiencing envy or guilt when I see other people's experiences on Twitter, which in itself can motivate me to put my foot on the pedal and work harder and harder. I have zero aspirations to become a Broadway tap dancer, and yet when I see a tenuous acquaintance got picked for the leading role in some reworked tap version of *Romeo and Juliet* I'm inexplicably envious. I can't dance, sing or act. A triple threat, I am not. But there's something about that permanent sense of guilt about never doing enough, and never reaching one's full potential, that will eat at me until the day I die.

We're all intimately acquainted with how social media can affect us: how it can affect our concentration, our feelings of self-worth and of self-loathing. And yet, those of us who have been with social media since its very inception (twenty-three years ago) can remember a world without those life-affirming red notifications. We remember there was a time before 24/7 keeping up with the Joneses. Sure, we used Myspace, and MSN Messenger, those fat little green and blue creatures that spun around in the corner of the screen when you were meant to be writing an essay, but we turned it off. You couldn't put a desktop computer in your pocket.

And everyone over thirty who had the privilege of internet access as a young person remembers how much effort went into names. Emo song titles written in cursive script could set you apart from the lame people. Statuses could be made or broken based on how niche your song title was – mine were always lyrics from Rage Against the Machine, Muse or, if I was feeling particularly creative, Rise Against.

Whatever emo song lyric you chose was always from the same band as whatever your crush was listening to. If they had a lyric from Muse's 'Butterflies and Hurricanes', then you would subtly also choose a Muse lyric. I doubt they noticed, but the hours spent agonising over this were undeniably worth it.

Then to get their attention, you'd log out and log in again to make sure they knew you were there. A desperate, attention-seeking tactic.

They hook you in young

We've moved on since those heady days of instant Messenger. Social media as we know it started with Myspace. It was the first platform to reach a million regular monthly users and for a hot second even overtook Google as the most visited platform. Then, puff! Myspace, Friendster and Hi5 were no more, and Facebook, with its sleek design and easy-to-use interface overtook them all.

Then, there's a clutch of Chinese social media sites. TikTok, a micro-video platform where users can share short lip-sync videos or funny sequences, is furiously used by Gen Z. Even millennials and boomers are getting in on the action, drawn in by the promise of short videos which we can scroll through during commutes/on the bog.

TikTok stars, like Instagram stars, are an advertiser's dream, and the young audience that uses the platform laps up the content. Stars include Nagmaa, Avneet Kaur and Asaas Channa, who have tens of millions of followers between them.

While it may seem like an alien subculture if you're not a regular social media user and/or under twenty-one, these 'stars' from online bleed into the very real world. Lisa and Lena, twins from TikTok, have since walked fashion show runways and even hosted the German Nickelodeon's Kid's Choice Awards ceremony.

Social media stars make the news, and although it's great that children and young people have a platform to express themselves, it can also be a place where children can drink in controversial opinions. Take PewDeePie, a YouTuber (someone who uses YouTube to produce and share videos) who helped to (allegedly accidentally) amplify an anti–Semitic narrative. PewDiePie, a video-game vlogger with 76 million followers (real name Felix Kjellberg) shared a link to an anti-Semitic site, E;R, which features white supremacist messaging and racial slurs. He pushed back, describing it as an 'oopsie' and said he was only recommending the site because he liked a review of a TV show on there.[1]

Joey Salads, another YouTuber, became famous for racist pranks where he'd carry an 'All Lives Matter' sign in a Black neighbourhood and comment that 'Black people get very emotional' when they accosted him about the sign. He also described Black people as violent as part of a 'prank'.[2]

Platforms are great to entertain and to share information and to talk about climate change and do fun dances and tell jokes. They give kids autonomy, allow them to take charge and be the boss, but that also comes with a little risk when moral and ethical considerations aren't fully thought through.

Kids are becoming brands before they finish primary school

Social media can exacerbate the pressure on kids to do more than post a creative video showing a new dance move. It can make children want to be marketable brands, to earn money and to chase followers and likes. Parents may be complicit in encouraging this. The pressure to be successful follows kids in their pockets. The apps to help them do homework, Duolingo, Netflix – everything is there and ready for children to learn and grow and be occupied constantly. Unwittingly, children have been exposed to the same pressures and stresses as adults, but don't have the mental development to switch off and say enough is enough.

Dr Sally Austen, a psychologist, explains that we all need time where we stop and do nothing. It's vital for our brains to process trauma and mend, she says. 'Social media is filling up the gaps of time where we used to do nothing, sitting on the toilet or train, or waiting for a friend. These used to be bits of time where we would do nothing apart from daydream, and maybe we'd run through to-do lists in our heads.

'All of that time is extremely valuable in terms of processing information. Processing information is impor- tant – it allows trauma to fade into our long-term memory.

51

Otherwise the memory of the trauma stays in our short-term memory or it's a constant flashback of terror.'

Dr Austen explains that there's far more to trauma than being in a car crash or being mugged, although these are obviously crucial examples of what trauma is. But little things that we get from social media also count as trauma. 'On social media you might get lots of "you're ugly, you're shit", which are all these little traumas, but we're also not giving ourselves time to process these. We need time to stand at a bus stop and think "Oh, I like her coat", or "I must phone my mum". It's so valuable but we're just not doing it.'

Our use of social media platforms is preventing us from healing, she explains. 'Being on social media also means we're not giving ourselves time to do other stuff either. One of the other ways to clear our heads if we're full of failure – for example, when we feel rubbish or terrible – is to think about all the other ways we can be a good person or fill our times with good things. Instead of Twitter, for example, fill your time with a constructive hobby. Rather than picking up your phone and opening social media, going for a run or doing some drawing could be a good start. Then you'll get loads of positive experiences that will cancel out the negative experiences on social media. For example, say you get some hate across social media, but everyone in the singing club you're part of was pleased to see you, then it should cancel out that angst.'

If we send a tweet and we wonder whether or not we should have sent it, it doesn't fill us with as much anxiety if we have richness in other parts of our lives. The thing is, Dr Austen asks, you wouldn't take a group of racist, rude, hurtful people into the bathroom with you, so why do you open social media on your phone in the toilet? 'You wouldn't let these people near you or your family, and yet we're letting them into our heads all the time.'

When it comes to children using social media, it can be especially damaging. On a broader level, a pressure to succeed exists that never existed before. If they're not blogging about being kids or starting a YouTube channel, but their friends are, do they feel pressure?

For about one week when I was a child, I remember being momentarily envious when a kid at school got a job in a car advert through an acting school I didn't even go to. The acting school was seen as more commercial and more musical theatre (skills, as I refer to above, I do not possess). I wanted the cash injection he had, but wasn't an actor, so it was sort of a moot point.

Being fourteen is really hard. Imagine being fourteen, the time when you develop your sense of self and identity, but you're also sharing your current version of yourself with other, faceless people online. The pressure to earn and compare yourself to others starts young: childhood is cut short. And childhood, says neuroscientist Susan Greenfield, is crucial for balanced brain development.[3]

Dr Austen worries about capacity assessment when it comes to children and social media. 'I work with people who are going on game shows or quiz shows, to figure out whether they're prepared for their exposure. If you go on this game show, you may end up rich and famous – best time of [your] life. Or, will you be the one that farts on TV [in front of] millions of people and you become known as Farty Fiona. Or there's a kiss-and-tell story.

'Kids just aren't best placed to make decisions about whether they want to be exposed to social media. I don't think when adults or children go into things like this [like running a YouTube channel or doing TikTok videos] they think what could go wrong. They don't necessarily think about what the impact of this could be in twenty years' time. Certainly, they don't have the same support as, say, a child actor who is appearing in a film, who has a chaperone at all times backstage. Who is talking this through with kids who are famous online?'

She says what she's most concerned about, however, is the impact on the average young child. 'Speech development is important at a young age. You need to have endless conversations with lots of different people. At the doctor's waiting room, you'll see kids on tablets while their parents are on their phones. Before, that could be ten minutes of rich conversational time. They could be playing I Spy or pretending to have a tea party with their parents. As we talk less to our children, we're going to see a significant wave of falling ability with our theory of mind, a skill much needed for empathy. Kids should be playing, talking, then playing – not sitting on phones.'

No matter whether you're part of a capitalist society or a dictatorship, it seems like we're all craving that feel-good boost that comes with seeing that little red tick hover over our apps or notifications tabs. In 2014, an article labelled our social-media-obsessed generation as Generation Notification: we keep using social media because we're addicted to that quick feel-good boost.[4] Feeling immediately desired by the community around us works wonders for that quick endorphin boost.

Social media has developed short-term, dopamine-driven feedback loops that are 'destroying how society works', Chamath Palihapitiya, former Vice President of User Growth at Facebook, told a group of students at Stanford University. He was responding to a question on how social media platforms exploit users, and Harvard University explored this idea in an online feature by Trevor Haynes, a research technician in the Department of Neurobiology at Harvard Medical School.[5]

While researching social media, every single result when I searched 'impact of social media' on search engines came up with negative associations. 'Why social media is ruining our lives'; 'Pushier notifications: how social media is getting more invasive'; 'Yes, social media is making you miserable' are just some of the headlines among 240 million search results about the impact of social media.

What's interesting is social media is still a fairly recent phenomenon. Although people under thirty probably couldn't imagine a life without logging on to some form of social media, those a little older can remember surviving well enough without it. It has changed the way we are and how we interact with our communities, friends and families.

It has also created a whole new way to overachieve, whether that's by feeling pressured to build your following or by showing how successful your life is to friends and seeking their approval at the same time.

It's not news that smartphones and social media platforms utilise the same techniques as slot machines to keep us hooked: those of us who use these platforms are addicted. Try blocking your social media apps and seeing how many times you pick up your phone and itch to open it.

Breaking the cycle of social media addiction

My vice is Twitter. I'll often scroll through a variety of conversations without posting or replying, but relish the opportunity to switch off from the mundanity of whatever I'm doing. Ironically, I just took a break in the middle of writing the previous sentence to do just that, and felt my focus drop and my brain pull in about fifty different directions. I saw three people I know well celebrating that their new shows had sold out (I felt good for them but also a kick of guilt because it's been nearly a year since my last play and I need to crack on and write another one). I saw a playwright tweet about emotional exhaustion and then chocolate and it made me want chocolate. I also felt more guilt.

Even though I spent about five minutes scrolling through Twitter, I can't remember anything else specific I just looked at. But the only reactions I remember were the negative ones.

This is why I'm away, trying to detox from my phone and trying to break the cycle of addiction.

Dr Sally Austen thinks the best way to deal with pressure from social media, or addiction, is by adopting her dad's phrase: 'Everything in moderation. If 100-per-cent-detox is easier, then go that way, but the first choice should be moderation. What's important is being conscious about what you do instead. For example, there's a good analogy in psychology where, if a child is running along the edge of a swimming pool, there's no point shouting "Stop running". You must say "Start walking" instead. If you don't know what to turn to instead, then it can be quite a complicated process for a young person to move to in their mind.'

Taking this into consideration, if you're trying to detox from your phone, it's worth planning what you're going to replace it with ahead of time. 'Try having a book to hand, or a sketchbook, and know that not being on your phone all the time will bring angst and anxiety at first. You don't want to put your phone down and immediately pick up gin. Instead, think about all the time you gain back. Create things you can be proud of.'

She mentions a type of therapy known as solution-focused brief therapy (SFBT). This is where people describe what their life is like on a scale of 1–10. Ten is miraculous, wonderful and superlatively happy. Most of us live in this moment just a few times in our lives. Most people say they'd be happy with a seven, she says, but they're currently at a five or even a two.

'I ask them what their life would look like if they visualise it as a seven. What would it take for them to get there? I doubt they'd imagine themselves on Twitter for three hours a day. Maybe they'd be walking along a beach with a partner, or finishing making a quilt if they're a little older. You must ask yourself, what is the vision of what you'd do instead? We've got derailed from our true selves. People think, "Oh, I'll just be online for a few more minutes and then back to real life," but this is our real life. We can't forget that. Our real lives have become social media. I don't think anyone wakes up and says, "Yes, I'm going to spend six hours today scrolling the internet.'"

Real life has become social media.

Although I don't think social media has been solely to blame for my mental health, being able to see WhatsApp and feeling pressured to respond and reply to people all the time made me very anxious. This was especially true when I was dating a guy in a US time zone, as I knew the timeslots to communicate were very small, so I felt intense anxiety if I missed texting him. Guilt kicked in and even if I was on another date in the UK, I'd slip into the bathroom and send him a message.

I'm also conscious that my entire life can be viewed on social media, so anyone I'm dating can immediately view my whole career history, from articles I've written about mental health to the time I got fired as a waitress for dropping a tray of drinks over someone's head. The nice things that make me normal and sane (like, I'm really into cooking and I give a great foot rub) don't tend to make it into magazine features.

The other thing that made me leave my smartphone at home for the two-week 'detox' holiday was the fact that my screen time was creeping up. Every day, my own phone, my worst enemy, told me my phone usage was 2 per cent worse than last week. Apparently, I spent an hour and fifty-six minutes a day on my phone. This included reading my Kindle (marked as a 'productive' activity by

Apple) but the majority of time was spent using WhatsApp and Google Maps. I'm going to put this down to having friends across the city and different continents, so I have to rely a lot on messaging services, but there's no excuse for using Google Maps so much in my own city.

Adults swipe their screens approximately 2,600 times each day, and we're so used to holding our phones as we go out and about – whether that's to the gym, grocery shopping, etc. – that we feel our phones phantom vibrate. We've become so attuned to receiving notifications that we imagine people are messaging us when they're not.

I neglect Facebook, and in return it has become demanding of my attention. Now, I get notifications that simply tell me: 'You haven't been to this group in a while' or 'Someone you don't know posted in this random group.' The little red attention-grabbing notification marker catches my eye and I click on it, holding me on Facebook for another ten seconds, enough time to take in an advert or two.

So what happens inside our brains when we use a social media platform?

Social networking sites are intense, targeted, mini human societies, yet they're also responsible for a clear uptick in depression, anxiety and sleep problems. If they're just a microcosm of the best things about human life, then why would this be the case?

The thing that gives us the same hit when we have sex or eat delicious food is called dopamine, and it's also released when we use our smartphones. Dopamine is released when we have a positive social interaction, which is why when we use a social media site we want to use it again and again, like the rats in the cage that get a positive stimulus when they nudge the correct lever.

In our case, the correct lever includes nice comments and likes on pictures. We all carry a goldmine of these dopamine triggers in our pockets now, so we can enjoy these stimuli whenever we want.

We start to crave likes. Just like addicts, we think about ways we can get more and more acknowledgement from our communities. We post funny videos or statements that express political ideas or sadness, but why? Because we're addicted to notifications and the social interactions these platforms give us, even when they start to get toxic.

At first, our relationship with social media felt benign. These big tech companies got us hooked. But now, even though we know we're carrying around these devices which advertise to us and make us feel miserable, we know we can't put them down. We're hooked.

And even though we might not realise it, many of us exhibit signs of competitiveness when we use social media. That friend who was posting about being exhausted because of too many creative projects: she may have just been innocently saying how tired she was, but why tell her 4,000-plus Twitter followers? Whether she was aware of it or not, she was showing everyone how successful she was, and perhaps someone who hadn't got a creative project commissioned that year read it and felt bad.

The person who tweeted the post wouldn't have done it to make anyone else feel bad; the person who read it wouldn't have been angry at the person who tweeted. But there is an emotionally negative exchange at play here. More likely the original tweeter posted it to ask for ways to make herself feel better, and the community dutifully replied, with pictures of chocolate and hot water bottles.

Here is the crux: – Twitter – or Instagram or even Facebook – can be an extremely supportive and useful platform, while also being a negative one when it comes to feeling like I should be pushing harder and doing more. I'm part of a group of Twitter female journalists and we've moved from Twitter direct messages to a WhatsApp group.

Ultimately, this group of mostly freelance journalists look to each other for support. I've asked them for quotes and ideas; we've all swapped tips when it comes to the worst late-payers or editors who haven't treated us well.

It's a great group and it creates solidarity. And that was birthed from Twitter, which I think equals a positive social interaction.

Those who make a lot of money from social media – the YouTube billionaires, people like PewDeePie – and kids who get free holidays and trips also seem to have positive interactions with Twitter. However, there are plenty of instances of social media stars burning out, despite the high pay cheques. The *Guardian* interviewed former YouTuber Matt Lees, who he said he slid into a 'bleak, lonely' place,[6] because he doesn't think brains are meant to be interacting with so many people every day.

'The audience expects consistency. They expect frequency. Without these, it's incredibly easy to slip off the radar and lose favour with the algorithm that gave you your wings,' he told the *Guardian*'s Simon Parkin. 'When you've got thousands of people giving you direct feedback on your work, you really get the sense that something in your mind just snaps. We just aren't built to handle empathy and sympathy on that scale.'

As a result of burnout, he developed a thyroid problem and slipped into depression.

What's fascinating is how Silicon Valley parents are so aware of the dangers of the apps and programmes they're working on that they ban their own offspring from using it. Nannies have even been asked not to use their phones in front of the children for fear it'll cement bad future habits.

Many tech stars like Mark Zuckerburg and Marissa Mayer rose to prominence in the world of tech when they were still young; Zuckerberg when he was a teenager, and Mayer at twenty-five. Now many Sillicon Valley entrepreneurs have families and they're starting to realise the damage that these apps can have on them, even when there's a television involved. One tech journalist and entrepreneur, Sarah Lacy, invited friends over but found that the other tech colleagues she was hosting were extremely anti-screen.

> I have a huge TV in my living room and I think we had a
> baseball game on in the background – we weren't even watching
> it or interacting with it. But then, something curious happened;
> [a] dad, 'another figure in the tech industry', was sitting on the
> couch, holding his baby, which began looking around the room,
> and its mother obscured its view of the screen saying: 'No,
> you're not going to see television at all until you're three years
> old.' She thought the baby being on this couch would be perma-
> nently damaging to her child.[7]

Tskenya Frazer, twenty-four, was quoted in the *Guardian* as saying that using Instagram and Twitter made her feel bad about her own life when she saw friends post about promotions or work or new houses or cars. 'As soon as I woke up, I would be on Instagram, scrolling through. I would be on a page with a girl with the most perfect body.'[8]

Social media can make us feel like we're not working hard enough. It can make us feel like we're not good enough, make us want to diet, or to splurge money on holidays we can't afford. I used to scroll endlessly through Instagram, before leaving the platform for good last year. I blocked an old friend because she would constantly post pictures of herself doing gym workouts. She was scarily thin and kept captioning her pictures with how well she was feeling and doing. It made me stressed because, firstly, I looked like all her 'before' pictures, even though I'm vegetarian, eat healthily and work out a lot, and secondly, because she was celebrating her skinniness, which made me feel uncomfortable and guilty when I chose to eat a pizza rather than a bowl of spinach (which she would photograph and upload to Instagram).

Maybe she was using it to validate herself, but like in response to the associate posting about theatre success, I felt dreadful. I blocked her, but it made me realise that it is on all of us to manage ourselves and our own usage of social media. There's no point simply chastising the big social networks for getting us hooked. The drug exists now, and we must learn how to wean ourselves off it.

It would be like an alcoholic being furious at a bar for selling beer, or an overweight person angry that shops had aisles full of crisps and chocolate. Yes, alcohol companies can be careful about advertising to children, for example, and fatty food companies can reduce the amount of salt and sugars in their products, but ultimately, if we can, and if we are aware and able, it is up to us to regulate our habits and manage them and restrict them as best we can.

Paying for a hotel to nanny us is one dramatic way we can curb our social media usage. Hotels that physically remove the problem are becoming more prominent as they give us permission to stop and switch off.

There are plenty of hotels out there.

Villa Stéphanie in Baden-Baden, Germany, knows professionals want to come and switch off on holiday. This is why there's a button in the room that can switch off all Wi-Fi and electronics whenever you want.

Five years ago, I was amazed that this sort of service existed. Editors snapped up articles about digital detoxing as we reached peak social media usage. On one trip where I was writing about the pleasure of digital detox for a glossy magazine, our PR was telling us how they'd pay Instagrammers £10,000 per picture, in addition to providing the whole trip for free. Despite being hugely grateful for my free trip to Cambodia, staying in a beautiful hotel and visiting Angkor Wat, it showed me, even back in 2015, the way social media would control the media industry.

At the Aleenta resort in Hua Hin, south east from Bangkok down the Gulf of Thailand, visitors are asked to hand over their phones and electronics on arrival. At Grand Velas, a large resort on Mexico's Riviera Maya, guests who have handed their phones in and opted for the digital detox package are given a T-shirt that says 'I am doing digital detox'.

With no phone, I suddenly have a lot of free time. I haven't told any of my friends I was planning to do a digital detox – I only decided after my hefty data roaming charges at the airport. I strongly hope they don't think I am dead, crushed to death in some horrific road accident. An earthquake struck the region a few days ago and I wasn't able to mark myself as safe across social media, but I logged on to my email and told my mum. Email doesn't count as social media, so I fired off a few emails to PRs and editors for work.

A few days after, a group of flights were diverted from the region because a huge storm lashed the coast. I again sent an email to my mother, and have presumed at this point my friends are assuming the worst, especially as, for some reason, both the storm and the seismic activity have made the front page of the newspapers back home.

When I browse the prices of some digital-detox retreats, it's shocking how much we're paying to allevi-ate the stress and anxiety that comes with the £700 cost of a phone. We're paying to make ourselves miserable, and then we're paying to detox from it.

When I stopped using my smartphone, I'd try to make friends using an old phone, the old-fashioned way: '7 p.m. outside the entrance to Palomar, you know the one in town, near Wholefoods? But yeah, give me ten minutes' leeway because I'm also estimating public transport time, yeah, thanks.'

Instead, they got things like – *7?, . . . Plmor? Xx –* because typing on an old (non-predictive-text) keyboard is like getting stuck on a roundabout with no exits.

When I got another, new iPhone, it felt like ice on a hot day. It was so necessary, and for the six days before I was mugged by a thirteen-year-old on a bike, it was joy.

What I realised during my accidental detox was that using a smartphone wasn't necessary for me, but it was for my friends, for my boss and for other people to get in touch. Telling a recruiter that I'd have to do the interview via my laptop via Skype, because I'd 'run out of credit', unsurprisingly did not get me a job as head of content for a FTSE 100.

Social media, and our reliance on it, and society's reliance on us using it, needs to end. I'm in my hotel room and I'm watching lightning flash across the sky. From my terrace I can see the white light flicker across the waves and reflect in the pool that stretches navy towards the white strip of sand, lit by every jolt of electricity.

Along the beach, I see the flash of cameras as hotel residents, leaning out from their balconies, snap the sky. When they get home, they will remember standing on the terrace, getting frustrated that their high-spec phone camera hasn't captured the heat, the tension, the headaches that the storm brought.

I know because I used to be that person, hoping that the sunset burning purple in my car's rear-view mirror as I sped Thelma-and-Louise-style down a long country road would look just as good on Facebook.

But then I stopped mid-upload one day. Who would want to see this picture? Who would feel bad because I had experienced a holiday while maybe they hadn't been able to take a vacation for a year because they were paying for childcare?

So I stopped trying to take the perfect picture, and stopped trying to share memories. Instead, I made myself put the phone down and try to remember them, not record them.

I no longer feel anxious about other people's lives, because even when mine is average and boring, I know it's OK, because the planet will spin around and it'll be my time again soon.

Career

I wanna get something off my chest. For the past 8 months whenever I see people I know, it's always "you seem to be doing so well! you're smashing it!!" (which is really nice, thank you!) but never a "how are you??" and this is one of the ways being online has ruined my MH . . . [Mental Health]

It seems like such an ungrateful thing to complain about!! but honestly since when does a career correlate with personal wellbeing? why are we so drawn to making this comparison? are we really all defined by our work? it makes me go into a bit of an identity crisis i won't lie

I feel INSANE even talking about this but in ways I feel more alone that I have before! people will ask you how you are but as soon as you start telling them how you ACTUALLY are they switch off! they refuse to believe the version of you they've built in their head doesn't exist

If we keep reducing people's worth to their online output or latest project, we're a) at a danger of dehumanising them and b) perpetuating the cycle of defining people by their status, career or material wealth. Think about this the next time you say "you seem to be doing well!"

Diyora Shadijananova (Twitter, Aug 2020)

You're at a gig. You meet some new people. You're dancing and pumped and want more of the music, more of the songs; you're vibing.

Then, out of the blue, just as you turn to face your new best friends, sweaty and beaming, you hear:

'So, what do you do?'

No matter where you are – the pub, walking the dog, queuing for popcorn in the cinema, standing idly on a street corner – someone will appear from nowhere, make some small talk and then hit you with The Question. Apparently, we're only as interesting as our job.

I've stopped asking people what they do, and this throws the room. Whoever you're talking to will spend ages trying to drop it in, mentioning their long hours, talking about a mythical 'client'. They often accompany the mention of 'client' with an ironic eye-roll, so you know they're a corporate wanker but they hate themselves for it.

What appears to be a casual, innocuous question is laden with supposition, and it can also be bloody stressful to answer it.

This is especially true if you're in a room full of paediatric doctors and someone asks you what you do, and you're like, 'Um, I'm a writer.' Then they go quiet and you know they're like, 'Wow, have you ever considered doing something less self-absorbed? Like, I've held an actual human heart in my hand. I've *saved lives*.'

There's the polite nod, the half-smile, and then they spot someone else over your head and wave at them, scarpering from what they imagine will be a light, flimsy conversation. The Bridget-Jones-in-a-roomful-of-lawyers conversation.

I'm also not a fan of this question because the converse is if you're in a room full of chartered surveyors (or similar), they'll think being a journalist is really fun and interesting, and will do anything to escape talking about chartered surveying. So, you end up becoming the entertainment for a while as people fire questions at you like:

'Have you ever met Obama?'

(No)

'Have you ever been to the Oscars?'

(No)

And so on.

For my friends who work in the creative industries, who do odd jobs to supplement their work as illustrators/ actors/photographers, and meet people who do not work in the creative industries, the question can feel all the more loaded as those who are schooled in 'polite conversation' try to make the best of a chat everyone knows is going nowhere.

'Oh, you work in a gym? That sounds interesting.'

'No, it's not really, I just log people in and out.'

'But you must get to do loads of fun workouts.'

'Not really, because I'm at work.'

If you've ever worked in the creative industries and you go to a party where, inexplicably, everyone works in banking, you can be sure you'll endure some patronising conversations where they think they're showing a real interest in your work as an actor/writer/singer, but you present zero opportunities for networking so you're not really worth talking to.

It can feel at times like everyone in London, Los Angeles, Hong Kong, New York or Sydney is career-focused, but perhaps that's because almost everyone who migrated to the world's most significant cities did so to work. Being asked again and again what you do can make you doubt who you are. No one cares whether you're a good person. They want to know if you can make money. They want to know if you've mingled with celebrities. They want to know if you're awesome. And frankly, what if we're OK with being good enough? What if we're happy not being promoted because our work–life balance is on point? Then we fail the 'dinner-party test'.

Failing the dinner-party test

The 'dinner-party test' is shorthand for constantly asking each other what we do. Its essence is: are you interesting enough to sit next to at a dinner party, or, when you mention your job, do the other person's eyes glaze over? It's not about money, because bankers, lawyers and anyone who has to wear shiny shoes to the office immediately fail this.

Last year, I decided to fail this test too. I decided to embrace failing it, celebrate failing it, because I stopped being a journalist, which is all at once a very cool job for passing the dinner-party test, but terrible at the having-a-comfortable-stable-life test.

There's an element of narcissism involved in staying with a job for so long because you don't want to admit that you're now doing what sounds like an extremely dull job.

When dreams come true, but they suck

I desperately wanted to be a journalist. Ever since I was a really young kid, I did what all baby journalists did: I wrote little books and fake newspapers for my toys. But the reality has never matched the dream. There's more rewriting press releases and copying and pasting wire copy into articles than non-journalists will ever know.

Over the past few years, I've drifted out of journalism proper. Instead, I dabble, writing the odd travel piece and theatre feature. I can't stop being a journalist. I have too many questions and I want to stay engaged with the rest of the world, showcasing stories and people and places. But I've also found that I crave working with people and, ya know, getting paid, so I began to look at working creatively in an institution. I've dabbled in advertising, social-humanitarian, tech and engineering, and know now that snobbery reigns. You become a sell-out.

Being a sell-out was the worst thing I could imagine for years. I used to speak to press officers as a (very) young journalist and think, 'God, they must hate their life,' because I was a snob. I used to be proud of working my ass off and putting every hour of the day into becoming a journalist. I made sacrifices and I looked down on those who hadn't, because I was an asshole. And then I hit my late-twenties and realised that this dream wasn't viable for normal people. I (obviously) had no trust fund coming my way, no pension and barely any savings, and I thought, very immediately, fuck this. I don't want to live the way I am now for the next forty years, because it's not worth it. It was a gutting, sad realisation that there I was, nearly thirty, grinding the dreams of young me into the ground with my heel, but if I didn't do it now, someone would do it for me later.

And seriously, fuck it. So, I sold out.

For the first time in ten years I have a pension. It only has £375 in it, but it's a real-life pension, which suggests (incorrectly) I am a grown-up adult. My 'boring' corporate job also affords me a parking spot for my bike in central London (if I join a year-long waiting list, but still, the thrill!). Finally, there's budget to throw into projects I actually want to do.

I'm also a sucker for random employee benefits, like the free breakfasts my old ad agency used to give us. Things like dogs being allowed in the office. Ironically, the private corporate life we all jeered at in newsrooms actually allowed a great work–life balance.

Most of my twenties were spent working in newsrooms which had no money, so also had zero benefits.

One office I worked in had no natural light, because the window blinds remained pulled down at all times. There was no microwave or kettle, so we had to buy food each day. When I worked there, I had to knock £20 off my day-rate to take the breakfast, lunch, snacks and coffees into consideration.

Another company I worked for, albeit for just seven months because there were myriad random issues, which included allegations that the magazine had connections with a controversial Korean Christian preacher who some have described as a sect-leader, didn't have a shower.[1] Arriving at 6 a.m. on some days to cover the Asia beat after a fifty-minute bike ride (my salary was so low there was no way I could afford the Tube and my weekly groceries), I had to 'shower' in the disabled toilet by wringing a face-cloth over my head.

For some reason, this particular publication, which had nothing to do with finance, was located in a Canary Wharf tower block, in London's financial centre. We shared a floor with an international consultancy, who offensively always had elaborate fruit baskets wrapped in ribbons waiting for them outside their doors. Not just mangos and bananas, but pineapples and dragon fruit. Real exotic stuff.

When we walked to the lift, we could see they had ping pong and, also, possibly a foosball table. In contrast, we had our summer party in our narrow-boat-sized kitchen which had no natural light.

Whether you get extra benefits or not, from my experience working across multiple industries, and for both the public and private sectors, it's clear that we're all working a lot.

Too much and too hard.

What would happen if we all decided to fail the dinner-party test and just decided to do jobs we actually wanted to do, rather than ones we thought sounded successful from a societal (or parental) point of view?

Catherine was one of those people who eventually said 'enough's enough'.

'When I was at university, I was like a demon possessed. I barely had any friends because I spent the entire time in the library, studying,' says Catherine James, twenty-nine. 'I'd go and see all my tutors all the time because I was obsessed with getting it all right. I always wanted to be a teacher, so I applied to Homerton, Cambridge after I got a first. I thought they might have given me an offer later by mistake, and when I got there, I was just surrounded by all these hugely intelligent people and I felt so stupid.

'When I started working as a teacher, I was getting into work at 7.30 a.m. and leaving at 7.30 p.m. I quickly realised that I wasn't the right personality for teaching. There was always something extra to do, whether to mark another book or add some graphics to a PowerPoint. It felt like my work was never done. My deputy head told me I needed to look after my boundaries, and I wanted to be a good teacher so much. But I quickly realised that a tired, exhausted, underweight teacher was no good for that job.'

Catherine had experienced anorexia since she was thirteen, and had been hospitalised six weeks into her A levels. She was starting to learn that periods of stress lead to relapses in her eating disorder, and she left her job as a teacher. 'I went into retail. I was no good for anything else. Professionals signed an intervention and said I needed to go back to hospital.'

She knew, like I did, that hospital wasn't the best place for her. 'Over time, with an amazing therapist, I began to see, for all my academic achievement, that I had failed spectacularly at the most important things in life. I'd never had a relationship because I was too busy working, never been on a girls' holiday, never got drunk, and I only had two friends from university. It became clear that I'd sacrificed the things that really mattered.'

Then gradually, with 'adequate nutrition and clarity of thought', Catherine realised that anorexia and high-achieving were no longer going to be her 'thing'. 'I realised that, after everything, after all the long days at work, and days spent in the library, I suddenly had no career and no job, despite all my hard work, no social life, and I felt incredibly lost. A bit betrayed. It felt like I'd been lied to by everyone, by school – that if I work hard now, I would get a good job later. I felt stupid for believing it. The thing is, as you get older, you see everyone else who didn't achieve at school, and they're doing fine now, and I'm not.'

Her therapy helped her realise some crucial things. 'On my deathbed, do I want to be known as the girl who worked really hard until she died? Or do I want to be known as a kind person who had time for friends?'

She's changed her job to a more 'average' one, and it's one she feels much more in control of. She's now a community navigator, working with frequent users of A&E to look at their social problems to reduce their attendance. 'With this job, I don't feel like I need to do more. I won't be staying after 16.30, and if there's something that still needs to be done, I'll do it tomorrow. I'm not anxious any more and I know I can do it tomorrow. There's always more time, and I realise, now, that my job is not my life. I enjoy it, I do it, and I do it well. But no one else is going to care if I've worked until eight.'

Catherine has acknowledged that her epiphany has probably come too late, but her priority is now on becoming a more rounded person. 'I know that working long hours and being stressed means I don't eat properly, so I need to look after myself. I will lie in. And I know I'm not a morning person. And I will take that time. And I am much happier, and I am much happier with my average life and job as opposed to being anxious and stressed and tormented.'

It is possible for us to overwork ourselves to death, which is all the more reason why we should take our foot off the pedal sometimes.

Karoshi – when we literally work ourselves to death

The first case of *karoshi* was recorded in 1969 in Japan, when a twenty-nine-year-old man keeled over at work. He'd had a stroke while working in the shipping department of a large newspaper company after working immense hours. The term was eventually coined in the 1980s after young execs with no prior history of illness dropped like flies as they died prematurely of heart attacks and strokes. The International Labour Organization (ILO), part of the UN, compiled a report that documented some key aspects of *karoshi*, in which it was identified that it's impossible to work seven days a week, twelve hours a day, without experiencing any negative repercussions.

Karoshi literally means 'overwork death' in Japanese. The cause is, unsurprisingly, too much work, and is a growing problem across Japan and other parts of Asia where the boss's word is law. Working hard is a matter of family pride and honour, in addition to a desire to do well: burnout across these cultures isn't uncommon. You only have to look at the dedication to schooling in Japan, Korea and Singapore, where students regularly spend full days at school followed by evenings at night college, to understand that this pattern of behaviour tends to follow well into the working life.

In Japan, other cases of *karoshi* the ILO found included Ms D., a twenty-two-year-old nurse, who died from a heart attack after thirty-four hours of continuous duty five times a month. Another described Mr B., a bus driver who worked 30,000 hours in a year and did not have a day off for fifteen days before he also died of a heart attack. To put this in context, if we had a 37.5-hour working week, and took no holidays, the average person would work just 1,950 hours a year. The ILO says the phenomenon is not a medical condition, but a social one. 'The media have frequently used the word because it emphasizes the sudden deaths (or disabilities) caused by overwork which should be compensated. *Karoshi* has become an important social problem in Japan.'[1]

They also refer to karojisatsu, or suicide as a direct result of overwork. Examples of work triggers include not being able to achieve the high demands set by the company, being bullied or forced to resign. The ILO cites the example of staff – previously loyal to the company – being forced to resign because of cutbacks.

And this certainly isn't solely a Japanese phenomenon any more.

According to a Gallup poll conducted in 2019, some of the most stressed countries weren't necessarily ones you might expect. Based on the question 'Did you feel stress or anxiety yesterday?', Greece tops the list of countries with the most-stressed population.[2] Its stereo-typical vibe of a relaxed, Mediterranean culture is evidently being affected by an uneven government, high unemployment and a refugee crisis bubbling away on its doorstop.

After Greece, the poll found that the Philippines, Tanzania, Albania, Iran, Sri Lanka, the United States, Uganda, Costa Rica and then Rwanda made the top-ten list of most stressed countries. Stress and anxiety have no boundaries: poor working practices, employment law and overwork can create cauldrons of stress among a country's workforce, leading to negative societal outcomes.

Fifty-nine per cent of us experience stress at work in the UK. While it's most prevalent for higher earners (those earning over £40,000), 21 per cent of us experience moderate to high amounts of stress several times a week.[3] And for what? Whose benefit? And why?

The bravado of long hours

In my first job, which was in the UK's civil service, I was, for some reason I can't remember now, required to get on my bike and cycle at 2 a.m. into Whitehall, where I worked on a speech I didn't understand. I can't remember if it was because my boss had a young child so couldn't come in, but I do remember being there in the middle of the night and having to wave my arms around to keep the lights from going off.

Even though it was just a one-off, I remember feeling physically sick the next day as I tried to navigate the tiredness, but also the smug sense of bravado of having come in to work at 2 a.m. Working long hours has always been, but hopefully won't always be, seen as a sign of success.

I dated a banker once who talked about the state of permanent exhaustion he lived in. The way he told it sounded macho – who could stay in the office longer? But then weekends would involve heavy drinking to try to forget about the week's brutal workload. By all accounts, it was a never-ending cycle where he needed to go crazy to shake off all the stress. His flatmates would drop hundreds of pounds on booze and gadgets just to achieve a sense of normality, leading to increased pressure to get the bonuses they needed to keep up with their wild lifestyles.

In April 2016, twenty-nine-year-old Michael Halligan typed 'I have cracked' on his phone, before jumping eighty feet to his death from City of London bar Coq d'Argent. The bar had become notorious as a jump spot for overworked businesspeople, despite Coq d'Argent employing security guards who questioned anyone who was alone and erecting six-foot-high fences around the periphery and making it very difficult for anyone to exit any other way than down the stairs or in the lift.

With main courses between the £27–£45 mark, it seems like an opulent and tragic place to make one's final stand. In 2012 a businesswoman leapt to her death, a restaurant critic jumped in 2015, and security guards were from then on told to question anyone they saw standing alone on the terrace.

Working in the City, where long hours and lack of sleep can drive you mad, coupled with boozy nights and drug binges, can lead to situations not unlike the Japanese trait of karojisatsu.

Hyper-productivity and the trait of 'always being on' has become the norm for many young professionals. As such, we're experiencing burnout at much higher levels than generations before us.

Speaking from experience, and anecdotally from friends, there's a real fear in saying 'no' to projects, in case you're not asked to work for editors or employers again, and it's often the case that multiple opportunities come at once, which can lead to spectacular burnout.

My very own spectacular burnout

In May 2019 I'd just had a pitch accepted by a production company for BBC Radio 4, I had to complete a book proposal, another book was out for consideration and was being turned down by agent after agent, I was working every weekend for a national newspaper and full-time during the week for a multinational company. In addition to that, I had a play about to be shown at a theatre in London and was trying to manage the press and marketing for it, and was also, on top of all this, trying to deal with a break-up and moving into a new house away from the flat I'd bought with my ex.

Careers are tough.

I delivered two bad pieces of work. One was a book and another was a proposal for a white paper.

Reader, I nearly died. And guess what? I knew they each had issues, but rather than asking for an extended deadline, I worked nights and forced myself to get something, anything, out.

I could feel the anxiety and pain building up. This is what it felt like to be successful – to have your projects accepted and for people to say yes. But what I really needed was to say 'Thank you, but no; would you consider me pushing the deadlines back by a few months?'

Like so many people who rely on two jobs (or more) to get by, I've never had a nine-to-five. I'm almost always working on projects in addition to what looks like my day job, either to pay the rent or to try to prove myself as a 'creative'.

We work too long and too hard in the UK, and there

are the stats to prove it. The TUC (Trades Union Congress) found that workers in the UK put more than two hours extra in each week than the next hardest-working counterparts. But just because they work longer, doesn't mean they work smarter. The UK, despite putting more hours in, lags behind Germany and Denmark in terms of efficiency.

The TUC found that it would take sixty-three years for workers to get the same amount of free time as other countries in the EU. Our average forty-two-hour working week is at direct odds with the thirty-seven hours worked in Denmark and thirty-nine in Holland, Italy, Belgium and France.

Sweden, commonly lauded as being one of the best places for work–life balance, also has, by law, something called *vab*, which is a day you take off if your child is sick. If any salary is lost during the day – for example if they're a freelancer or contractor – the state will reimburse them for 80 percent of any lost earnings.

Shared parental leave has also been a little misunderstood by foreign press, who celebrate Sweden for having very generous leave packages. New parents are given 480 days, which can amount to nearly two years of workdays, and there are 'three so-called daddy-months, which can only be taken by one partner and are lost if not taken'.[4]

One worker who moved back to Sweden, having

worked in Dublin, said in *Our Chemist* magazine: 'I didn't feel that parents could leave before 4 p.m. in Dublin. I get the feeling that it's much more relaxed here.

'I think we are much more efficient during the day. There's so much more lazing around, especially in the United States. They put in a lot of work hours, but they're so inefficient.'[5]

Britain has another fun clause that is designed to make our working lives hellish. The forty-eight-hour opt-out clause. If you've ever worked in the restaurant business or a company based on shift work, you may be aware of it. If you're over eighteen, you can be offered the chance to work the EU maximum recommended forty-eight hours a week. Now Britain has left the EU, who knows how many hours British workers will be expected to put in, but there's always going to be an expectation that they'll be expected to push far more than the average.

The forty-eight-hour opt-out is voluntary and must be done in writing.[6] When I worked as a waitress for Strada, I opted out and frequently worked sixty-five-hour weeks, which included double shifts. I did this in addition to my MA and I was tired, but the low hourly wage gave me so little cash it would have been almost pointless working for any fewer hours.

Plus, although allegedly there can be no threat of being

fired if you don't sign it, I've worked for one restaurant where the fewer hours you worked, the worse tables you were given, so you never received tips. As a nineteen-year-old server relying on tips rather than the £30-a-shift pay cheque (for seven hours' work), that can feel super-demoralising.

Anyone who gets squeamish when they think about how many hours they work shouldn't look to London. The average Londoner works for three weeks longer each year than other Brits, simply by putting in more overtime.

The average working week, taking into consideration part-time workers, is thirty-one hours; in London it's thirty-three. This is due to the concentration of highly skilled professionals who tend to get drawn in to working longer hours because of an intense working culture. And Londoners don't just spend more time at work. They also have the longest average commute across the UK, with an average of seventy-five minutes each day.[5] It should come as no surprise that during the Covid-19 lockdown, not having to commute to the office made many people's lives more bearable, as commutes have been found to negatively affect our wellbeing.[7]

But is it worth it? Are we getting the success we feel we deserve by putting the extra hours in? Is working until we literally drop dead going to make us feel more content?

However ridiculous and rhetorical that might sound, the answer is actually . . . maybe.

Way back in 2006, researchers from the University of Gothenburg published a paper that revealed the secret to happiness might actually be hard work. Working towards a goal can bring more life satisfaction than actually achieving it, the study found, but what goes hand-in-hand with that is a strong relationship. I know that when I was ploughing on with my first book, I was deeply interested in the project. My mood felt better, I felt like life had more purpose, and as soon as I'd submitted the draft there was a significant gap. I'd reclaimed my evenings and weekends, sure, but it had taken up so much time (it was a book on hiking and swimming so I had a lot of places to check out) there were a few weeks when I was browsing websites wondering if I should take up ice hockey as a new hobby.

We probably remember those languid summer-exam periods, tapping our pencils on the tables in the library as we urged the calendar to click forward so exams would be over. When exams were over, although there was a feeling of elation, do you remember the feeling of phantom guilt?

Where you'd suddenly feel panic that you should be studying but then remember that exams were over, and you were off school/university/college for eight more weeks? Was there any better feeling? Similar to accidentally setting your alarm on a Saturday morning and then realising you actually have nowhere to be.

Bliss.

A world happiness poll which took information from 150 countries in 2017 concurred with the earlier Gottenberg study. The study explored a concept called 'subjective well-being', which, in layman's speak, is simply 'happiness'. Pollsters Gallup used the Cantril Ladder, which measures happiness from 0–10: the top rung is where you're smashing life and super-happy, while the bottom of the ladder is where your subjective well-being is wavering precariously.[8]

Those working blue-collar jobs tend to rank lowest on the Cantril Ladder, while those in white-collar professions rank highest. This is hardly surprising, as blue-collar jobs tend to have more precarious shift patterns and lower pay than white-collar professions. And yet, during the Covid-19 crisis, other than NHS workers, blue-collar jobs were seen as most important and most vital. What the study found was that having a job is far more important to a person's well-being than not having one: unemployed and self-employed people tended to respond more negatively to questions. Working hard boils down to fulfilment, researchers found. Dr Bengt Bruelde, lead researcher at Gothenburg University's philosophy department, determined: 'The important thing is to remain active: From our research, the people who were most active got the most joy. It may sound tempting to relax on a beach, but if you do it for too long it stops being satisfying.'[9]

This goes some way to explaining why, when I'm working in a job where there's little to do, I derive very little pleasure from it. In fact, it's more likely to send us into a state of anxiety or frustration than not.

Professor Sir Cary Cooper, CBE, 50th Anniversary Professor of Organizational Psychology and Health Alliance at Manchester Business School, University of Manchester, has found that being underworked is just as detrimental to mental health and happiness as being over-worked. 'Underload can be a problem – you don't get the stimulation you need. Pressure helps you up to a bit – we all have different pressure points, but a little is useful.'

He explains that underload, or not having enough to do, may affect you because you lack stimulation and you feel as though there's not enough pressure on you to achieve a task, which can be debilitating. 'If the workplace doesn't challenge you enough, and they give you a routine job that equals high levels of underload, in turn you may feel less valued, less challenged, and you may also stress about things like losing your job. After all, if you're not working, should you keep your job?'

So, hard work is shown to increase fulfilment, but does hard work ever really pay off? We've already seen that countries like Germany and Denmark work fewer hours than the UK and yet have greater efficiency, so is there any point in working to exhaustion? What do we want our gravestones to say? That Joan sent 200 emails an hour or that she was loved by her family and friends?

People who do too much hard work, which includes working overtime and working in their free time to meet demands (as half of all EU workers do), are less happy, more prone to stress and anxiety, and, crucially, experience lower job-satisfaction. According to authors of a report published in the *Industrial and Labor Relations Review*, employees who invest more effort in their work report receiving less recognition and fewer growth opportunities. And they experience less job security. So increased work effort not only predicts reduced well-being, it even predicts inferior career-related outcomes.[10]

The authors of the report found that overtime doesn't pay because you have less time to recover and work at your highest level if you're always putting overtime in. Plus, they make the point that bonuses are often awarded by looking at how well your colleagues are doing too, so if there's a culture of overtime then what's going to set you apart?

Excessive long-term effort is exhausting and means you often can't perform at your highest level. When I burned out in May 2019, I didn't get good feedback on some of my projects and I was struggling with my day job. I handed in an article with a sentence that didn't finish, and even though I'd edited it twice, my tired eyes had just completely missed it. For a longer project, where the paper's structure was key, I was unable to take a step back and work out what needed to be done to it.

When even Uber, the company who wants us all to clock off from job one and onto job two, changes its slogan from 'work smarter, harder and longer' to just 'work smarter and harder' you know something's up.

Most of us know that working for long hours is detrimental to our health. We know it doesn't reap rewards and we know it could cause long-term physical and mental health problems. Yet why do we all keep going? Why are we all so proud to tell anyone who'll listen how busy we are?

Anyone whose salary has quickly increased knows that money is less of a motivator than we think it should be.

Josh, a friend living in Bristol who earned £25,000 when he started work and is now on £77,000, says he barely notices the difference. 'The thing is, I've upgraded my whole life. When I was twenty-two, I took the bus to save money and now I drive. So I have car costs. I was happy to [house]share with four other men/boys and live in squalor. Now I need my own flat. I have a mortgage in a nice area. When I was twenty-two I ate pasta, I think, for every meal. Really basic stuff: penne and tomato sauce, maybe with some ham if it was reduced. Breakfast was whatever was in the cupboard at work. Now I go to a fancy gym, need to fill up on higher-protein items because of it, and I go out a lot during the week, paying for dates. Basically, I have about the same disposable income now as I did when I was twenty-two, and I don't feel any happier about the big things if I'm honest.'

Speaking from my own experience, I think it's because we're all trapped in this cycle that's been created for us from birth. We are so used to the rhythm of clocking in and out from age four (or even younger, if you went to nursery) that it's understandable few of us know a different way to live.

We work hard because when we worked hard as children we were praised: we like praise. Work and the rewards cycle is our very own Pavlov's dogs situation, where we crave being told we are doing well and being rewarded, whether that's financially, with a more senior title, or the addition of a corner office.

Our careers, promotion and financial advancement fuel our need to consume and to buy. We need to buy a house, so we need a stable job. There's poor infrastructure in so many areas and cities around the world that we need to buy a car, and to buy that car and pay the monthly repayments, you guessed it, we need a steady job. This isn't rocket science, or even anything new, but I find it helpful to have an occasional reminder that we're working so we can spend and consume and keep big businesses alive, many of which thank us by not paying tax.

If this sounds bleak, maybe it is. We consume because we get a warm, happy feeling when we buy things. It can feel, at times, that the impulse to consume is in our DNA. In the US, consumers spend $5,400 dollars a year on impulse buys, and 70 per cent of that is on food.[11] In Canada, that's around $3,000, while a study conducted by Nielsen found that 52 per cent of Thais had also made a big impulse buy, followed by 44 per cent of Chinese. This can be seen on Black Friday, the big shopping day after American Thanksgiving, when hundreds of thousands of people storm the shops, picking up 'bargains' that most probably only decided they needed on the day.

It comes from an innate survival instinct: fear of scarcity. When we were on the plains, if we saw something delicious in a tree, we needed it there and then, even if it wasn't what we'd gone hunting for. Who knows when the next kill would be? Ryan Howell, an associate professor of psychology at San Francisco State University in California in the US, told CNBC that the impulse to buy is a survival method. 'If you see something that seems to be running in short supply, you're going to get it,' Howell said. 'When we see a "50 per cent off" clearance price tag, that scarcity impulse kicks into gear.'

Over $13.6 trillion is owed on credit cards in the US;

in the UK, the average person has £15,400 racked up on theirs.[12] Debt can kickstart anxiety like nothing else. Friends in debt have taken on second jobs to try to reduce their credit card bills, only to find themselves aware of the extra money in their accounts tempting them to spend it. We work to spend, and many of us spend to cope with the daily drudgery.

Hey, I never claimed this was going to be a book filled with hilarity.

It's not just physical attainments either. For many of us, our sense of identity is built into our job titles. We 'work in media' or we're 'bankers'. For most people, jobs can be a shorthand for personality: they give us stereotypes that we lean into and find ourselves emulating. The work-hard-party-hard stereotype propagated by the media isn't helped by clock-off Friday drinks in ad agencies, or the constant evening drinks and events you get invited to as a journalist.

Do we know whether we are kind people? Do we know whether we're dependable or caring or loving or evil? Do any of us, between rushing to meetings, friend-dates, meeting a deadline, have time to know who we are? Or are most of us caught up on this wheel which has the inevitable ending of not knowing who we really are, but pretending to succumb to stereotypes and what society expects of us?

Maybe it's time to start a revolution. Maybe it's time to ask why, in the twenty-first century, when engines and machines and AI and technology were meant to make our lives so much simpler, we're still working the same way as we were in the 1930s, complete with the same-length day and the same-length week? Back in the 1930s, John Maynard Keynes predicted that one day some countries would be so rich that each man would be able to work ten to fifteen hours less a week.

Of course, that hasn't happened.

Even after the Covid-19 lockdown, which showed we were all perfectly capable of working from home, The Office retained its (false) aura of productivity. We were hurried back there, because in the modern world, that's where we've always been.

We work longer hours and our countries and companies get richer: that's just how capitalism works. In turn, sanitation has improved. Our health service, literacy rates and child mortality rates have all improved. In fact, it's also how communism works, as even Karl Marx believed that living well meant working well, too.

We choose to work doggedly, relentlessly, because sure, we enjoy it, we enjoy the feeling of being busy, but we're also trapped in a weird work prison. Work is everywhere, and the opportunity to work is so tantalising we can't get enough of it. Our smartphones ping through the latest work email that we feel the need to reply to instantly, then more reports and studies and tasks come in on top of that.

A few pioneering companies understand that a four-day week is possible. Technology is making our lives easier, say tech companies. But the vast majority of businesses – whether that's a drill factory in Manchester or a printing company in Teesside – are still working on a five-days-a-week, nine-to-five mentality. Within those companies there will be people doing overtime and there will be people pretending to look busy but who can't be fired because they've been there for twenty-seven years and they'd 'have to get the unions in if they want me to leave'.

Is it because work is more of a habit than a necessity, and we've got trapped on a treadmill that feels impossible to get off?

Gaining perspective helped me to stop panicking about deadlines.

When I worked at my old company, my boss used to say: 'We're not saving lives here.'

No doubt he meant this as a jocular Hey, don't stress about the deadlines, it doesn't really matter. But in fact, it made me despair as I had a melodramatic crisis: what is the point of me and my job?

And realising that the answer was there isn't one, was terrifying at first. When I started out as a journalist, all I wanted to do was uncover human rights abuses. It's very fair to say I no longer do that. Occasionally, I'll file a piece about a great ice-cream parlour, or why Baltimore is actually a fun city to visit.

But other than bringing a little joy into people's lives if they like ice cream, my life has no real global use or function.

If there's anything more likely to tip you into a chasm of despair than realising your job is completely pointless, it's that.

But also, it's helpful. Because I really do stress less. So the head of department needs to see a report on what font to use for a report due in two weeks, like, by 3 p.m.? Why? I do the work and I do it well, but I'm not going to stress because it's totally irrelevant. Instead, I've pledged to try to change the system. Rather than writing a report on why we should change the font, simply changing it and giving reasons after would save a lot of time and agony.

I've realised, working in a corporate environment, that everyone is very consumed by very small things that don't really matter. And I'm one of them now. And actually, it takes an extraordinary amount of pressure off life, because really, most of us have totally pointless jobs.

All you're doing is making someone else richer. Relax.

OK, so you're using your Harvard degree to redesign a logo for a tech giant? Excellent, but everyone will hate it, and the end result is . . . that tech giant just gets richer anyway.

Surgeon, supermarket staff, delivery driver, teacher, nurse, plumber? You guys carry on.

If this sounds depressing, see it as freeing instead. You get a salary, sick pay, a team of (probably) fun people to work with, and a sense of identity created for you by your larger workplace. And I'm not being facetious – it's been a huge pleasure for me to go from the world of self-employed to a big business because I am part of the whole, rather than the beginning, middle and the end.

And if there's anything better than relieving your anxiety by knowing your rent will be paid even if you file a deadline ten minutes late, it's working as part of a team.

For the last nine years, I've never been able to switch off. I've always had to reply promptly, refile, hunt for new images, find a new angle, rewrite a standfirst, pitch and everything else that would help me pay rent.

I may not have that dinner-party cachet now, but honestly, the next person who looks over my shoulder when they ask me what I do because I'm not cool or interesting enough, that's fine by me. Because I'm actually, I think . . . happier.

Mental Health

If you haven't sliced your wrists with a champagne glass at your boyfriend's best friend's wedding, and then had to fly home early and spend three days alone, then you haven't lived, folks.

Remember that month I told you about? May 2019? Well May 2018 was nearly as bad. And at the end of it was a wedding in Italy, full of people I didn't know. I was on the cusp of a mental breakdown, brought on by a growing to-do list and an inability to say no to friends, projects and people. On my knees in that hotel room in Italy, I mopped at the blood, my brain fizzing like it had short-circuited.

Looking back at that day a few years later, I realised that I needed someone to take me, hold me, let me sob it out, and calmly tell me everything was going to be OK until my brain stopped fizzing.

Since the wedding in Italy, since standing on a bridge in London, I know how to recognise what feels like brain freeze pouring over my head the second anything gets too much. To know that that's the moment I need to step outside, away from the situation, and that sometimes it's OK to just walk away, breathe and deal with the weird repercussions later.

Mind, the UK's biggest mental health charity, explains that the number of people with mental health problems hasn't altered that much, but the number of people who report them and the way people try to cope with them is changing.[2]

The number of people who self-harm or attempt suicide is increasing too: our ability to cope with what the world throws at us is impoverished.

But the world is difficult because, as we've seen in the chapter on nepotism, it just doesn't work the way we ever expected it to or thought that it would.

Perhaps with social media, a twenty-four-hour press and people sharing their lives through a flurry of books and TV shows and plays, we are more aware of society's failings. The media shares stories of corrupt bosses and pulls back the curtain on companies not paying tax, and exposes the prime minister taking an expensive holiday on a tropical island while more people than ever rely on food banks.

Whereas these incidences have always happened; they've happened behind closed doors. Now racists are being called out, gender-pay inequality is being plastered across front pages and NHS funding shortages are laid bare. This leads us to challenge those who have rarely been challenged in the past, at least in the UK and US.

This fuels anger and frustrations, which can in turn contribute to eroding strong mental health. An anger we've seen tip over and burn into phoney politics, where the disenfranchised fight back, doing things like protest-vote to leave the EU and vote for ridiculous politicians who claimed to represent those people with quieter voices.

These pressures tip into mental health issues, when we start to work out how we can reflect and cope and fit 'making ourselves better' into our busy lives.

Every seven years the UK government conducts a mental health survey to see whether there's been a change in the number of people who are experiencing mental health disorders. In 2016, the most recent survey, 5.9 out of 100 people in the UK had anxiety, 4.4 had PTSD and 1.3 out of 100 experienced OCD.

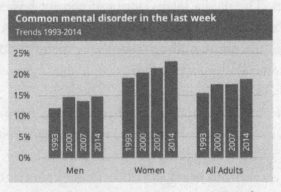

Chart from House of Commons Library[3]

Bipolar and borderline personality disorder tend to be measured over a person's lifetime, according to Mind, as you can't just 'be cured' but learn how to live with it.[4] Two in 100 people have bipolar while 2.4 people out of 100 have borderline personality disorder.

These figures only comprise people living in private housing, however. They don't take into consideration those living in prison, spending a long time in hospital, those in sheltered housing or homeless people. Rates among these groups of people, who may lack stability or who are dealing with a bigger picture, tend to be significantly higher.

Twenty-six per cent of women in prison were seen for a mental health condition while incarcerated, while 25 per cent had symptoms that seemed like psychosis, the Prison Reform Trust reported.[5] According to the Harvard Public Health review, the rate of suicide among homeless people in the US is around nine times the average of the general population.[6]

Mental health is still taboo, especially among the older generation. There's a silence that shrouds a conversation whenever it's mentioned.

When my dad had depression, family members, although extremely supportive, would talk about his 'illness' as though he had flu. This was as recent as 2004/5, and although my wonderful mother initially talked about depression as being 'just a state of mind' and that being happy is just 'mind over matter', she now knows it's a real thing.

This is all about education and changing society's narrative, which is increasingly relevant as more of us drop like flies as the world throws challenges that feel impossible to overcome.

Among contemporaries, if I'm not feeling up to going out because my mind is all over the place, I no longer say it's because I feel sick or because I have period pains. I say it's because I'm having a horrible mental health day. On days like that, it can be hard to lift myself off the couch, or do anything other than plug into a podcast and walk down to the Thames, pacing along the river as I will my brain to just pull itself together and be more sociable.

Those days aren't great days, but I wake up the next day, so there must be something right working up there. My extraordinary friends have got me through the last year, no doubt.

After coming out of hospital there was a whirl of meetups, of theatre shows, of going to see absolutely terrible films, of conversations about nothing and no one, trying to pretend the world inside my head didn't exist. I didn't give myself time to dwell for too long on why, just a few weeks earlier, I'd wanted to step out into nothing and fall to my death.

Making mental health less taboo

Mental health has always been a taboo subject because it means you're brushing up against the expected way of thinking, and nobody likes that. For thousands of years, mental health has been understood as a form of demonic possession or a way of being punished by God. It also supposes a baseline – a normalcy that is in itself difficult to define.

In ancient Greece and Rome, mental health was seen as an imbalance of humours. William Harris, editor of the book *Mental Disorders in the Classical World*, says that in ancient Rome, one of the remedies for a mental health episode would be to go and spend the night in a temple of the healing god Asclepius, who would maybe tell you how to be cured. If no cure could be found, then the mentally ill person could end up on the street.[7]

In the ancient world, the focus of treatment was physically restraining the ill and providing counselling, and it's quite startling to think how similar our treatments are a few thousand years later. The first person to acknowledge that the mentally ill might need more than a quick visit to a temple was Hippocrates, who sampled how changing their living environment or surroundings could improve the mental state of the person who was sick.

Hippocrates is one of the most prominent figures in the field of medicine. In fact, his moniker is 'The Father of Western Medicine'. Despite being born in 370 BC in Kos, Hippocrates has continued to influence the West with his teachings. Doctors today still swear the Hippocratic Oath, vowing to do their best for the patient and to help them make a full recovery: 'Make a promise to help, or to do no harm.'

Hippocrates' key theory was that we are made up of four humours. The idea of the four humours is seen by some as a precursor to modern-day psychology. His teachings on the humours described how we are formed from black bile, yellow bile, phlegm and blood. If someone had more of one humour than another, then our temperament would shift. A physician in ancient Rome, called Galen, developed Hippocrates' ideas and conducted more research into the area of emotions. 'If you have too much black bile', he wrote, 'you're likely to be melancholic.' If you have yellow bile, you'll be quick to anger. Too much blood, and you're likely to be happy and 'sanguine'. Lots of phlegm, and rather than be sad about this, you'll be thoughtful and wise.

A thousand years later, and there's been little progress in the field of medicine. Unless you include the addition of even more leeches. In the Middle Ages, leeches were used (with varying degrees of success) to purge the sickness, but then again, most ailments were 'cured' using a leech, including a leech to the penis for erectile dysfunction and a leech to the eye for blindness.

TV shows have opened our eyes to the poverty of care afforded to the Victorians when it came to mental health. Some of these shows might seem melodramatic in their depictions of mental health institutions – and there was probably a lot less ambling around in public corridors and a lot more restraints – but depressingly, they're not far off. From shows like *Penny Dreadful* to *Vienna Blood*, we can see how patients were drugged, chained and sedated in the cities' premier mental asylums. Straitjackets were *de rigueur* and electric shock therapy was still being trialled – a therapy that continues today in some US states.

Conditions in Bedlam, in South London, or Bethlem Royal Hospital, were bad enough for it to be entertaining, and it became a popular tourist attraction. Visitors would pay a penny to be taken around the wards by an orderly, and then observe life within from an elevated walkway, staring at women and men in chains deemed 'mad' or 'not saveable'. This would be a fun day out for the late-nineteenth-century courting couple. Bedlam was so famous a landmark that it would be included on tourist itineraries alongside London Zoo.

The original Bedlam was founded in medieval London in Bishopsgate and was designed by Robert Hooke so beautifully that it was described as being as 'opulent as Versailles' by visitors. It had a 540ft-long facade with Corinthian columns, earning the moniker 'a palace for lunatics'. Inside the building was a different matter, to the extent that the word 'bedlam' soon became known as a byword for chaos or madness.

Two large statues on the outside of the facade hinted at the horrors within. One, called Melancholy, was calm, while the other figure, known as Raving Madness, pulled forcefully against his chains and seemed furious at his lot. Mental health has never been a tasteful subject, and although the conditions of the building were bad, nothing could compare to how the people were treated inside.

Those with learning disabilities, physical disabilities and mental health disorders were all crowded into the space. One form of therapy was 'the rotating chair', where a patient would be placed in a chair and then suspended from the ceiling. The chair was spun quickly, perhaps as many as one hundred rotations in a minute, causing the patient to throw up. This would be seen as a good, wholesome way to get the madness out.

Today, Bedlam has changed. No longer a place of torment or tyranny, it's now located in a peaceful, green space close to Croydon. Features include a swimming pool, gym, chapel, crafts workshop, restaurant and a patient library.

Perhaps the closest I've come to a modern-day Bedlam is the Maudsley Hospital in Camberwell, where all of my care work and visits were meant to be. I had to go and pick up some medication one day, and they threw in a big, yellow stress-ball with a large, happy smiley face on it. It was my third day of medication and I wanted to throw up, but luckily there was a woman outside the Maudsley screaming at a car, endlessly, which was obviously very reassuring and made me feel great about my future.

Is there a link between smarts and poor mental health?

It can feel like it's a bit of a leap to say that those who are perfectionists or constantly striving to succeed are more at risk of mental health disorders than others. But when something feels so out of your grasp, and you have no idea what the correct path is, and you put pressure on yourself to graft, and throw yourself at the wall – whatever your definition of success is, even if that's just learning how to ride a bike, aged forty – an ounce of failure can hit you hard.

Maybe there's a reason why people like Einstein are called 'mad geniuses', or successful writers are known as eccentrics. People with brilliant minds who find it hard to slot into society may be labelled as brilliantly insane, or crazy.

Studies show that intelligent people might be more

prone to mental illness, and certainly the number of famous intellectuals who experience mental health or personality disorders would support this. Virginia Woolf was severely depressed and killed herself; Stephen Fry has talked about having bipolar disorder. Ernest Hemingway once wrote, 'Happiness in intelligent people is the rarest thing I know.'

Obviously, there are many, many people who struggle with depression but have a low IQ, and just because you have a high IQ does not always mean you're a striver.

Studies show that entrepreneurs and CEOs are both at higher risk of experiencing depression than the 'average' person. This has as much to do with long working hours and demands placed on them by the board and share-holders as anything else.

Ted Turner, founder of CNN, has spoken about living with bipolar disorder, while a University of California San Francisco researcher, Michael A. Freeman, found that 49 per cent of entrepreneurs who founded compa-nies also experienced mental health problems. A *University of Cincinnati Law Review* study conducted in 2005 found that CEOs may be more than twice at risk of developing depression as others. J.K. Rowling has spoken about her depression and anxiety, while 68 per cent of UK musicians have also had depression or anxi-ety, according to charity Help Musicians UK.[8]

So the stats back up the idea that those who throw

themselves into work, especially creative work, can struggle more – but why? Wouldn't it be easier, or even possible, to take our feet off the pedal and stop striving, to save our mental health?

Professor Sir Cary L. Cooper is luckily on hand to talk about this supposed correlation. He agrees that there's some evidence this may be the case.

'I've done lots of research on people who are very successful entrepreneurs – John Harvey-Jones, all these people. And what you find is that they're, number one, extremely driven, and number two, workaholic, and number three, resilient. One thing you'll find is that failure doesn't tend to bother them. They just tend to pick themselves up and sort themselves out.'

He adds that another interesting thing he's found is that many successful people tend to have very low self-esteem. 'This usually stems from an event in early childhood where they're trying to prove themselves. And what causes possible mental health issues is when they have that single focus on their business, they start to lose other things around it, like relationships and friendships. If you're working all hours God sends, and if you have children or other responsibilities, then ultimately, those [relationships] can break down. And that leads to anxiety and depression problems. The question successful people need to ask, is how do I balance those parts of my life? You need a coping strategy that works.

'Striving for success, or being ambitious, doesn't automatically mean you're going to have mental health problems, but it is a personality trait, for sure. Whatever happened to you in childhood created that need to be successful, whether to prove something to your parents, to your teacher. What's interesting is how you experience that breakdown as a Type A, success-driven person. It might not be a mental health problem, but you could [have] a heart attack instead. People who are very success-oriented have six times the rate of heart attacks than people who are more laid back and have greater balance in their lives.'

Well, isn't that swell.

Just after the First World War, a man called Lewis Terman wanted to see how people with a high IQ could help the war effort, so he started a study, gathering 1,500 children with IQs over 140 in Californian schools to explore the impact of their intelligence over their lifetime. He wanted to better understand how their IQ impacted their day-to-day, and one thing the study found was that although many achieved success and wealth, many others gravitated towards 'more average' jobs that don't need extraordinary IQs, like the police force, teaching or becoming a typist. They seemed relatively comfortable with their choices.

These very smart people married and committed suicide at similar rates to people who were not endowed with enormous IQs, but they all had one thing in common: they were plagued by unhappiness that they had not lived up to their potential. This group of people felt less accomplished than maybe they would have done had their IQs had not been so high. When intelligent people make a mistake, they might be harder on themselves than other people because they know they're capable of doing better. High expectations tend to go hand in hand with a high IQ.

We've all made bad career or life choices at some point. Perhaps you've taken a job that seemed to offer a great opportunity but you actually realised you'd be stuck in a dead-end situation with no chance of progression. For smart or ambitious people, perhaps that can tip them into some kind of despair, wondering how they're going to get out without upsetting the balance of perhaps a mortgage or family responsibilities.

On the occasions I've ended up in jobs where I'm spending two hours a day working and six hours a day wondering how to look like I'm working, I've tended to tip into an anxiety-driven panic, wondering existentially whether 'this is it'. I am a living embodiment of being chronically underworked, and feeling stressed about this.

In some offices I've worked in (and, as a former contractor, I've worked in many) there's a mix of people who seem very happy, relish not working too hard and leave on the dot. They tend to have a brighter, airier disposition, as though they understand that work isn't everything.

On the other hand, all of us have worked in offices where there's a clear bunch of workaholics, those who stay late, don't set boundaries and answer emails at midnight on a Saturday. Maybe that's you. In some jobs, that's definitely me. In others, I'd like that to be me, but I just genuinely do not have enough work to stretch it out that long.

And when that job doesn't provide me with a meaty enough project to get my teeth into, I start to wonder what I'm being paid for. And then I start to spiral into an anxiety loop, wondering whether I'm good enough to be doing what I'm doing, and whether there's something else that should be eating all my time.

Another chunk of research exploring this was conducted by Raj Raghunathan, at the University of Texas Austin's McCombs School of Business, who has explored the subject in a book called *If You're So Smart, Why Aren't You Happy?*.

In an interview with the *Atlantic*[9], he talks about happiness among successful people not being sustainable. Mostly, he says, there's a level of dissatisfaction among successful people. Once you've scored a hit, you immediately want the next one.

He says:

*If you get a huge raise this month, you might be happy for a
month, two months, maybe six months. But after that, you're
going to get used to it and you're going to want another big
bump. And you'll want to keep getting those in order to sustain
your happiness levels. In most people you can see that that's
not a very sustainable source of happiness.*[10]

Raghunathan also explores the idea behind why we're so
driven to succeed, and why that can lead to greater
incidences of unhappiness among successful people. He
looks at how two different states exist in society, one
where there's scarcity and one where there's abundance.
It makes sense in a time of scarcity (e.g. a warzone or a
famine) to strive and to push oneself hard to guarantee a
greater chance of survival. But as humans, why are we
pushing so hard in times of abundance? 'I think our
evolutionary tendencies might be holding us back . . .
quite a lot of studies [show] that you actually perform
better if you don't put yourself under the scarcity mindset,
if you don't worry about the outcomes and enjoy the
process of doing something, rather than the goal.'

Ultimately, he says, a large part of life is that if you see
a mountain in front of you, you want to climb over it.
And when you do, it turns out there are more mountains
to climb.

It's not just anxiety . . .

And it's not just anxiety and depression that plague those who are more successful or ambitious. A study by Pitzer College researcher Ruth Karpinski and her colleagues, published in the scientific journal *Intelligence*, found that those who belonged to Mensa and had high IQs were more likely to have more serious disorders too. This includes bipolar disorder, obsessive compulsive disorder and even autism. Interestingly, Karpinski's studies found that those with the highest IQs also tended to have higher rates of allergy: 33 per cent versus 11 per cent of the general population.[11]

In her analysis, she put this down to smart people suffering from 'overexcitabilities', which is an unusually high reaction to an insult or external stressor. This in turn tends to lead to more anxiety if you get a negative comment from your boss, for example, as you tend to overanalyse the comment. This can stimulate physical responses to stress too, creating a double whammy of physical problems and mental health issues.

Everyone but the very happiest of us will have lain awake at night stressing about money or promotions or career progressions or similar. The darkness seems to mock our suffering, closing in on our thoughts and making time stand still, so it is always 3.30 a.m. and we're stuck in a loop where we get sucked down into the whirlpool of anxiety, we check back in with the clock (still 3.30 a.m.) and then we return to our loop of anxiety.

If this sounds bad, then if you're Black the situation is much worse. According to the *Mental Health Bulletin*, 12.7 per cent of Black people already in touch with mental health services spent at least one night in hospital with mental-health-related problems between 2014 and 2015, which is more than double the number of white people.

A *Guardian* article by journalist Anni Ferguson explored why Black women tended to be beset by mental health issues more than white women. 'Aside from mental health problems, we all have one thing in common: we are all Black women in our twenties and thirties, and we can all testify to being tired.'

Ferguson started a WhatsApp group to encourage her friends to speak openly about their mental health situation and what they believed was causing it. One of the women who responded, Michelle, aged twenty-seven, said: 'Why do I have to change who I am so that people don't find me intimidating or aggressive? It's tiring to have to always conform to get ahead.'

Another, Naomi, who works in the City, said: 'I have to prove that I can do the same thing as a white person. Often what I say will be ignored, then someone who is not Black will say it and all of a sudden it makes sense!'[11]

My friend Ali, whose parents were both born in Jamaica, agrees with this. She also uses the word tired to describe her general day-to-day emotional attitude. She's been diagnosed with clinical depression and has been sectioned before. 'I feel like I have to prove myself so much more than my white friends. Like, work twice as hard. When I was at school my family would put pressure on me because they didn't want me to conform to a "Black racist stereotype" of kids dropping out of school young and doing drugs, and when I got older I felt like I had to work twice as a hard in the office so people would respect me more. Maybe it's all in my head, but if I talk to any of my sisters, they say the same thing. It's the twenty-first century!'

Chloé Elliott, founder of Odyssey Box, a subscription box for luxury natural hair products, says she found out about the Black attainment gap at university. She invested considerable effort into working to help change this by becoming Equality and Diversity officer at her Russell Group university union.

'I've always grown up with the mentality to work twice as hard for half as much. You could call me any name under the sun, but if you call me lazy, that's where I get off. When you're in school, there's a direct reward because you work hard for a test, but it was so disillusioning when I got to university and with the same work ethic didn't get to where I wanted. My whole experience was to try as hard as I could, yet I was always falling short. It wasn't until I connected with other Black people at university, I realised we were all experiencing the same thing.

My uni life could be summed up by saying: I could try as hard as I could and still only get sixty per cent, and so I thought 'What's the point'? I studied French and German, and in my second year, I thought I'm not even going to get to work for the EU anymore because my government has removed that option from us. I even kept getting told my English wasn't good enough, despite it being my first language and growing up in London and Hertfordshire.

I went on my university year abroad in Germany – working in school as an English language assistant. There was prejudice there too. I just thought, "I keep trying so hard to win the system, I'm now going to spend the year doing something I want."'

*

A number of organisations, from NAMI (National Alliance on Mental Illness)[12] to Mental Health America,[13] suggest significant stigma exists towards mental health in some African American communities, which can make it harder for people to ask for help, compounding the problem.

The mental health crisis seems to have penetrated into all sections of society. I feel it at home, and I feel it when

I'm on holiday. Many friends have been to see therapists. Family members have said they've experienced depression, stress and anxiety.

I recently devoured *The Coddling of the American Mind* by Greg Lukianoff and Jonathan Haidt, which gave me a fresh perspective on our mental health situation. What Lukianoff and Haidt's book found was that on American campuses there has been a significant number of students 'no-platforming' speakers. They describe this movement as a rise in safetyism, where students are protected from mental-health-triggering situations by well-meaning adults and institutions.

The authors argue that students will be unable to thrive outside the safe campus bubble if they're constantly protected from alternative viewpoints which could trigger their mental health issues. They hypothesise that Generation Z, or iGen, those who were born after 1996, are 'obsessed with safety, including emotional safety'.[14] Requests for safe spaces accelerated after iGen started university in 2013 onwards: these aren't millennials, but those who have known nothing but the internet. This is relevant to our exploration of never feeling good enough, because it shows that we've been so crippled by our need to please and do well that we struggle to step up and say no to the structures that have kept us in line for decades.

The final point of Lukianoff and Haidt's introduction

sums up the current situation on campuses across the world. Children and young people must be exposed to stressors and challenges, or they will fail to mature into strong, emotional adults. 'Safteyism is a cult – it deprives young people of the experiences their antifragile minds need, thereby making them more fragile, anxious and prone to seeing themselves as victims.'

This book heavily resonated with me. It made me stop and question my right to be angry at society. It made me think hard about whether I had actually been ignored or passed over for things in the past because I'm a woman, or whether the dominant narrative right now is 'unfairness', so I just assumed I had.

In the first chapter of this book, I wrote about feeling disenfranchised because of lack of privilege. But is that even accurate? Are we blaming our perceived lack of achievement on others, rather than taking responsibility for it ourselves? And, consequently, am I, by asking this, adopting a neo-liberal, conservative viewpoint?

I think the answer is no – I don't just believe that there is inherent misogyny and racism in society: I know there is. Thanks to prejudice and unconscious bias, there's clear evidence that people with Black-sounding names are more likely to be passed over when it comes to job interviews. There is also clear evidence that women of a childbearing age may be rejected for work too. This only adds to our levels of emotional anxiety: minorities, women, gay people, are already more at risk of experiencing mental health problems. We are disadvantaged before we set foot outside, thanks to the patriarchal society we live in.

Walking down a street in New York's Lower East Side last month, I passed two separate couples, hands loosely linked, both talking about mental health. What they said stuck with me because it was so intense: 'I feel like I'm in crisis,' one woman was saying to her boyfriend, who didn't so much as turn his head.

The other, a few blocks on, was another young woman telling her very tall boyfriend angrily that: 'You have no idea what it feels like to be this sad.'

Our life can feel bleak, and like it's impossible to succeed.

Perhaps we feel like there are so many obstacles in our path, whether that's gender, class or race, that we are gradually worn down, like a badly-acted soldier in an action film shot first in the shoulder, then in the knee, and finally in the head.

Some of us go down slowly, some of us the bullets skip by our heads, some of us take the gun and fire back, roaring into the enemy's onslaught, while a few of us eventually fall, never to clamber up again.

Mental health is something we all have – it can be good or it can be bad. But one thing that's helped me over the past year has been realising that it's OK to be good enough. I don't need to be the best or the smartest. Channelling average and cutting myself some slack to just be 'OK' has helped. It means I hope I'll be able to clamber up again and again and again.

Sleep

Since last August, I've been waking up at 3 a.m.

Often, I wake up at three, check my clock and think: 'Ah, 3.30 a.m. is the most common time for people to die,' before immediately falling back into a light doze when I'll wake up at 4 a.m., as if to check I'm still here.

If there's one thing a depressive needs to kickstart their day with positivity, it's knowing they survived the night.

Those of us who struggle to sleep, who lie awake in the dark wishing that dawn would break and soak into the curtains, understand the fears that night can bring. Those in relationships feel alone as the person next to them breathes steadily, lost in a beautiful slumber. Those who are single have no distractions from being awake, and it's easy to sink lower and deeper into sadness.

I often lie in my white, wide bed, which is filled with books I was reading, books I'm about to read – pages turned sharply at the corner – and books that I must read, piles of decorative cushions that look great during the day but fuck my neck up at night, and Arrow, my yellow knitted duck, who has kept me company better than any bedfellow ever has, held close, and feel the night close in with a sigh. Night for me is anxiety. It's a time where I can't distract myself, and I long for day.

Sometimes I run through all the things I've done wrong. I've found, since August, that that has included the ways I've tried to end my life. Why it went wrong every time. Why the things I tried to do didn't work. And sometimes, how it could go better next time. Sometimes I'm frozen in fear at night and I wake up soaked in sweat thinking of that drop in front of me on the bridge, of that vast emptiness below, wondering if the painful memories I feel now are worth it. If anything's worth it.

And when I get to this stage, I fumble for the light, knowing that the brightness of my Lumie lamp will pull me from this mindset into daylight. No matter what time it is, I'll stretch for one of the books on the bed, which is always the world's driest: a 450-page epic on the history of the Jewish peoples which is so impenetrable, so dry it crumbles between my fingers each time I pick it up, that I'm still stuck on page twelve, the bit where another academic says how much this book changed his life – most likely because it improved his quality of sleep like no other device could.

Despite being awake for most of the night, I'm also a very early riser. There's something delicious about waking up early, but also something smug. I love the feeling of getting things done before the 'real' day begins.

This feeling of smugness goes hand in hand with relief that I have the privilege to choose whether or not I get up early, that my job doesn't rely on me taking the bus at 4 a.m. to clean an office. I'm sure that feeling of deliciousness would crumble after day three, and I'd start to crave a lie-in.

But an obsession with losing sleep and burning the candle at both ends is growing. Perhaps it started with former British prime minister Margaret Thatcher, who famously boasted that she (allegedly) needed to sleep for just four hours a night. If motivational magazine articles and TED talks are anything to go by, the last two decades have seen an escalation in the number of 'successful people' getting up early in the name of ambition.

I get up early, but I'm always exhausted by 10 p.m. Some mornings, when I've pushed myself at the gym too hard, or tried to do too much before 9 a.m. (I'm currently writing this on a Saturday morning at 7.13 a.m.), I've had to bail on friends in the evenings. What fun is that? At my friend's carol concert, where I was meant to meet his new girlfriend, I ended up saying some hasty goodbyes at the interval to avoid passing out on the pew.

As I get older and my evenings are packed with *things*, I realise that trying to burn the candle at both ends of the day is pointless. And yet, being able to hack staying awake still seems to be seen as a sign of success.

People are busy. We're always busy and it feels like we're becoming busier. In a world that was meant to become more efficient as we adopted smartphones and tech, our lives often feel overwhelmed by tasks, people and notifications. Drinks with friends you rarely see; socialising at the office; swinging kids from activity to activity.

Once I've made dinner, seen a friend, sent some work emails and tidied the flat, there's enough time for me to collapse into bed to read a book chapter. Rarely a month goes by when a magazine or newspaper doesn't post an article shouting about all the crazy things you could achieve in your day if you just chose to push yourself a little harder. The message is clear. Successful people don't need to sleep, and they use that extra time in the day to make more money and fuel their productivity.

Michelle Obama famously woke at 4.30 a.m. when she was First Lady to get her gym on, while Jennifer Aniston wakes at 4.30 a.m. to meditate. From some quick googling, it appears that tech CEOs are the biggest fans of not sleeping, and, as many people want to become tech CEOs, it's unsurprising that there are lots of people trying to copy the habits of the rich and famous.

Maybe it makes sense to wake up and work out at 4 a.m. if you're so famous that you have paparazzi lining your driveway as soon as the sun rises. Or if you have a multi-billion-dollar business to run. I'd want my CEO working eighteen-hour days too.

But is there any point in trying to emulate this way of living? And does it work for the rest of us, who don't have butlers, chefs or personal trainers?

Let's look first at how much sleep you actually need each night. Adults need between seven and nine hours every day, but there are outliers: some need just five hours while others get grumpy if they haven't had their full ten. The amount we sleep declines as we age. Newborns need between seventeen and nineteen hours a day because they're growing, while teenagers still need up to eleven hours a night because their brains are developing.

As adults are fully formed people with brains that finish developing around age twenty-five, we don't need as much sleep.

Lose sleep to become successful . . .

Yet sleep has turned into a competition, and, despite the amount you sleep being completely personal, the success mantra has transformed anyone who sleeps past eight into someone who is lazy. If you don't set your alarm for 6 a.m., you're not go-getting enough.

Entrepreneurs are falling over themselves to wake up earlier than the next. Not being a slave to sleep is seen as an aspirational state of mind. Sleep is for those who have nothing better to do.

Martha Stewart, broadcaster and businesswoman, gets up at 4.30 a.m. every day. She does this partly to catch up on the news and partly to feed her menagerie of animals. Stewart has horses, donkeys and over 200 chickens to feed. 'It's an exhausting lifestyle, and I always say sleep can go,' she told WebMD. 'It's not important to me right now.'[1]

This sort of dialogue has the potential to be damaging. It is also a very privileged position to be in, and failure to acknowledge that does it no service. For most people who wake up at 4.30 a.m., they wake up then because they have to. They may have been priced out of more central housing so have a long commute to work; they may work difficult, long shift patterns that require unusual hours.

To be able to spend three hours of your day feeding chickens, meditating and doing a six-mile run like Twitter's Jack Dorsey is a position of complete privilege. Are they only able to invest so much in themselves because people around them are doing the heavy lifting?

Few people in these public positions acknowledge the extra support they get with keeping a schedule like this. Michelle Obama said that it was only thanks to being in the White House that she was able to keep up with an early morning routine.

If you're one of these extremely tough, hard, ambitious

people, no doubt you'll have read about these early starts and wondered if you should be adding them to your life too. An early start is made to sound fabulous by people who have a strong support network and can cope with it.

I choose to wake up early in the morning, but it's not so I can get a head start on my day: it's so I don't feel guilty if I can't finish everything. Well, at least I've tried, I can tell myself.

But I'm fascinated by all these different elements that the world's wealthy and successful commit to every morning. I want to see if punishing ourselves first thing in the morning will transform us into a tribe of successful strivers.

Tennis

Vogue Editor Anna Wintour plays tennis at 5.45 a.m. I'm always intrigued when I read articles about people who get up early to play tennis in the morning, because this requires you to know somebody else who also wants to knock a ball around at dawn.

This particular habit of the rich and famous feels like it requires a lot of planning. I half-assed text some of my friends about going to the tennis courts in the park and I get blue-ticked by all of them.

At 10 p.m. I set my alarm for 5.15 a.m. and prepare my

bag for the next morning. I am determined I will start the day like Anna Wintour and finish the day feeling like I've put an edition of *Vogue* to bed. Too late, I realise I don't have a tennis racquet so pack my squash racquet instead. I don't have a tennis ball either, but have found both a yellow smiley-face stress-relief squidgee and a squash ball, so I throw them both in, reminding myself it's about the drive.

I check my phone again. None of my friends have replied and I turn off the light, trying to channel positivity. London is full of ambitious people reading articles about successful people. There's probably a whole host of people down at the courts in a park in Vauxhall on a Tuesday morning in December.

I go to sleep feeling more optimistic and wake to rain. It's a thirty-minute walk to the tennis courts so I call an Uber. This is what Anna Wintour would have done, I remind myself, furious that I've already spent £11 and it's not even 6 a.m.

The Uber driver doesn't make small talk. I get the feeling he thinks I'm unhinged, travelling to a small park thirty minutes from my home in winter. I've worn gym clothes but I'm clutching my squash racquet like I'm about to bludgeon someone to death with it, because I don't have a case, so he avoids my gaze and pulls away so fast his tyres squeal.

One thing you must always do if you decide to channel

Anna Wintour is check your local tennis courts are open. Or, at the very least, if the park is open. Neither were, so I consider hitting the stress ball with my squash racquet a few times on the pavement and then get splashed by a Megabus driving through a puddle, so decide it's time to walk home.

When I get back home at 6 a.m. I take a hot shower and go back to sleep. I wake up an hour later feeling frustrated that I've missed my gym session and also angry that tennis before work is sold as an aspirational thing. A plea to magazine editors in the UK printing these 'successful before 7 a.m.' claims: unless you have your own floodlit, heated, covered tennis court and a robot friend, you will never, and I mean never, play tennis before 6 a.m. Just do a quick subedit and replace it with 'pilates' if you must.

Liquids

It probably comes as no surprise that Apple's current CEO Tim Cook wakes at 3.45 a.m. Although he rises at an obscene time, he does normal things, like drink coffee, work out and send emails. While researching this book I had the pleasure of checking out some absolutely wild claims, which unfortunately meant I'd have to try them to get a jump on my day.

Dan Lee, founder of standing-desk company

NextDesk, imbibes a lot of liquids. I'm poised to follow his routine to see how it sets one up for the day, so I set my alarm for 3.30 a.m. Because I have a semblance of a life, I'd only got home at 11.30 p.m. and was in bed at twelve. Getting up at 3.30 a.m. felt like a joke and I was extremely sluggish.

Blearily, I checked what else Dan Lee does in the morning. According to an article published by Business Insider, he then drinks two litres of water and two cups of coffee followed by a smoothie.[2]

I would feel uncomfortable drinking this volume of liquid at any time of the day, but at 3.30 a.m, when my body wanted very much to be asleep, it was torture. After 500ml of water, I brew two cups of coffee and blend a smoothie with whatever leftover bits I have in the fridge. That's some brown kale, half a banana, some orange juice that I'm pretty certain is past its sell-by date and some strawberries. I've run out of milk, but no shops are open for another three hours, so make it with water.

I'm already bloated from drinking just a quarter of the volume of water Dan Lee puts away, but I force the disgusting smoothie down and sit, staring in glum silence at the two cups of steaming coffee. I already need the toilet, and it's only 3.50 a.m. I also want to be sick, so I go to the bathroom, try to drink some more of the two litres of water he apparently downs, and check down at the list of things he does pre-work.

Now, he plays with his dog for thirty minutes. Aside from the fact I can't believe anyone could physically move after this much liquid, I don't have a dog, so I get back into bed and fall back asleep for thirty minutes, something that's considerably harder to do when you've had so much water. After thirty minutes with his dog, he does an hour of reading. He doesn't specify what type of reading he does, so I choose the news. It's exactly the same news I read when I went to bed because nobody at the newspaper I read is mad enough to update the homepage at 4.30 a.m. I get sucked into the sports and business sections, two areas I never read, so this morning I end up learning a lot about player transfers.

There's still three hours until I have to be at my desk and I'm ready for lunch. I drink the remaining liquid as I read and then note Dan Lee goes to the gym for an hour between 5.15 and 6.15. My gym opens at 6 a.m., so I pull my trainers on and go for a long run instead. I can feel the liquids as I run, and my workout is consequently very relaxed. When I get back to my flat, I note that Lee then spends an hour shaving and showering, and it's at this point I really feel like something's gone wrong here. Even if I shave both legs, I'm in and out of the shower in ten minutes. I don't need to read the news for an hour before work when it's the same as the day before. And I certainly don't need to drink this much liquid before the sun rises.

I can't deal with any more of the routine, so I give myself another hour in bed, and by the afternoon, want to pass out.

Surely one of these slightly mad morning routines has to work. My attention is drawn to Ellevest CEO and co-founder Sallie Krawcheck, whose morning sounds brilliant.[3] After getting up at 4 a.m., she has 'creative thinking time'. This lasts until she starts work, and she makes herself a pot of coffee and keeps the lights low. The only random thing she does is light a fire in the hearth: I have no hearth, so I light a candle instead, something I usually only do in the evening after work.

After a slow wake-up while staring at the screen, I sip my coffee in a restrained way. There's no downing cup after cup of liquids in Krawcheck's morning. The first twenty minutes are tough. I find myself flicking between Twitter and the news until I realise no one is updating the news and nobody is posting on Twitter.

So I open a blank document and write an article I need to do for work. I already have the case studies and transcriptions, so the piece is written by 6.30 a.m. and filed to the editor, after a quick proof, by seven. I'm in the gym by 7.15 a.m. This routine is a success.

We actually need sleep

Sleep is crucial. We spend about a third of our lives asleep, and there's a reason why babies sleep so much. It's all about growth and repair. Without sleep, we can't mend. Essentially, by refusing to go to sleep, you're denying your body the chance to recover.

If you're sleep-deprived for long enough, you can die, and it's no coincidence that in the Russian NKVD secret police, one of their methods for getting prisoners to agree to anything was by keeping them awake. Thousands of people attested to being kept awake by this torture method in the hope they'd confess to made-up crimes invented by the government so they'd be declared enemies of the state.

NKVD methods, later also used by the KGB, were pretty effective and simple. They were copied across the world, by Khmer Rouge interrogators during the Cambodian Civil War in the 1970s, and by the United States in the aftermath of 9/11.

In Soviet Russia, prisoners were kept in small, isolated cells. These cells were unbearably hot or bitingly cold depending on the time of year and in which area of Russia's vast land they were located. Lights were often on at all times, so if the prisoner tried to fall asleep, even for a few moments, the bright lights would sear into their minds.

Berlin's Stasi prison had cells that were too small to even sit down in, and prisoners would be so exhausted they'd try to sleep standing. Sleep deprivation continues to be a common torture technique, and one used in former prisons from Tuol Sleng, operated by the Khmer Rouge in Cambodia, to Budapest's House of Terror, to the Solovetsky Islands on the way to Murmansk in Russia's Arctic.

In other secret-police-run enterprises, each time a prisoner fell asleep, they'd be roughly shaken awake by guards who were on watch to make sure they could never sleep. Constant light and lack of access to daylight meant that people were so sleep-deprived they didn't know what time of day it was. Losing their circadian rhythm made them more pliable and damaged the way they thought, which is one of the reasons why people who live in the very far north have extremely high rates of depression.

A report in the journal *Proceedings of the National Academy of Sciences* found that sleep-deprived prisoners are four and a half times more likely to falsely confess to crimes they didn't actually commit.[4] The report found that 50 per cent of those involved admitted wrongdoing even if they were innocent, while just 18 per cent of those who were not sleep-deprived did.

This goes to show that no matter how driven or ambitious you are, without good sleep your mental faculties are damaged. Reaction times are slow and the ability to make good judgements and problem-solve goes out the window. So, should we really be celebrating entrepreneurs and celebrities who eschew sleep, or are they just helping us turn into a society of sleep-walking zombies?

Lucy Yi works in banking and when she started her first job, at a big American bank in Chicago, it took her just four weeks to fall into depression.

'I thought I'd found my dream,' she says. 'I got the job at the bank I wanted after doing an internship and then a three-month summer placement. I was prepared for the long hours and the managers seemed supportive and friendly.'

She joined in September and by October she realised she hadn't seen daylight for a month. 'I felt tough, you know? Like I was smashing it. The lore is everyone in the office gets up at 5 a.m., works out, then comes to work. It's what you do if you want to be successful.'

Yi says it so matter-of-factly, I almost believe it to be true. She pauses just long enough for me to wonder if she'd forgotten about the email subject-line she'd sent to me – 'Breakdown' – and then she smiles. 'Yeah, so I was going crazy. I was so tired I was drinking about ten cups of coffee a day. I slept at work in the bathroom, and you know, at that point, I didn't care if there were germs, I just needed to sleep.'

After six months, Yi left the bank. 'I'm still afraid I'm not tough enough, that I gave up too early. Maybe you think I did. We all know people who are still there, who you never see, and they just disappear because they get sucked into the corporate bubble. For a few months that was me and I felt like I'd died. I'd make mistakes, then get anxiety about making mistakes, and then I wouldn't sleep. My heart would race super-fast and then it would feel like it skipped a few beats.

'I was averaging about four hours' sleep each night, and then, because I had created a weird sleeping pattern, I'd wake up in deep panic every weekend.'

Yi said she wasn't exaggerating when there were some mornings she thought she was going to die.

We've seen how sleep can help us to stay sharp, but how can sleep physically kill us? In 1989, a scientist at the University of Chicago called Allan Rechtschaffen conducted a sleep-deprivation experiment on ten rats. It took eleven days for the rats to start dying, and by day thirty-two they were all dead. Post-mortems showed how, physically, there was nothing wrong with the rats. They just died from exhaustion because their bodies couldn't function.

The CIA also subjected dozens of prisoners in Guantanamo Bay to sleep deprivation back in 2008. They were tightly shackled, dressed in nappies, with their hands tied close to their chin, and every time they dropped off to sleep, the prisoners would fall forward and be jolted awake by falling on their chains. After keeping some of the prisoners shackled and awake for eleven days, medics reported finding no physical ill-effects on the body, but mentally there were problems. One prisoner, Mr Jawad, was put in isolation for thirty days. He was woken up every three hours, night and day, for two weeks. It broke him, and today he has PTSD and flashbacks.[5] The amount of time it was permissible to keep prisoners shackled and without sleep reduced to a week after this experiment.

But what happens when you start missing out on sleep intentionally? If you've ever pulled an all-nighter to finish a college paper, or not slept on a red-eye, you'll know just how bad one night without sleep feels.

You might feel dizzy and a little sick, before feeling like you're coming down with some aggressive flu (minus the phlegm). Life feels like it's floating around you, you become irritable and more prone to sadness. By the afternoon, most of us have crawled our way to a couch and dozed off.

But if you were to keep pushing, it would be a different story.

After twenty-four hours with no sleep, your cortisol levels rise. Cortisol is a stress hormone released by your adrenal glands, and when your cortisol levels increase, your blood pressure can rise too. According to a *Slate* article, your body stops metabolising glucose properly, which in turn leads to you craving carbohydrates.[6]

Anyone who has been exposed to any sort of diet advice knows this isn't a good thing. After a few more days, body temperature drops, the immune system is suppressed and, at least if you're a rat, after thirty-two days you'll die.

Researchers believe that death caused by long-term sleep deprivation could be as a result of brain damage. A good night's sleep will reverse the immediate danger, but in the long-term, poor sleep has been found to cause heart disease, obesity and diabetes. Professor Jason Ellis, Professor of Sleep Science at Northumbria University and director of Northumbria Sleep Research, has spent his career looking at the impact of sleep on our lives. He says sleep is all about quality not quantity, to the extent that some people really do thrive off just four to five hours' sleep. 'However, there are very few of these people. Look at Ariana Huffington. She said she used to follow the "you snooze, you lose" mantra, but actually, she saw the benefit of getting a full night's sleep and said sleep really boosted her productivity.'

Dr Ellis says even a night or two of compromised sleep can harm our immune systems. 'There are changes in mood or performance, memory, perception and problem-solving. In the longer term, we've seen sleep deprivation can lead to obesity, diabetes, etc., which is caused by the disregulation of the hormone that helps us to regulate eating.'

However, he admits more work needs to be done on whether rising very early can be damaging in the long term. 'We all have our own chronotype – if you're working within the framework of what your body wants and needs, and if that's waking up at 5 a.m., then you're going to be fine. However, we've seen shiftwork can be very damaging. Humans were not designed for shift-work, and studies show it can lead to higher cancer risk, stomach problems and obesity.'

He points out that the biggest problem with trying to burn the candle at both ends is that our productivity will suffer. 'You may be available more, but that's it.'

And if you're still struggling to sleep, allow me to recommend you the doorstopper of a book *Ten Million Years of Jewish History*, font size 6, with paper so thin you could roll a cigarette with it. Works every time.

Leisure Time

I was browsing Twitter recently, procrastinating from writing a report on gas pipelines, when I saw a comment calling for the end of the side hustle. *'Women don't have hobbies or leisure time any more, we just have side hustles.'*

A side hustle is something you can monetise. It is a project that could catapult the doer to success or stardom, far away from their 'mundane' life commuting to a job in insurance. A side hustle is borne of the world of *The Apprentice*, and the word 'hustle' originally means to move hurriedly along, which gives a pretty good indication of how unrelaxing these 'around work' activities can be.

A 2018 study conducted by the University of Reading found that more than a third of British people aged 16–34 have a project on the side of their regular job.[1] The project, or side hustle, might not be making much money, but for many it's their future. The side hustle is the way out.

And although this seems quite benign – surely it's great to have multiple interests and ambition – the reality is that your evenings and weekends also become work. And that's ignoring the large number of people who are required out of necessity to work a second job to simply afford rent or food, for example.

Worse, your hobbies might become something else you can fail at.

Side hustles, to give them their cute millennial moniker, or 'monetising your leisure time and contributing even more as a tax-payer to the economy', to give them their sceptical, socialist title, can be anything that brings in a little cash on the side.

It might be making jam to sell at a local food market each week. It could be baking cakes to sell online, or making headbands to sell on Etsy. Someone I used to work with would cross-stitch hoops and sell them on her Etsy store for £40 each. I bought one and it still hangs in my study today.

Another former colleague makes prints of endangered British animals which he sells on his website, which also doubles as his very impressive journalism portfolio.

I spoke to Emma Gannon, podcast host and author of the brilliant *The Multi-Hyphen Method*, which explores the pleasure that can come from having so many different strings to your bow. 'The term "side hustle" has become a buzzword of late, but really all it means is "passion project". A voluntary project that you want to do on the side, either because it allows for fun or creativity, or you want to start some sort of low-risk business while keeping your main income stream.

'There are stories of entrepreneurs getting up at 4 a.m. to do their side hustle, like Emily Weiss, founder of Glossier, who now owns a billion-dollar company, but these are also the rare success stories. Side hustles can be incredibly fulfilling but can also lead to burnout, and they are certainly not a "necessity" to get ahead. Side hustles are great because they can grow organically. I spent thirty minutes on mine a week and it grew from there. Every individual is different, but having a side hustle does require some element of sacrifice on your time, especially at the beginning.'

Side hustles, in this case, do tend to be more of a job that can form part of your income stream. Gannon adds that they're extremely useful (once lucrative) for when one project or client falls away. 'One of the main benefits is having multiple income streams. If one project or client falls away, I have others. I also love how many different people I meet beyond colleagues in an office, and how I am learning new things all the time.'

Gannon thinks that we all have strengths, and maybe even one super-strength, but that we are 'average at pretty much everything else. There is definitely a power in embracing our mediocrity, but also celebrating our strengths. Discovering our strengths is key to juggling a portfolio career, and outsourcing tasks also. There's a section in *The Multi-Hyphen Method* called "Hobbies are not the same as side hustles". Adding a side hustle can simply be a new hobby, space for self-growth, a creative act that no one will ever see. Side hustles don't always need to be a Career Thing. If you love baths you don't need to set up an Instagram page selling bath bombs.'

The closest I've come to having a side hustle is producing theatre, where I did a run of new-writing nights focusing on politics. But this was completely because I love theatre, and not because I ever thought I'd earn money from this hustle. I haven't tried to start a real side hustle because, ultimately, I'm not very good at anything that people would want to buy. I can't craft cute things into even sweeter things. I have no ability with carpentry or metalwork. Cake decoration bores me and, anyway, none of my cakes have ever risen.

I have largely managed to steer clear of the side hustle because of my extreme lack of skill and ability, although I have strongly thought about training as a PT. Yelling at other people to do burpees is probably my only genuine marketable skill, but let's face it, it's hardly unique.

Having a side hustle isn't bad: it can be fulfilling and really pleasurable. But it can be exhausting. It's a very real feeling experiencing the need to be constantly switched on. Waking up at 4 a.m. to send jars of award-winning honey (for example) out to buyers before going to work as a trainee human-rights lawyer might sound glamourous if you talk about it at a dinner party, but this could soon cause burnout. Being good enough could just be about loving the bees, harvesting the honey, eating it, and then giving it to friends and family.

If we count making theatre as a side hustle, I spend a lot of time sending out logistical emails. When I'm running a new-writing night, so much time goes into reading and reviewing scripts to ensure I have the most exciting new writing to share and present. A new-writing night will live or die on the quality of scripts, no matter how brilliant the actors.

Hours and hours are spent reading over brilliant submissions while I scratch my head figuring out what could work with what. It's some of the most pleasurable, hard work I do, and in many ways more challenging than my day job because people throw their life and creative soul into this writing.

Anyone who has spent five minutes in theatre knows that theatre is possibly the least lucrative profession of all time (not to mention the rehearsal spaces and venues that need to be rented, marketing costs, and paying the light and sound technicians).

Getting bums on seats is tough, especially in an apathetic city like London. I've had nights where I've literally said yes to three things and gone to none of them.

If you live east then getting west is a pain, if you leave work at 5 p.m. and have to wait around for a few hours, then a 7.30 p.m. start is a ball-ache. Support is hard, and side hustles to do with theatre can live or die based on your willingness to market the show so effectively that people will feel FOMO if they don't come.

When I had my own show on, which was a full week of just my work for one and a half hours, it triggered a total meltdown. Even though the show had a wonderful producer, Laura Furner, and director, Anastasia Bruce, the pressure of writing it, of tweaking it, of my work being on show for everyone to see was absolutely exhausting. I could do nothing other than stare into spare for about a week after and I haven't written a new play since.

Benjamin Myers, author of prize-winning novel *Beastings*, reflected on his own anxiety with writing in a recent article for the *Guardian*: 'Last summer, in the midst of promotional chaos surrounding my new novel *The Offing*, I cancelled my own London book launch and instead drove to the Chatsworth Estate in Derbyshire, a place I had never previously visited, and jumped in the river right in front of the very big house. It was not entirely an act of self-destruction or a plea for help . . . it simply seemed like a more obvious thing to do than trying to persuade members of the public to buy my book.'[2]

Doing anything creative can be hugely draining, especially if the subject or project is challenging.

People who have side hustles are absolutely slaying it, because it (quite literally) crippled me. I attended my very own press night, when all my friends were there, when there were meant to be reviewers coming, when it was sold out, and I sat downstairs, outside the theatre, completely blank and feeling extremely low because two people hadn't shown up. I was exhausted and I couldn't enjoy the finished product.

Why side hustles can be great

Let's start with the positives. A side hustle lets people follow their dreams without giving up the day job. Yes, it can mean quite a few extra hours' work each week, but it can be worth it to get a sense of creative satisfaction.

Simon Naylor spent twenty years sweating it out in the restaurant business. Based in Sheffield, he worked his way up to managing restaurants, but a few years ago decided that he wanted a new challenge. 'I've been working for a big Swedish furniture company for the last couple of years. It's full-time and I love it, but it's been a big career change after twenty years in catering and hospitality.'

For a man who manages kitchen fittings, he is remarkably at home co-running a bar and restaurant in Sheffield's now-trendy Heeley district.

'We sell vegan pizzas,' he says, 'but there's an option to use vegetarian cheese if you want.'

Pour (also, pun-intended, dog-friendly), which Naylor co-runs with two friends, is his side hustle.

'The furniture job is full-time,' he says. 'But they're really good to work for and flexible, and my manager is very understanding.'

The thing is, although he loved his new job, Naylor didn't want to lose the opportunity to make use of his twenty years' experience in catering. 'So, eighteen months ago the opportunity came along to invest in a bar project, cooking up some food on the side. I was renting a flat above the pub, which was next door and owned by the same landlord. It had been an Italian restaurant that had gone bust, and the landlord knew another guy, Ed, who was a brewer. Between the three of us, we made it happen.'

Despite working full-time, Naylor manages to fit in working there every Wednesday and every other Friday. His full-time work is based on shifts, which includes evenings and weekends, so he fits his side hustle around it. 'I do prep and make dough. I make sure the kitchen manager knows what's happening and I meet with my partners if necessary.'

In the bar in Heeley, there are some excellent beers on tap and adventurous pizza options – Naylor has put his years of skill and passion in place to help Pour succeed. And it's doing well. Just over a year in and they're breaking even. He hopes this year he'll be able to turn a profit.

Naylor has a full-time job, also works as an actor, and has a family. He explains that it triggers feelings of guilt sometimes because he can't give as much time to the business as he'd like, and he thinks if he had more time to put in they could be a few steps further ahead than they are now. 'But it's important for my mental health to be balanced, and I find myself being quite protective over my time. I've worked on jobs that have fifty, sixty, seventy hours a week, and you realise that that's a long time and it doesn't necessarily benefit the business.'

Naylor says a lot of people he knows in Sheffield have something on the side. 'About a third of people I know have side jobs,' he says. As well as creating something fulfilling, he thinks life is about more than just having a job for life. 'There are barely any industries around where you can say that, so I think people are creating safety nets for themselves with multiple jobs. I think it's important to look at the skills and experience you have and what you can do with them.'

Yes, it takes up time, but Naylor says he likes the fact he has the opportunity to do this. 'I look back ten to fifteen years and I was doing one job and not much else. It's been nice to diversify, and it's a good feeling.'

So could the problem be not with us, but with our jobs? Maybe we feel the need to maximise our leisure time because our nine-to-fives aren't hugely stimulating.

In an overstimulated world, where we have distractions coming at us from our phones, laptops and real people, perhaps our jobs haven't yet caught up. According to a report by global consultancy firm McKinsey,[3] around 50 per cent of all jobs could be automated by 2030. This indicates just how dry some of our roles are, whether that's tax law or shelf-stacking. Even teaching is at risk.

In a recent article for news and features site Refinery29,[4] Naeema Pasha, director of careers at Henley Business School, University of Reading, who conducted research into side hustles, thinks that one reason people are more at ease with a side hustle than in previous times is because the workplace is less secure. 'Companies that used to offer steady, "life-long" careers are no longer offering the security that previous generations experienced.'[5]

As house prices rise and salaries stagnate, it can seem smart to try to monetise every second we have. How else will we afford that elusive house, which is now estimated to be worth around fourteen and a half times our annual salary, compared to three times our annual salary in 1995?

Everything not only feels more expensive – it is more expensive. In the film *Little Women* (2019), Jo is awarded $100 for a story she writes in the late nineteenth century. I have been paid similarly in the early twenty-first century for my work. Something doesn't add up.

New revenue streams are opening up, and people are jumping on them: being Instafamous or being a YouTuber are genuine revenue streams. Few people set out to work full-time in these industries, but if you make it, and make it big, you can easily make a career out of it.

That people can succeed and earn money by posting make-up tutorials, or videos about brushing their hair, can inspire others to try the same. Podcasts, which can be recorded in a quiet room on a phone, have taken off. Clips showing a recent travel experience hiking up a mountain might be bought by an outdoor adventure brand, and suddenly your world takes flight.

A whole ream of side hustles that don't rely on physical space are born. Our interest in work on top of work increases.

A shift I work every Sunday for a national newspaper pays for my gym membership.

It all might sound like a win-win situation: earning extra cash for doing something you love. But the reality is, it leads to burnout faster than you might think. A side hustle is more than doing an extra job, like cycling for Uber Eats. It's defined as something you enjoy doing too. If you can earn money while you're doing that, then this sounds like a GOOD THING.

But studies show if we leave no time for recovery, no time for just chilling out, we burn out. And put in black and white, is that surprising? Of course not.

Multiple studies have found that working for longer than thirty-nine hours a week can cause big problems. Not just when it comes to stress and mental health issues, but also physical problems. More people have bad backs than at any other time in history, and at least a little of this is owing to being slouched at desks getting the hours in.

According to a recent survey conducted by the Chartered Institute of Personnel and Development (CIPD), one in five of us are exhausted by our work. A quarter of us find it difficult to switch off, and two thirds of us have experienced health problems related to work, such as anxiety. The study found that more than a quarter said their profession had a negative impact on their personal lives.

Adding a side hustle to our work stress just doesn't feel sustainable.

What happened to hobbies?

One way to enjoy a side hustle is to reclaim the word 'hobby' and learn how to enjoy our leisure time. I've found that the way to do this is by picking up hobbies I could in no way monetise (such as my sub-par piano-playing, or singing unmarketable choral music in a local choir).

I really enjoy cooking, and once a friend recommended I apply to the TV show *MasterChef*. I was flattered, but I also found it interesting that the immediate response to enjoying something was to try to professionalise it. My hobby, the few hours I get to myself in the kitchen every week, would become all about learning how to set custard and make choux buns from scratch.

Hard pass.

What happened to the good old-fashioned hobby where we just have fun? Even computer gaming, which was previously just something to kick back with, has turned into a multimillion-dollar industry known as e-sports.

Shaynee (not her real name) is twenty-seven and admits to feeling exhausted by her leisure time. She has asked not to be named, because she is cautious not to come across as though she's ungrateful for her opportunities. 'Truth is, I'm tired. I spend all my time doing things. I'd like a break, but I feel guilty. I spend a lot of time seeing my friends' plays because I'm proud of them, and I can network also; I run a podcast; I write a newsletter which has hundreds of subscribers and if I'm late with that then it gets a bit stressful. I feel like I've built a rod for my own back.

'These things are all my choice though, I know that. I just spend so much of my time doing things for my career, but I worry it's not enough. I won't do a hobby that isn't about progressing my career. I feel guilty saying this, but that's just how it has to be right now. There's time to relax when I retire.'

There's nothing wrong with lifelong learning. It's something to be celebrated. It's why we read or watch documentaries or go to galleries or museums. Humans are inherently curious. We care very much about what's around us, and there's a reason children spend a lot of their childhood asking 'Why?'.

After all, as Plutarch once said, 'Education is not about the filling of a pail, it's about the lighting of a fire.'

Learning and growing constantly throughout our lives is vital to a happy and fulfilling present. But do we need to take 'developing ourselves' with us on holiday or every weekend away from the daily grind?

Time off is vital for our brains to breathe and hopefully to reach a squishy, jelly-like state, while we also eat lots of delicious food. We may (naturally) want to throw a little culture into the mix. Pushing up against the growing craze for being perpetually busy, is time that calls for idleness. 'Recharging' sounds like a very hippyish and twenty-first century need, but scientific evidence does show that elements of idleness are crucial to get the big idea.

Why else do good ideas always come from having a long shower?

After all, a change is as good as a rest. There's nothing wildly controversial about this statement. Even the most ardent workaholic knows that they probably *should* switch off. Many dazzling thought processes occur when we're taking part in some form of downtime. Taking a little time out can replenish focus and motivation throughout the day, whether that's just staring out of the window or going for a short walk around the office. In turn, this boosts our productivity and creativity, which not only helps us to complete basic tasks, but also helps us to succeed.

So, in effect, without relaxation or downtime, the brain will fight on, but it won't be working at full capacity. According to an article on brain downtime by Ferris Jabr, writing in *Scientific American*,[6] 'moments of respite may even be necessary to keep one's moral compass in working order and maintain a sense of self.'

In the article, Jabr quotes a meditation expert and writer called Michael, who took ninety-two days out of modern life to try to switch off. 'Currently, the speed of life doesn't allow enough interstitial time for things to just kind of settle down,' he told Jabr. 'When you go on a long retreat like that, there's a kind of base level of mental tension and busyness that totally evaporates.'

Few people can simply choose to take ninety-two days out of a year to live in silence and meditate. But there are ways you can encourage your brain to recharge without going to an extreme level.

There's a reason my apartment is full of books and cooking equipment and paints, and yes, reader, even a PS4 and TV screen, hidden away in a big cupboard so I don't always have to look at them. But there they are. I know I am likely to work more hours than I should, so I purposefully go overboard with distractions.

I bought some candles to light when I get in from work, hoping they'd make me relax. Instead, I now do work to the cloying scent of 'Fireside Treats', which flickers in a big glass jar, casting ominous shadows over my workroom as the night draws in.

Buying what essentially amount to toys in a bid to make myself put my laptop down is extremely depressing. And, before I feel like a total loser, I know I'm not alone. I'm one of the first to leave the office, so I might look like a slacker, but if I'm not going anywhere that evening, as soon as I get home I open my laptop, refresh my emails and try to get back on top of tasks that skipped my attention during the day.

Chloé Elliott, founder of Odyssey Box, feels the same way, and she's only 23. 'I don't have a hobby that doesn't make money or go on Instagram. I'm probably a prime example of someone who has got sucked into it [the capitalist system]!'

She explains that the hobbies she no longer does are the ones that aren't profitable. 'I've been knitting since I was 6 years old, but you'd have to sell things for £100 to make money. I crochet my own clothes. I used to play all sports: rugby, swimming, gymnastics, and that's time taken away from earning money. It feels like I'm on a treadmill and I'm running towards financial freedom, even if that means spending the whole of my twenties doing it.

I do feel like I'm not living in the moment, and lots of people, from the age of seventeen to early thirties feel the same way. We think our lives and jobs will be better when we're in our forties, so we're not living it now, or making the most of it now. I feel very low sometimes, I worry when I don't have sales, and wonder what the point of the whole week was.'

Chloé had burnout when she was just 22. 'I was off work for six weeks, and for those weeks I had to just lie in bed and stare at the ceiling. That's also when I founded Odyssey Box, because that made me feel better and get started again. Even now, I don't drink or sit in the park with friends. It feels like if you're not on board, then you're slowing me down and you're getting in the way. I feel most at peace when I've completed something.'

But at least if we have the means and ability to book a vacation we can choose to get away from it all. Right?

Wrong. ABTA (The Travel Association – formerly known as the Association of British Travel Agents) has forecast a rise in working holidays. A recent report said that 'holiday-makers are looking to ensure they maximise their expenditure and leisure time. This is driving the "hard-working holiday" . . . [which includes] the added benefit of coming home with a new skill . . . [This] holiday mindset is set to continue for years to come.'[7]

When I was younger, I used to love travelling long distances because it was the perfect excuse not to reply to emails. Today, putting a quick out-of-office on saying 'might not be able to reply because I'm boarding the plane' is truly freeing. Recently, I've recognised that my brain needs a hefty break, so I've tried to resist the temptation to sit down and use the journey for anything other than pulling the blanket up to my chin, taking a sleeping pill and passing out for ten hours.

But what about the people who strive to succeed even when they're on holiday? I'd like to propose that it should be mandatory to have at least one really average holiday a year. And I would bet that if you're lucky enough to have two holidays, you'll enjoy the crummy, budget, raining one more than the one you splurge on, any day of the week.

Perhaps you are one of those people who has a big, disposable income. The kind of person who thinks that they've worked really hard that year, put in some pretty long hours, and they deserve a holiday. Rather than booking two weeks in the Maldives to hang off a sun lounger, there's an enormous rise in people booking holidays where they're challenged, sometimes by other people shouting at them to run up hills.

And if I had a spare five grand, I probably would too.

What's excessive is just how expensive these holidays are, and how there appears to be a growing trend to deny yourself any fun or relaxation time whatsoever. Take Third Space, which also happens to be my gym. (Disclosure: I'm a massive fan, but even I, a total fitness fanatic, balk at spending money on my holiday in a similar way to my everyday.)

This year Third Space is running two retreats. One is based in the Sahara and offers a marathon-training session. According to its blurb, for £1,600 you can spend your holiday doing a marathon distance, split into running, biking and kayaking. 'Physically challenging, an element of training is needed to get yourself ready for this one.'

It's important that I keep sticking my hand up and admitting that this sounds like a really fun trip for me, and, if I had some spare cash floating around and a sunburn death-wish, I'd probably sign up. But a tiny voice inside my head is saying: 'This isn't a good way to spend a *holiday*.'

Our lives are neurotic and chaotic and can be laced with anxiety and deadlines and stress. For many of us, keeping fit is tacked on to a long list of 'things we have to do'. The beauty of taking a holiday is being able to decide that actually, today isn't the day we decide to work out. It's about having a lie-in, or trading your 6 a.m. daily HIIT class for a strenuous hike later in the day.

As well as challenges, Third Space's escapes also include a holiday called 'Restore', which promises daily yoga, HIIT and workshops. The price is around £2,000 for the week. Going on holiday is one of the few times in the year I grant my body some time off, and although there's definitely a lot of running, hiking and the odd foreign spin class thrown in, even a fitness obsessive like me can see the danger in making ourselves push every single day of the year.

We probably don't want to spend our entire holiday in a museum or reading lengthy books about niche history on local metallurgy, for example, but it's good to mix and match. More average holidays that will probably restore our bodies and mind far better are as follows.

A phone-free week at home

Buy an enormous stack of books/magazines/paints/a Netflix account – whatever makes you relax – and put your phone in a bag. See friends lots by writing the appointment times on a physical calendar. This has the added bonus of making you excited to speak with them and hear their news because you've been away from the 10 million group chats you belong to.

Camping

Studies have shown that being outside is great for your mental health. So is wild swimming, stroking animals, being with friends and waking up with the sun. Camping in the height of summer in a field by a river will tick off all these things. Pack a rucksack, hop on a train on Friday evening, and find somewhere to put a tent up for two nights. Grab some bagels and fruit and you've got some basic meals sorted so you don't even need to splash out and buy a stove. Sorted.

Camping in France

As above, but more exotic and more-guaranteed warmth.

A cheap flight to somewhere with a beach

After a global pandemic, jumping on a flight to anywhere feels exciting. Having a cheap and cheerful holiday is a great way to do this, and reducing huge costs will make the trip feel way more relaxing. Staying in cheap hotels that actually turn out to be amazing will feel great, whereas splashing out on a five-star hotel only to discover it's a bit shit is guaranteed to make you regret your life choices.

*

It's easy to pour scorn on holidays where you skill up rather than relax, before you realise that, for many, the alternative is just logging on to work email. The first thing I've seen people do when they get to a hotel or a restaurant (or even a beach) is connect to Wi-Fi. A torrent of emails and messages, some from colleagues and others from friends, pours in. Switching off is almost impossible as soon as you're online.

This is why the whole concept of learning holidays is probably quite a good one, despite the fact, superficially at least, it just sounds like more of the same. After all, if we find it almost impossible to switch off, why not keep our brains on and make the most of our capacity to absorb as much information as possible? Entrepreneur Deirdre Bounds founded a travel company called

GoCambio, which connects people who can teach languages with those who want to learn. Speaking to *Director* magazine, she said: 'By immersing in something new, you're forced to put your phone and laptop aside and focus on the task at hand, even if it's only for a few hours. It's a fast and effective way to switch your mind into holiday mode and at the same time stimulate your brain with something that is completely different to work.'

She adds that execs are the main customers. 'Exec-level people are, by nature, high-achievers, and this doesn't stop on holiday.

'One activity is never usually enough. Things that combine surf and yoga, for example [are most popular], hiking and canoeing, cycling and cooking, and so on.'[8]

Although this undeniably sounds exhausting, it also, if you're the sort of person who hates lying on beaches, sounds fun. But surely we have to avoid the temptation of just moving from one state of busyness to another?

We can convince ourselves that it is relaxing, but surely there's some pleasure in just being average. In just saying: 'I don't need an exec-level holiday. I just need a break.'

After several years of spending holidays speeding from one town to the next, attending language schools, volunteering programmes and surf camps (I once spent a really miserable two weeks helping to build a child's adventure playground in Brussels which, looking back, felt like slave labour), I'm trying to take easier holidays.

My laptop still comes with me, but I'm taking pleasure in revisiting cities I've already gone to. Hunting down that old coffee shop down a side street you once found, or going to a restaurant where staff look at you with a glimmer of recognition; these are ways to have an enjoyable holiday without feeling stressed about not making the most of your time there. There is a solid handful of cities and places I've returned to tens of times, and it's going back to these places, rather than always pushing myself to go off the beaten track, that is actually surprisingly relaxing. Budapest, Bologna, LA, New York, Tel Aviv, Lima, Bangkok, Hong Kong. I love these places, and there's such a pleasure in returning and not feeling like you have to go to every museum and every hot new opening because, to some extent, they feel familiar.

I'm learning (gradually) that it's fine to take a holiday to exactly where you've already been, and walk familiar yet different streets, enjoy the shaft of sun that catches you in a net of warmth when you round a corner, having a glass of wine at a pavement cafe when the feeling takes you. This, I'm learning, is a holiday. It's not one for everyone – thankfully we're all different.

But hopefully someone out there will hear the message that it's not crucial to post the whole experience on

Instagram; to hit bigger holiday targets; to tick off every country in the world, as if they're just names rather than living, breathing places.

Call me boring, but sometimes it's good aiming for a 'good enough' on holiday. Good enough can equal contentment, which is what you want from a rest. Eschew that fourteen-day scientific cruise to Antarctica, and go to Edinburgh instead. Have a piece of shortbread, sit in front of a cosy fire and dance the night away at a ceilidh. Bliss.

Education

Give a child a box and it becomes a palace. The upended cardboard box on the multicoloured rug is the seat of the Duke of Chester and he's hosting a ball. The courtiers arrive by zebra. Playmobil and Lego figures are the glitterati and they ride zebras and lions, which the child swears blind are dazzling white palominos.

A few hastily drawn windows in felt-tip pen and some scissors attacking a door-shaped hole, and you have the palace realised in all its glory. As the guests arrive, each has likes and dislikes. Some decide to fight, others complain about the journey time. As children play, their imagination grows, their communication skills improve and their creativity blossoms.

For the past twenty years, there's been a clear growing trend across parenting to structure our kids' early years. Playtime becomes scheduled time, which doesn't really work as a concept when children don't know what it means to diarise.

Education has always been contentious. Parents are convinced that their way is always right and that they know the best for their children. But clearly, something's going wrong. Children's mental health is being described as an 'escalating crisis'. According to a BBC article, the number of children seeking help from Child and Adolescent Mental Health Services (CAMHS) in England has more than doubled over the past two years.[1]

The way we educate, test and allow children to explore and play is clearly impacting the way kids feel. A recent exhibition at the Wellcome Collection showed that today's children preferred 'quiet play', 'educational fun' and 'digital play' compared to previous generations. This suggests that what exists now is more subdued play. Have we, without realising it, returned to the 'seen and not heard' school of child-rearing?

While I write this, I'm sitting watching three children play. The first is bossing her younger sister around. They are carrying rocks between two pieces of paper, speaking Spanish, and are creating some kind of magical universe. Occasionally they scream loudly to their mum to get her to come and look. When she doesn't come immediately, they scream even louder, and one gets quite upset.

At the same time, their younger brother, who looks like he's about to hit four, sprints around the pool, apparently pretending to be a tractor. He has been running non-stop for the last twenty minutes, chuffing and panting as he goes. He does not seem to notice that there are no grown-ups also doing this. He does not care.

His biggest concern at night is probably that monsters will nibble his toes while he sleeps, and he is probably terrified by that. He, like many children under the age of four, believes that there are no limits to what type of evil monsters can dwell in our wardrobes or linen closets.

Acclaimed neuroscientist Baroness Susan Greenfield suggests that 'small children seem to live on an emotional roller coaster. With miraculous rapidity, heart-rending sobs give way to gurgles of delight at the sight of a chocolate bar or a cat walking past . . . if such intense emotions were displayed in an adult, they would presumably be seen to be indicative of some inner state, such as bereavement, so extreme that it would have to pervade the individual for far longer than the seconds for which it streaks across the face of a child.'[2]

It's thought that the average child laughs around 300 times a day, while for adults it's as little as fifty times. We, as adults, live life in a significantly more melancholic way, or an emotionally stable way, depending whether you want to spin this loss of the display of emotions into a positive or negative. And yet, despite this happiness and lack of understanding, and lack of ability to place any experiences into a contextualised reality, children are beginning to experience mental health problems at an astonishing rate.

Mental health rates among children are climbing

There has been a 'sharp rise' in the number of under-elevens getting mental health treatment, data obtained by children's charity the NSPCC reports.[3]

Schools across England have made a total of 123,713 referrals for various pupils to seek mental health support, a figure which has risen by a third since 2014/15. The rise has been blamed on a number of issues, the most pressing, say researchers, is pressure put on young people at school. It's obvious that our enforced pursuit of success is leading to an extremely high number of children feeling stressed out and anxious, conditions that used to be mostly the preserve of adults.

According to a survey conducted by Barnardos, school is the biggest stressor for under-twelves. The survey reports that nearly half of twelve-year-olds in England (48 per cent) feel sad or anxious at least once a week. By the age of sixteen, 70 per cent report feeling this way at least once a week, with more than a fifth (22 per cent) having negative feelings as often as once a day.

Journalist Lucy Clark has written extensively about the pressure put on children in the Australian education system. She was inspired to write her book *Beautiful Failures: How the Quest for Success is Harming Our Kids* after her own daughter struggled with the educational system. Speaking to ABC News, she said: 'This drive to achieve a number at the end of twelve years of schooling has become a kind of mania,' she says. 'Overriding so much that is wonderful and exciting . . . about being educated.'

She explains that kids who achieve are suffering just as much as kids who fail. The main problems with the education system? 'There is too much focus on academic outcomes and a very narrow view of success, with a one-size-fits-all approach that negates individuality. There is too much testing and too much competition, and too much comparison between kids.

'The whole system is geared towards achieving better outcomes rather than getting kids to love learning, and consequently there is a hierarchy of pressure, with kids right at the bottom.'

Anyone who has children at school in the UK, or who remembers being a pupil recently, will probably recall the kick of nerves, the feeling that there was always work, no matter how much of it you thought you'd done.

Every evening there was more homework, more

learning that couldn't be crammed into one day at school, and the itchy endlessness of being asked to sit down by a different teacher every hour, who didn't know how much you wanted to sit and daydream and just stop and take it all in, but you had to keep going and plugging every part of your new brain with details of osmosis and Pythagoras and *Coriolanus*.

And for what?

That continued sensation of guilt when you're not working, right the way into adulthood.

The feeling that when you're not sitting at your laptop trying to come up with pitches, or replying to an email at breakneck speed, that you're going to fall right to the back of the class and have to start at the beginning of the CGP revision guide *How to Be an Adult*.

I reckon that's why so many of us are such highly-strung-out adults – because many of us never felt like we had the opportunity to press pause.

My parents never put pressure on me, ever, but even so, I recall the first computer games I was bought being educational ones, books set in historical time periods that made me obsessed with people like Mary Queen of Scots, and even watching TV shows like *Blackadder* encouraged me to write whole new scripts which I made my friends perform in the school yard (sorry Autumn and Ella).

Life can be wonderful and full and busy, but as the

majority of kids grow up in the city, there's less time and space for them to hang off trees or dig holes to Australia.

One in eight children today have a mental health disorder, and research by the NHS found that one in five children acknowledged they'd been victims of cyber-bullying. Emotional disorders, which include bipolar disorder, have also risen, from 3.9 per cent in 2018 to 5.8 per cent in 2019. Imran Hussain, the director of policy and campaigns at Action for Children, told the *Guardian*'s Haroon Siddique that these figures revealed the true scale of the children's mental health crisis in this country: 'Sadly, this stark rise in children and teenagers suffering from a mental disorder makes it clear current government plans are failing to grasp this reality.

'Every day, our frontline services see children and teenagers struggling to understand how they fit into the world. They have to contend with things like intense pressure at school, bullying, problems at home, all while navigating a complex 24/7 world with constant stimulation from social media.'[4]

The introduction of screen time

I was one of the first generations of children given their own screens. When I was ten, my parents, unusually, bought me a computer for my room. I used it mostly for late-night MSNing (instant messaging) friends, but also doing homework on and playing around with Paint. I also spent hours and hours immersed in *The Sims*, *Age of Empires* and *Stronghold* like the geeky teenager that I was. Sure, I enjoyed sports and going out for walks, but I found it hard to resist the allure of building my own world, just . . . virtually.

All play is good play, and, as a child-free grown-up, I am the last person to judge the way kids choose to chill out. But what can't be ignored is the rise of stress. Kids start school young in the UK (around four years old) and the majority continue until aged eighteen. Because of work demands on parents, some children may attend nursery from just a few months old, which means by the time some kids hit eighteen, they've never known life without structure.

According to the American Psychological Association, around 83 per cent of stress felt by young people results from education. This isn't hugely surprising, because most kids don't have to pay rent or be nice to their horrible managers, but it's definitely concerning. Other than during exam time, there's no reason why school should be so stressful. In an ideal world, school should be interesting, creative, inspiring and educational. Stress shouldn't come into it.

In addition to the stress of school, the same study found that 67 per cent are stressed about getting into the right school or college.

In 2018, the NHS conducted a survey of nearly 10,000 young people which found some startling statistics. The study found that between eleven and sixteen, both sexes were equally likely to have a mental health disorder, but when they reached seventeen to nineteen, girls were more than twice as likely to have a disorder.[5] This could be because more pressure is put on girls than boys.

The transition from play to education is a tough one. All of us can remember the day we realised we were mortal, or that our parents would one day die, or that we would have to eventually leave our homes and pay rent. As a child, when the world is overwhelming and big and scary, these are not easy things to wrap one's head around.

Growing up is hard, and while we're trying to contend with studying for exams, realising that we're actually terrible at physics and trying to figure out what we want to do with our future, we have to learn to navigate real life too. Body image issues; racism; bullying – it's not surprising that kids at school are overwhelmed by reality. We grow up fast and it's easy to see why so many children feel so overwhelmed.

Now, through our phones, we have access to videos that show terrorist attacks in the Middle East, we hear about children being abducted and murdered in other cities and are also aware of the constant chime of politics, racism, immigration. Kids are smart. Our intolerant world will bleed into cartoons and kids will get a sense the world is a troubled place. The anger, the fear and the anxiety: they'll absorb it from friends and family but also try to work out what's happening so they can manage it too. Adults have a tendency to wrap older kids in cotton wool, urging them to focus on school and friends.

But 'it doesn't concern you' doesn't wash any more. Not now they have access to the world from their smartphones. They follow Greta Thunberg and hear her crisis call. They see the hashtag #BLM (Black Lives Matter) and ask what they can do. Celebrities hashtag #MeToo and it becomes appropriate to discuss sexism.

Thanks to phones and the internet, childhood is focused more than ever on the external, which can be extremely overwhelming when you only know half of the story. And the issue, says parenting expert Liat Hughes Joshi, is we're losing sight of what education should be about.

Learning for pleasure or for gain?

Anyone who has spent time in a big supermarket recently, or walked down a town high street, may have noticed the boom in extracurricular tutoring. Explore Learning centres, which offer extra maths and English tuition, can be spotted at the back of hypermarkets and on high streets. They offer an extra hour of tuition at the end of every school day for children as young as four.

Once the preserve of the firmly middle class, private tutoring is now rising, and it's becoming more accessible than ever before. It's still out of reach of many, however, where even the most basic courses at centres like Explore Learning cost £124 each month. And despite being marketed as 'accessible', critics say such centres are fuelling social inequality: how can anyone whose parents can't afford extra tutoring expect to compete with somebody with additional help across the board?

Extra tutoring isn't dominated by white middle classes either. Statistics show that tutoring is actually more prevalent among non-European families: White European (25 per cent of children are tutored), Indian (45 per cent), Chinese (35 per cent), African (41 per cent), Other Asian (29 per cent), Pakistani (28 per cent), Caribbean (27 per cent), Other White (27 per cent).

When I was a child, the only people who were tutored were those who had learning disabilities or who really weren't going to pass their exams and had families with a high disposable income. I appreciate that inner-city Sheffield probably isn't the epicentre of private tutoring, but a *Guardian* article from 2018 highlights that this idea has probably changed too. In it, the author, Sally Weale, spends time at an Explore Learning centre in Bradford.[6]

Children at the centre come from all walks of life, she says. She writes: 'There are families from Latvia, Poland and the Philippines. The parents talk about giving their children "an edge", the "leg up" they never had.'

One of the parental case studies is Ijaz, and he acknowledges just how competitive schools are in the area.

> I warn my kids they should be top – or among the top
> five at least – in class. They are doing well. I don't mind
> paying extra. I'm investing in their future. I know the
> importance of education. My kids love it.

It's great that Ijaz's children sound like they love studying extra hard to please him. But what if Ijaz's children weren't academically inclined? What if education and childhood is about more than being picked up from one learning establishment and driven to another just to make the top five?

Education through nature and play isn't a new concept. Jean-Jacques Rousseau, in his treatise on education, or *Emile*, written in 1762, celebrated the need for one's mind to be opened and enhanced through play. In his book, he describes the steps one must go through to become the 'ideal man'. Up to the age of twelve, he should be exploring a state of nature.

Children must be 'free of swaddling clothes' and allowed to play outside and all the rough and tumble that goes with it. Next, just before puberty, Rousseau argues that children should be taught a trade or handy skill, like carpentry, and only once puberty has commenced should they start their formal education. A child should only learn what is 'useful or pleasing', because then he will learn to love education.

This is all well and good for the son of a French landowner, but you'd be hard-pushed to expect a child living in an inner-city tower block to spend their childhood scooting to the local grass verge looking for ladybirds.

There has to be balance between what Rousseau wanted children in his era to achieve in an educational sense, and what is available in ours.

The pressure we put on children today starts young, and not just among the four-year-olds hoping to improve their maths after school.

'More harm than good'

From a young age, we're told how special we are, and this can actually be quite damaging. It's good to remember that we are (almost all) destined for quite average lives, something Liat Hughes Joshi reminds us. Joshi is in the middle of writing her seventh book on how to raise a functioning adult. She is a slight forty-something, with clear energy and a passion for education and children. She also tells it like it is. We're talking about the risks of overparenting – the type of helicopter parenting where every element of a child's time is controlled by parents. 'While it's generally well-meaning, it can often do more harm than good,' she says. 'The purpose of parenting, in my view anyway, is to help your child become a well-functioning, happy adult, and to do that we have to look at more than just A grades or music. We've lost sight of that a bit, I think.'

She feels one of the biggest issues with 'tiger parenting', and indeed schools telling children just how special everyone is, is that the majority of kids 'are around average. Tiger parenting is about getting kids to strive to be A-grade superstars and they can't all be that. Just accept who your kid is. We all want our kids to do well, but we also have to accept that it's not just about grades and certificates.'

Liat shares some real talk, which is a refreshing change

amid the plethora of people celebrating their baby's milestones with 'Oh, he can walk. He's going to be a mountaineer.'

Joshi adds: 'It's quite harmful as a society for kids to always be told that everyone can reach for the skies. You hear phrases like 'You're a superstar', but frankly, our children are destined for quite ordinary lives.

'Setting them up to expect to be celebrities or captains of industry is damaging: we're setting them up to feel like failures in later life. To actually teach them or encourage them, to help them learn that they're going to be mediocre and their life could be fairly dull at times, is far, far more useful. I really don't think we're getting the balance right at the moment.'

What we should be doing educationally, she says, is to tell children that they should try to achieve their dreams, but here's how to cope with it if you don't.

The way our education system spits out children is by teaching them to expect instant gratification. 'You get these young graduates going into the world of work with completely unrealistic expectations of what they should be doing. Young people have lost the ability to delay gratification and expect immediate success. People now feel like they should be running the company from day one, and I don't think we're equipping children well in this respect.'

As kids at primary school in the nineties, we were

never told we were special. You would be told you were 'bright', and to be labelled bright you had to do something really extraordinary, like win a city maths prize or write a poem that was published in a magazine. Most of my school reports said 'Conscientious'.

At the time, my parents seemed pleased with this, and I had no idea what it meant. If they were pleased, then great: I got chocolate.

Looking back, I still have no idea what conscientious meant in the context of a six-year-old, but I remember it being a strong feature of my report all the way up to my going to secondary school. So much effort was put in to avoid the 'c' word (clever) that it felt at times even parents didn't have a clue whether their kid was thick as a brick or probably going to manage to get a few A levels.

Being honest about children's capabilities and grades feels as obscure now as it did in the 1990s and 2000s, according to some teacher friends I spoke to. The risk is alienating the child and stopping them from loving learning, says teacher Chris, who works at a state school in a deprived area. 'The trick is knowing how to motivate a child when their parents might not be interested in education, and being told that they're average won't help that.'

That said, a bit of realism would help his job a lot. 'We get some parents saying that they're practically bankrupting themselves tutoring and asking why they're not doing better. They tell me they should be top of the class.'

He admits that some kids just aren't academic and it's often parents who refuse to accept this.

The last twenty years have seen the substantial growth of both tiger parenting and helicopter parenting.

Parents have always wanted the best for their children, but in 2011 a new book hit the shelves: Amy Chua's *Battle Hymn of the Tiger Mother*. In her book, she describes the tough love tiger parents use to inspire and motivate their children. Chua, a Yale professor, described tiger parenting as more of a Chinese phenomenon.

She says: 'The Chinese believe that the best way to protect their children is by preparing them for the future, letting them see what they're capable of, and arming them with skills, work habits, and inner confidence that no one can ever take away.'

Conversely, Western parents, she says, try to respect their children's individuality, encouraging them to pursue their true passions, supporting their choices and providing positive reinforcement and a nurturing environment.

Since the book's publication, the idea of tiger parenting has taken off in a big way, especially in middle-class households. In the US, tiger parenting was almost totally the preserve of Asian Americans, and indeed, says Liat

Hughes Joshi, many immigrant families in the UK really invest in their children in this way too.

It's all about tough love and setting very high goals for your children. If they fail, they're scolded. An article in *Good Housekeeping* magazine quoted Hazel Rose Markus, a professor of psychology at Stanford University who wrote an article on this. She said: 'Parents in Asian and Asian American contexts often direct children to recognize their fundamental connectedness to others, especially parents and their obligation to them.

'One of the most important obligations is to become an educated person so you can provide for the family and contribute to society. Being a good child means living up to parental expectations.'[7]

Our lives are very much shaped by how our parents treat us. Even in the womb, a baby can feel the effect of chronic stress. From day one, the choices our parents make, from whether they decide to respond to our every whim and cry or leave us to fall asleep alone, will dictate the way we react to future events.

So it is with education. Many demands are placed on parents, such as 'If you don't read to your child, they will grow up to hate learning' or similar. But reality defies these blanket, fear-mongering statements. It helps, for sure, but if your child wants to read, they will find a way to read. Haven't these people seen *Matilda*?

The rising cost of living, more people than ever having

multiple jobs to put food on the table and an increase in both parents working means there's rarely as much one-on-one time with children as there was fifty years ago. Something that affects women more than men, at least for now, is the expectation that we will be wonderful mothers as well as successful in our career. Perhaps we'll keep a side hustle going alongside our pregnancy and maternity leave; and, anecdotally, it seems women are still the ones to remember everyone's birthdays and what everyone at school is allergic to.

Among friends who have had children, there's a lot of 'When we decided to have a child, we agreed to split everything equally. But his salary was higher, so he went back to work and I stayed home. It just made economic sense.'

Ultimately, until we crack the gender pay gap, this workplace imbalance is never going to end. But I digress.

Good enough education

Education has been successful if a child can read, write, tie their own shoelaces, make a cup of tea and do some basic addition and subtraction. Anything else is a bonus. I've worked alongside people at work who couldn't tell me when the Second World War ended or what the capital of Germany is, but were remarkably good at campaign strategy. Sure, they're never going to be the go-to person for the office pub-quiz team, but while understanding Hitler's rise to power is interesting, it's hardly an essential skill.

I studied history at university, so typing the last paragraph was painful. But it's also truthful.

Sometimes we just need to unclench our teeth and accept that some people are very disinterested in the past. I share similar disinterest in their campaign spreadsheets, and we rub along just fine.

So why, over the last two decades or so, has there been a real explosion in extremely intense parenting? At its most base level, parents ensure their children receive an education partly because, by law, it's required, but also because we know children need skills if they will ever stand on their own two feet. With more people than ever going to university, children need a way to stand out.

Just as a penguin makes sure its offspring can fish for themselves before letting them become independent, humans do the same with their children. We all roughly know what we need to be desirable employees. We need to have some social skills, it helps to be clean, and hopefully an ability to just sit down and get the job done. Seven hours at school a day since the age of four should hammer that home.

Education for education's sake sounds like a no-brainer. But then why, when it transpired in a remote, very misogynistic part of India that educating girls had economic value, were parents suddenly happier to invest?[8] At first glance, investing in education to make a return sounds like an extremely crude thing to do. In *Poor Economics*, authors Duflo and Banerjee found that parents investing in their child's education does pay off – eventually. Parents do the investing and children get the benefits, and in poorer countries it's then assumed that children will dutifully look after them in old age.

The authors of *Poor Economics* found multiple cases where parents were not convinced about the investment they'd get back from their children, so they sent them back to work. They also cited a fascinating study where they had organised a parent–child collage session in rural Udaipur, India, and asked parents to cut out pictures of what they thought sending their children to school would bring them. The pictures they produced were covered in gold jewellery and new cars.

The collages showed that parents thought their children's education would secure wealth for the family. In Madagascar, parents thought of their kids' education as 'a lottery ticket, not a safe investment'.[9]

70 per cent of parents asked from a group of 640 in Madagascar thought that finishing secondary education would be enough to get a government or teaching job. In fact, just 33 per cent of children who finish education might be qualified for such a role.

But how is Madagascar relevant to 'tiger moms' in

DC or North London? A recent study found that even in the US, eight out of ten parents hope that by signing children up to extracurricular activities they'll achieve a higher future salary.[10] Seven hundred parents who had children participating in sports and musical activities thought that the more they spent, the more money their children would earn in the future. In 2019, a study conducted by insurance company COUNTRY Financial found that 56 per cent of parents would be willing to get into debt to put their children through school, and that 60 per cent of parents had already enrolled their children in a hobby that was 'financially taxing'.

If it's not, to put it crudely, about immediate financial gain, then it might be a longer-term investment. A survey conducted by the University of Michigan found that 55 per cent of parents thought that their kids' extra-curricular activities would lead to entrance to a higher quality of university. And it almost goes without saying that the same study found that the children of parents from lower-income households were less likely to partic-ipate in extracurricular activities.

Consultant clinical psychologist Emma Citron spoke to me about really listening to young people. 'Communicate with the youngsters. If they say they don't want to learn violin, then we can't force them to. The thing is, most parents are really very good parents and they know their youngsters well and they don't want to make them ill with stress or pressure. Some people know with a little more focus or encouragement or homework time, their children could achieve their potential better and so they nudge them appropriately.

'Then obviously, on the periphery, there are those who perhaps don't think they themselves have done enough, or achieved what they could have done. Maybe they want to live out their unmet ambitions through their offspring – "Look at my son or daughter and look at how brilliant they are", which allows them to bask in reflected glory.'

In the UK's capital, the average cost per hour of an after-school activity is £21. The minimum wage is just £8.21 an hour. If extracurricular activities are as important to entry – in order to prove rounded characteristics – as universities say they are, then I think we have the answer to why social mobility in the UK has stagnated for so long right here.

After all, children who cook and clean for their brothers and sisters because their parents work nightshifts don't get a certificate for being well rounded. Kids who care for a disabled relative every hour they're not at school are rarely praised in a school assembly.

Success is hard to quantify, but extracurricular activities, which are clearly a middle-class phenomenon, are one way of helping kids stand out from a crowd. But other than flying a flag to show that you can afford to pay £40 an hour for piano lessons, are extracurriculars really that vital? Does every child have a desperate urge to play piano, or do they want to play because a) you want them to play, or b) their friend Cindy plays and she's very good?

When I was a child, I begged my parents to let me learn piano and, after much nagging, they relented and let me learn. It was a hobby that kept me going from age five through to eighteen, but it was one that also required an enormous amount of work. I enjoyed my extracurriculars more than school (because they were fun). I also know how privileged I am to have felt stress from extracurriculars (yes, eye-roll at me, I deserve it); but I remember panicking that everyone else who did music lessons was progressing faster than me. It caused me my first case of genuine anxiety, aged around six, and that's because I had a cassette tape of the *Life and Times of Wolfgang Amadeus Mozart*.

I wanted to be Mozart so much. Sadly, I am very much not.

On the tape, Leopold, his father, was teaching his sister. (Who, by the way, was also exceptionally gifted, but did we ever hear of her again? Nope.) Wolfgang wanted to play and muscled in on his sister's lessons. When he did start playing, he apparently copied what his much more advanced sister Nannerl had been playing note for note.

So I wanted to get a piano because I wanted to be

Mozart, and then quickly realised I was only going to be playing 'Jelly on a Plate' for the next year. (C, D, C, D, C ,C, D, C, D, C; C, D, E, C, D, E; C, D, C, D, C.)

My friends, if you ever want confirmation that you are indeed not Mozart and are in fact very average, try playing a tune whose lyrics are 'Jelly on a plate, Jelly on a plate, Wibble wobble, Wibble wobble, Jelly on a plate.'

The stress surrounding extracurriculars was real. When I got older, I did athletics and had to compete at weekends. My friend Ellen and I would walk around after our races making ourselves sick by eating too many sugary, green chewy sweets as we toured Yorkshire's athletics grounds, but in reality we were both nervous and cared about doing well in our respective sports. There's something terrifying, at fourteen, about crouching down on the blocks and listening to the countdown followed by the shot of the starting gun. There's nothing relaxing about that.

We're constantly encouraged to be brilliant at everything. Don't play football? Well you're probably missing out on teamwork. Can't afford piano lessons? Your poise and coordination will be poor for life.

So much pressure is put on parents, and on us as children when we're actually at school, that it's possible to feel real guilt if we choose not to do extracurricular drama or get a tutor in maths. How can we possibly hope to succeed otherwise?

Let's be frank for a moment. Other than having fun and making new friends at the time, has being on the netball team ever been crucial for your happiness in life? Or for your success?

Plus, kids need to be bored. Emma Citron tells me: 'We know the brain needs downtime to do better. We've seen that a child does better in terms of concentration and mental health when they have times they're not being stimulated at all. Being overstimulated can result in burnout and leave them not wanting to do anything at all.'

She acknowledges that some children might love being busy all the time. 'A parent might say if they don't have their afterschool activities then they get bored – for the child, that could be the highlight of their week. That's what gets them excited.'

And it's clear that some people are willing to go further to push their children even harder. For some middle-class parents, their child's education starts in the womb.

Plenty of evidence exists that suggests babies start language-learning in the womb. For the last trimester of development, unborn babies can understand their mother's voice, and any strangers' voices their mothers speak with.[10] Babies prefer languages with similar tones and rhythms to those their parents speak, says Anne Cutler, a professor at MARCS Institute for Brain, Behaviour and Development at Western Sydney University, Australia.

A website called Motherly published an article titled 'Five ways to awaken your baby's senses in the womb'.[11] One piece of advice is to establish 'good habits by reading books to your soon-to-be babe. They may get a kick out of it – and you might just get one, too!'

This shows that pressure on babies starts even before they're babies. Experts say foetuses can understand speech from sixteen weeks, so parents who dream of success for their little one aren't wasting a second while their kid is in the womb.

A quick glance at a Google search shows pages of results for educational consultants who will help to get your child into the best private school for them.

Lucullus Educational Consultants say they have 'successfully placed hundreds of children from around the world into boarding schools, day schools and universities in the UK.' They add: 'We understand that every child is unique, and our approach ensures that each child has the best start in life at the right school through to the right university.[12]

Websites for these educational consultancies are full of pictures of happy, blond white children who have enjoyed 'especially tailored plans for your child's future', and, at the other end of the age spectrum, advertise experienced career-mentors who assess which career a child should take based on their 'personality and ability'.

If you can afford it, there's probably nothing wrong with hiring an educational consultant to propel your child through a decade and a half of education. But this is where I, with my predominantly state-school education, get the last laugh, when I realise most of my colleagues are privately educated and spent at least 80 per cent of their childhood on skis and/or horseback.

All that education and consultancy and womb bragging just got your kids to this: a small apartment and a mediocre gig in a corporate consultancy.

Is that really the aspiration? That someone spoon-feeds you the whole way, knocking down the pins of every obstacle in the path, to end up in finance, or law or marketing? With all the resources on the planet, is this where people want to end up?

Prince George, the child of Kate Middleton and Prince William, started learning Mandarin at just four years old at his fee-paying school in Battersea, London. The connected and the wealthy know that Mandarin is the language of the future. Swahili, another language Prince George is learning, is also seen as a vital language, especially as East Africa is home to some of the world's fastest-growing economies.

China is a global powerhouse: in the dying days of Western colonialism, China is asserting itself. Want to be a diplomat, lawyer, banker, teacher or doctor? Then learning Mandarin could future-proof your child's career. Sage parents have the ability to plan ahead and understand what skills to equip their child with, or even consult coaches about what their children should study.

Joshi says: 'I think loads of parents out there feel the pressure these days – there is a whole industry encouraging and fuelling helicoptering and tiger parenting, and it's only later on that lots of parents realise all that Kumon and clarinet lessons don't really matter that much.'

Trying to understand our educational system, and the way children are brought up, is fundamental to understanding why the current generation experiences more mental health issues than ever before, and why we put so much pressure on ourselves to be more than average.

If this sounds angry, it's because I am angry. We should be angrier about the way we're educated and the way we're restricted and how narrow our educational channels are. Why are apprenticeships so undervalued? Why are we so snobby about arts subjects?

Those in power tend to have followed a traditional route – they've studied politics, philosophy and economics (PPE) and they've usually gone to an elite university; it's rare that you'd find someone in charge who did a plumbing apprenticeship.

So, there's some good news to finish on. Because if you went to a top fee-paying school, then Oxford, studied PPE, yet managed to fail all your exams – don't worry, you'll probably still end up leading the free world because your family connections will be standing by!

Friendship

When I post a bunch of letters, I like to drop them in one at a time and wait for the thud of them hitting the bottom of the empty postbox. It's always an empty letterbox because, without exception, I remember to post my letters five minutes after the last collection of the day and arrive sweaty and manic watching the red Royal Mail truck pulling away.

So I end up taking my time.

I think about how the letters will travel across the world.

In my hand, there's a letter for my friend Alexandra in Prague who I met in Naples doing a workcamp when we were eighteen, stroppy teenagers who bonded over our hatred of budget Italian fashion. One for Glen and Maggie in San Francisco who have just found out they're having a baby girl. Another friend, Laura, who I met doing my master's degree in London. She's a brilliant, dedicated journalist and writer.

Another letter is for Adam, who lives a mile away from me, in Camberwell – that's a quick bike ride across

Burgess Park and down Britain's most potholed road. Another for my friend Ana in west London, whose house I've never visited because it's past Ealing and yet she makes an incredible effort to always meet in town, something I'm not sure I've ever thanked her for. One for Bobbie, who just inherited an allotment and is getting married this year and is the brightest, most sparkling person I know.

Another is to Autumn, my oldest friend, who I met at primary school in Sheffield and has drifted closer and closer towards living in London when she actually moved just four miles away. She is inspirational and cycles everywhere, and I think she's one of the coolest people I know, but I don't think I've ever told her that either.

There's one to Ellen in Sheffield, who I don't speak to nearly enough but wish I lived closer to so we could pop round and have a natter and catch-up like the (very) old times. One for Kitty, who kept me sane but since she had a kid I've not been in touch with much; and one for Sarah, who was my editor on the student newspaper but moved back to Australia a few years ago to be a grown-up and have a baby, and we cried with the realisation that we wouldn't see each other again and I miss her being around.

One to Helen, who is also getting married and lives in India; one to Elen, who I met at school and has the driest, most wonderful sense of humour.

There's a handful more, for people who mean a lot to me, who maybe don't know how much they mean to me, who I think I should tell how much they mean to me.

And this is a big ol' result of 'being too busy'. Let's just let that sink in for a moment.

We lose people and we let them leave because there are emails to answer. And there's always rain.

Have you noticed on the days you make plans to see friends it always rains, or you've always had a long day and you just want to cancel and lie in bed and stare at the ceiling because it seems easier? But you realise it's only water and you pull on all your waterproof clothing, grab an umbrella and get out to see them, because actually hanging out with friends is good.

I'm standing at this postbox in south London because last year was one of those years that was hard and soft in equal measures. Some brilliant things happened. I met some wonderful people. My first book was published. Two more were commissioned. I lost a long-term boyfriend and welcomed new people into my life. I met a person who treated me like crap. I'm still angry. But on the whole, it was good, because I survived it, and a huge part of me surviving it was down to my friends.

They listened patiently. And they sat with me and kept me company when I was released from hospital, cooking with me, going to see films with me, nervously sitting next to me when I'd run out of words and tears, just being there.

Sending a text saying 'Thanks for being there' doesn't really feel enough.

In fact, nothing feels enough. But over the last few years, in the months spent running between meetings and running myself into the ground, I've definitely put friends second. Because there's always something else. They have boyfriends or girlfriends or whatever friends; housemates, family issues, dog issues too. A new baby. But maybe they want to talk about something that's not nappies or poop, or they don't want to just hear their boyfriend muttering about his difficult client meeting.

And that's why I'm sending letters, because it's a little more than a text.

Even if I get no replies, it felt wonderfully cathartic and I felt full of love and gratitude for this loose network of people that ebbs and flows around my life, some playing a bigger role in some months, while in others we don't speak for a year. And that's OK, because I know they're there, somewhere. And at the right time.

And yet, would it surprise you to know that friendship seems to be going the same way as the local boozer?

The number of close friends we have has fallen.

According to a report published by Matthew Brashears at Cornell University, the average American had three confidants, or very close friends, twenty-five years ago, but that number has dropped to two.

James is thirty-one and confirms this. He's what I'd call an old friend and casual acquaintance. We meet annually, and when we do meet it's mostly for a big catch-up session. Then we don't see each other for another twelve months. When we sit in the park post-lockdown and socially distanced, he tells me it's nice because the only people he really hangs out with now are old uni friends or people from work. 'We go out and get drunk like old times, but we don't talk. There's no real connection any more, we just move in the same pack. Everyone I know has got married or has kids, and we can only get together once or twice a year now. It's sad. It does make me sad, honestly. They're great lads.'

And yet, thanks to social media, our communities and friendship groups feel expansive. The average Facebook user has 338 friends, although this fluctuates wildly depending on country, internet usage and age. Those who adopted the social-networking site later in life will probably have fewer friends because they're less likely to be part of a big community. Whereas if you start using Facebook at school, like I did back in 2007, you get almost an instant friendship group of the whole school year, all your sports clubs and communities, then university, where there's another deluge, and then new work friends, and then you've suddenly got, like, 800 friends.

Post a picture or a status today and it's liked by maximum twenty-two people.

Half of those people I guarantee you haven't spoken to for ten years.

It's not that the people at the other end of the computer screen don't care about you – it's that they don't know who you are any more.

The number of friends we have and need is called Dunbar's number. Robin Dunbar was in the middle of looking at some other research when he hit upon the idea of using the size of our frontal lobe to determine what size social group we'd be best in. He'd concluded that primates had big brains because they had to deal with a big group of other animals. Social interactions require a lot of brain power.

So he thought: Ah hah! Maybe this could work with humans too. Being a genius scientist, he went away, crunched some stats about mean group size and neocortical size, and came back with the figure of 150. This is the number the average person can have in a single social group.

One hundred and fifty people sounds like a lot, but his research showed that any more people in our 'casual' friend network and we'd be unable to process them all.

Dubar's number runs like so: 100–200 people are your casual acquaintances. If you were hosting a big wedding, these are the people you may ask. They may run to your best friend from nursery and the kind woman with a spaniel you met through BorrowMyDoggy.

He then used the rule of three to decrease the number of friends, thus increasing their importance. For example, he calculated that you might invite fifty people to a group dinner, then there's fifteen friends who you contact frequently, and then, finally, the final five close-knit circle of people. These people (even the five) may be fluid and change year by year, he says.

An article in the *New Yorker* by Maria Konnikova,[1] who was reviewing Dunbar's work, found that there were plenty of ways Dunbar's theory had been proven over time, throughout history.

For example, Dunbar found that Roman legions were also organised in this way, with companies being arranged in larger groups of 150, but broken down into smaller units of fifty and then fifteen. Among hunter–gatherers the average size of a 'pack' was 148.4.

Social media enables us to replicate (and double or triple) this size, but we lose that in-depth connection with people. In the *New Yorker*, Konnikova says: 'The amount of social capital you have is pretty fixed. It involves time investment. If you garner connections with more people, you end up distributing your fixed amount of social capital more thinly so the average capital per person is lower.'

But if we're not being fulfilled by our social media networks, then why are our real-life social lives shrinking when they're clearly so important? In the Cornell study, Brashears found that 64 per cent of his respondents stopped meeting up with people because they had 'nothing to talk about'. Just 36 per cent of people had no one to turn to to actually have discussions in the first place.

How to have bad but necessary chat

As a Brit, this is an astonishing figure. We have invented weather for this purpose. Many conversations start and end with 'Gosh, it's such a cold/hot/wet winter,' which then inevitably leads to discussions about cold winters and where we were when snow settled in 2012, and honestly, these Americans should try it. Weather chat is unfulfilling but can fill up at least twenty minutes if you work at it.

Throw in Brexit and some intergenerational angst and you have at least an hour of riled, angry conversation berating either the government and/or other people before you both tip your hat and go your separate ways.

It's simple.

In the US, replace weather with cars or 'how dirty the subway is'. Or Trump/Elizabeth Warren/Iran/How global warming is fake news. Done.

In France, weather can be replaced by 'dogs pooping on the street', a touchy and stressful, but still enjoyable, subject matter to while away twenty minutes, then bam, straight in with strikes and Macron's policies for that last hour and you're done.

It's natural for our friendship networks to ebb and flow depending on what we need and what we have to offer. If we're short on time, like most of the population, we might crave an old friend who can hop into a bar with us after work for an hour, have a quick chat about the state of things, and then dash back home.

If we're retired, maybe we need a friend who is happy to spend the whole afternoon together watching a film, cooking together and maybe going out for a long cocktail.

Our needs change as we age or enter different stages of family life, but the one thing that's consistent, despite our hundreds of friends and interactions across social media, is we're all getting lonelier.

Is loneliness actually a big problem?

According to a YouGov survey, around 2.4 million British people experience chronic loneliness (where there is no respite from feeling lonely). The government report, which was commissioned by MP Jo Cox in 2016, and continued after her murder, found that loneliness could be considered an epidemic. Apparently, being lonely can eventually lead to premature death, because it exacerbates the likelihood of becoming an alcoholic, smoking too much or having an eating disorder. The report found that being lonely exacerbates early death by 50 per cent.[2]

So why are we becoming lonelier, and why does it feel like we're losing friends who matter? We're busier, or at least feel busier, so we have less time to see friends. We may live further away from our pals; there's rarely a tight-knit community we all live and die in. Our community bonds are loosening.

While before, our existence may have revolved around a place of worship we would attend religiously every week, now it's rare in the UK to find somebody who does attend a service, especially if they're young. Just 722,000 people go to church each week, and most of those people are over the age of sixty-five. In fact, the number of people attending Church of England services has been dropping on average by 0.3 per cent a year.

Clearly the church needs to find ways to appeal to millenials, but the thing we lose, as the church as an institution becomes less significant, is community. Not so long ago, the church was a place everyone in the community met up once a week. There were crèches for kids to play in, Sunday schools, choirs, talks and advice. It was a place to get together and natter while your kids ran screaming around the church hall playing tag as you ate digestive biscuits and dunked them in your lukewarm tea.

In 2018, just 2 per cent of young adults (those under thirty) were affiliated with the church.[3] Today, our community has been replaced by online forums, social media and, quite depressingly, work. The future of work, at least until Covid-19 hit, seemed to be about the office aspiring to be everything for everyone. It's a home from home, a pre-built community where you can play sports, attend talks, enjoy free lunches, dinners, after-work drinks and even get advice on yoga technique.

Pubs are closing down at a rate of eighteen a week, according to the Campaign for Real Ale (CAMRA), and Covid-19 will further threaten social spots, so we're losing a further vital part of our community where we can hang out and have a good time.

Communities will always change, but for those who no longer work, there will be fewer places to go. When community falters, loneliness can kick in.

John Cacioppo, who conducted the report on loneliness with trailblazing MP Jo Cox, argued that the root of loneliness went deeper than any catch-all suggestions like too much time online or fewer people going to church. Instead, he wrote that evolution caused loneliness, that 'modern society is worlds away from the community-based life for which we're designed. It makes no more sense to be a human in isolation than it does to imagine a bee forging a life for herself without the support of the squad.'

Cacioppo points[4] out that until very recently, separation from our tribes – from our caregivers, hunters, food-providers, rent-payers, emotional partners – would have meant a very quick death. Being cast out would have meant not having a roof over our heads or being able to eat, unless we could somehow encourage a new tribe or community to adopt us.

It's for this reason, Cacioppo argues, that social rejection hurts as much as physical pain. Our brain is hard-wired to have friends to avoid loneliness. He cites brain scans that show that social rejection stimulates the dorsal anterior cingulate cortex, the same region of the brain that also reacts when the body experiences physical trauma.[5]

Being a loner isn't the same as being alone

He also points out that being a loner isn't the same as being alone. Meanwhile, people in hospitals are surrounded by people and yet those who stay for long periods of time may experience loneliness. Simply putting people together doesn't cure loneliness. In some ways it can exacerbate it, he says in an interview with Olga Kazan[6] for the *Atlantic*, because we realise that we urgently need to connect.

He says: 'Loneliness motivates you to repair or replace connections that you feel are threatened or lost. So people pay more attention to social information because they're motivated to reconnect.'

This can result in over-reading social cues and experiencing hostility that actually might not exist. It's true that, fundamentally, we're a social species, and that means we need people. But is there any reason to think we should flip this on its head and look at whether there's really anything wrong with being alone sometimes, if that's what you prefer? Does everyone need stimulation all of the time? I know sometimes I just want to close the door on the outside world and sit in my slowly darkening apartment with the lights off after work, watching the sky turn from pink to inky blue, and I like to do that alone, once in a blue moon.

Because doing that with somebody else there is weird as fuck, and they'd probably call for some sort of psychological care service.

But actually, sitting in a high-backed armchair, listening to the sounds of the city quieten, is a great relaxer.

Maybe a week of Netflix is fine, and a weekend spent

seeing a friend for a quiet coffee is all we need. And obviously, depending on our different personality types, that might be *all* we need. After all, an extrovert enjoys being around others and takes energy from them, whereas an introvert finds being with people exhausting. They need time out to recover.

Perhaps the issue isn't with lack of friends, it's society's obsession with loners being weird. Those who enjoy their own company aren't seen as team players, although it might be harder for them to lift themselves out of their own personalities. Psychiatrist Anthony Storrs, in his book *Solitude*, talks about the pleasures of being by oneself, of the skills you can only really learn if you're alone.

After all, you're going to be hard-pushed to find someone (however loving) who wants to sit through 10,000 hours of you learning the bassoon, or sitting in silence learning how to paint with oils. Some things are best done in isolation. Judy Garland and Marlon Brando were both famously loners.

My friend is an actor and said that, although he wins over a roomful of hundreds of people with his speech and actions almost instantly, he spends countless hours alone learning lines and doing character study.

'When people meet me offstage, I think they're surprised I'm not more outgoing. But I know when to turn it on, and I do it when it's important. When I'm on the screen in front of a camera or on the stage, it's my job. I can't just not talk. In the same way if you're in an office, you can't just put your headphones on and pretend you're not there.'

The issue is that being a loner gets bad press. In *Loneliness: Human Nature and the Need for Social Connection*, Cacioppo's book, co-written with William Patrick, he points out that crazy people are often ascribed the moniker of 'loner':

> When a deranged man named Russell Weston Jr stormed the US capitol in 1998, his picture appeared in Newsweek under the headline 'The Loner'. The media also ascribed that same judgement to the Unabomber, Ted Kaczynski, to President Reagan's assailant, John Hinckley, and to the Virginia Tech mass murderer, Seung-Hui Cho, and to any other socially marginalized individuals.

Friendship is inevitably important, but if it's so important, then why don't we value it more?

It can feel at times that friends can drop to the lowest-priority rungs.

A busy week at work? If you're single, chances are you'll prioritise seeing your housemates if you have them, doing some 'self-care', like going to the gym, and watching a lot of TV. If you're in a relationship and you're working late, guilt that you're abandoning your beloved will kick in, which means you'll probably choose to see them rather than go to the effort of travelling across the city or to another town to see your friends.

There are lots of reasons why we lose friends, says Dr Tina Tessina in an article for *Bustle*. It's natural for people to drop friendships when they leave school or college. You literally spend all day, every day, with the same people, all focused on the same goals. Your hours are the same, you have similar routines and you still live at home. You have the same dreams of success and failure, and being sixteen is fun, it's thrilling, there's still lots of new things to look at and explore.

Then there's the inevitable coupling up, which all of us will have been both guilty of and have experienced (however much we deny it). I have one friend who starts seeing a new girl and immediately spends every night with her: every conversation is about her, and he always has to leave early because he has to go and see her. Luckily, this stops after a few months and he turns normal again, but it's a pattern I've seen again and again.

Other reasons are having kids, moving to different cities, and, a weird one that I've noticed recently, income disparity. I have a rough knowledge of what all my close friends earn: by this I mean I know that to suggest dinner and drinks would be blow-out, or if it's best to go for a walk by the river or, if things are a real stretch, I love hosting them at mine for wine and a meal.

As a writer, that's been me, too. People working in creative industries go through feast and famine, and famine is tough when you have friends who are much better off than you. 'I'll get dinner,' they say, and you don't want to admit you can't even afford the Tube fare there.

I'm grateful for having had that income disparity because I know how hard it can be, not to mention embarrassing. I was once friends with someone who always ordered us bottles of wine for the table. She had a generous spirit and I really liked hanging out with her, but she'd reorder another bottle without asking me if it was OK. So one night the bill came to £75 for two bottles and she asked me to split, and at that time (I'd taken a year out to write plays and was living on about £300 a month) half of £75 was my food costs for the week.

Something that sounds so petty was enough to really harm our friendship, because it happened multiple times to the point I couldn't afford to go out with her. Even when I only ordered lemonade, she'd assume we'd split the bill, and in the end I had to avoid her because I was too British to just admit our friendship was costing me a fortune.

The assumption that our friends will always be there for us, until they're not, definitely exists. The narrative of having to work at our friendships feels like a relatively recent one, and it's one to celebrate. Some therapists also offer therapy for friends: I tried to persuade my friend to do it with me to see what it was like, but she refused.

'I don't want to cause a rift in our friendship when there isn't one already, just for your book,' she said, pointing at some of the questions we had to think about before going to the session.

What is your friend's most challenging characteristic?
What do you think he/she could improve on?
Tell me about a time your friend hurt you and why.

To be fair, I'm glad we didn't go through with this.

I wonder, in the world of self-help and self-care, whether sometimes the role of friends is changing. Do people sometimes see our relationships as essential ingredients to be happy? For example, magazines, experts and influencers tell us that friends are necessary in order to be happy, but perhaps this means we lean on each other a little too much.

In 2019, a tweet by Melissa A. Fabello went viral when she suggested that busy people sometimes needed to set boundaries with their friends.

So far, it all sounds completely fine. Making boundaries and being clear with them is part of making and maintaining friends. After all, you wouldn't expect any relationship to be without boundaries. I would be irked if each time my friend saw me they tipped their drink over my head. I'd say the unspoken rule is that we do not do that.

But Fabello's suggestion went a step further, clearly showing the way that friendships are changing. Putting yourself first has become something to aspire to – a desirable trait.

She recommended a template people could use if they have needy friends in their life: *Hey! I'm so glad you reached out. I'm actually at capacity/helping someone else who's in crisis/dealing with some personal stuff right now, and I don't think I can hold appropriate space for you. Could we connect [later date or time] instead? Do you have someone else you can reach out to?*

The message is clearly that she is busy, and she cares enough about her friends to put the time in for them, and this is her way of dealing with them. That's fine and I respect that.

But what was interesting about this tweet for me was the way it re-established who friends were. What friendship meant. Not just for the author of the tweet, but for the countless people who liked and replied to the tweet, absolutely supporting this take.

Is friendship really now a transaction? A commodity that we book into the diary and trade? What about being a friend for life who helps you out even if they are 'at capacity'. Also, is your 'personal stuff' really more important than helping out a friend?

If the 'personal stuff' really is that all-encompassing, surely you'd have already told your friend?

However, the tweet called out that emotional labour is real work; that listening, giving advice, thoughts and suggestions is actual work. It requires effort that can be quite exhausting, and is about asserting the fact that, for years, women have often undertaken emotional labour in a caring capacity with no consideration that it's actually quite an exhausting job.

Yet, sometimes you just need to vent, and that's what friends are for. Friends are there to be there for you, and as journalist Coco Khan points out in her *Guardian* column, sending this friendship out-of-office 'would have resulted in friend-relegation . . . or maybe a glass of rose to the face'.[7]

Khan hits the nail on the head when she says: 'I don't begrudge, but I can't help but cast a suspicious eye at our collective creep towards extreme, capitalist thinking where we see ourselves as a scarce resource, we see our relationships as transactions and where solutions for community problems are put down to the individual. Because, as necessary as self-care is, it is also an individualistic quick fix.'

Being busy is a problem. We're all too busy sometimes, and when we tell somebody else how busy we are, it can feel like there's an implication that the other person absolutely isn't busy at all.

I'm somebody who tells other people I'm busy, and it's my worst trait by far. Firstly, I have to remind myself that the other person almost definitely doesn't care: everyone has their own shit to deal with. Then I have to remind myself that being busy was my choice.

This is why being told how busy someone is is extremely boring (unless they're never usually busy, in which case it's actually interesting because your interest is piqued, and it turns out they're participating in some sort of extreme gardening event which is actually fascinating).

Being busy, or being 'at capacity' with other things, is often self-imposed. Parents are busy because (shock!) they decided to procreate and keep their day jobs.

Someone who is writing a book on top of their day job is (shock!) also busy because they're trying to do something nobody sane would want to do.

Somebody trying to work out at the gym more often is (shock!) busy, because he feels more exhausted than usual when he gets home from work in the evening so needs to recharge.

Someone working two jobs and caring for their disabled brother is extremely busy, because they're being a remarkable human being.

For the most part, being busy is a privilege. It implies that somebody wants you enough to be their employee or likes you enough to be their partner. It suggests you have enough money to afford a gym membership or to take up new hobbies, or that you've been lucky enough to be in the right place at the right time to get a book deal.

For a bleak six months, my life was dominated by deadlines. It was all I could talk about. To any friend who asked, I was 'busy'. When I made it out with friends (after much cancelling and poor planning), I'd get a stressful email and have to run home to make edits. Sometimes I'd tell them how busy I was, and it bored them. It bored me too.

Looking back, I've been an utterly lousy friend at times. I missed my oldest friend's thirtieth birthday party because I couldn't make it out of the door. In comparison, I hosted a dinner party and a friend, despite being broken up with the night before, still made it. Even though my oldest friend gets it and told me not to worry, I'm never going to forgive myself for that.

Because real friends are there for you. They don't send you a text saying, 'Hey, man, I know you're like, shit, but I'm super-busy. Please return next week, like, when I have more capacity. I'll send you a doodle poll!'

If it wasn't for my friends after my time in hospital, going on walks with me, sitting with me, taking me to the park and resting with me in the sunshine, I don't know if I would have made it through.

So my attempted suicide was a wake-up call. It thrust

me straight back into an appreciation of my friends. It was a reminder that it's better to be average and surrounded by love, than successful and surrounded by nothing, and although I can't guarantee I'll always be there for every single person I know, I'm damn well going to try.

Homemaking/Food

It's Sunday afternoon and I'm lugging a white plastic carrier bag along Bond Street. It's raining, and it feels like I'm carrying two golden retrievers in one hand. By the time I get home, my skin is so dented that it takes more than a day for it to spring back to a normal palm shape.

The bag I dragged along Bond Street until my hand felt like it was going to bleed is a Magimix food processor. I have wanted a Magimix since I was a child because I'm ridiculous. Fourteen attachments! Pulverises onion in seconds! Makes dough with no kneading! Basically, it's the answer to all my kitchen questions and is a tool that will absolutely change my life. It's also extremely heavy.

Instead, it's an attempt to improve my relationship with food and try to use up as many leftovers as I can, mostly because I have been guilted into feeling bad about food waste. Not that I eat badly (if you ignore the occasional chocolate binge, and whatever you do, don't leave Jaffa Cakes within ten metres of me because I will find them) – if anything, I am too worried about eating well.

I'm not orthorexic: I don't drink herbal tea, really dislike quinoa and would definitely not describe my diet as 'faddy'. But I am worried and anxious about doing the 'right' thing, and feel, like all of us, we're bombarded with different messages, each advising us to give up something else or try a new supplement. I spend a lot of time reading about food and thinking about what to cook, to the extent I'm wondering whether it's just too much. Why do I always feel the need to do more than just make a sandwich for lunch, or have scrambled eggs for supper? I need to learn eating is not a competition and buying a shop-bought cake rather than whisking one up in a Magimix at 11 p.m. is fine too.

There are so many questions about what we need, and what the world needs, right now. Should we be vegan, and prioritise animal rights? Should we be environmentalists, eating what's local to us, and protect the planet? Should we eat seasonally, and rely on swedes and turnips for the whole winter, unable to vary our diet but feeling great about reducing our carbon footprint? Or should we just throw our hands up and say fuck it all – as emancipated people, we're not slaves to the kitchen – and pop a ready meal in the oven after a tough day at work?

I started thinking about my relationship with food as I

unpacked my Magimix. Had I been conditioned from a young age to want a great food processor? But how else was I going to make pasta dough or great bread? How else could I julienne some carrots so I could make a great papaya salad?

The main reason for buying a Magimix was so I could make my meals more interesting as I tried to reduce food waste and focus on eating sustainably. There's only so much soup with root vegetables you can eat, so I was determined to make eating sustainably easier by buying something that would happily shred my food for me.

Over one third of the food that's produced globally is thrown away. That's partly you, yes you, binning that old bag of lettuce you only had a handful of. But mostly, it's supermarkets. These same supermarkets who refuse to allow any oddly shaped vegetables to grace their shelves. Whole fields can be left to rot because the potatoes are oddly shaped. Each year, an area bigger than China is used to grow food that's never eaten.[1]

I think we should all be worried about our relationship with food and the way we treat food. Even the coronavirus lockdown probably won't see us eating more carrot tops or bags of wilted greens (although I live in hope). Instead, food fashion dictates that we scatter handfuls of pomegranate seeds over salads, and add a handful of wilted spinach to soups. The rest of the container, uncalled for and unused, is left to fester in the fridge and then thrown away. The three white sacks of baked goods and yoghurts I was dragging along the road in King's Cross were all from Gail's Bakery, a cafe that sells fresh bread and if there is food left at the end of the day, Gail's carefully sets aside leftover food and distributes it to over 40 charities across London, Oxford and Brighton.

Food is wasted for thousands of different reasons. For single people who live by themselves (like me), it's a big ask to get through a massive bag of spinach before it wilts. I also don't have enough freezer space to store a great deal, so each time I buy a new item, I have premature guilt about not being able to finish the vegetables currently in my fridge.

Recently, there has been growing fear over the rise of ultra-processed foods (UPF). These are things like the ready meals that bear little resemblance to real kormas and jalfrezis, but are stacked in our fridges in their little plastic boxes, cellophane wrappers and cardboard sleeves. Ready meals were originally created to help busy families out: as women went to work, there was less time to cook, so ready meals helped to save women – who were still expected to be homemakers too – time in the kitchen.

Every book, journal or article calls ultra-processed foods out for being the devil's spawn. They're packed with salt! And sugar! And carbs! And carcinogens! So we should all avoid them, quit our jobs and stay home baking bread. Anyone who tried that during the Covid-19 lockdown will recall the defeated sourdough starter and poorly-risen loaf sitting in the rubbish bin. But UPF had a place and a role to play in the post-World War II world.

After the war, as family structures changed, a focus on getting food on the table fast became the goal. Artist and photographer Ed Ruscha took a series of pictures in 1961 called *Product Still Lifes*, which captured some of the American myths of a bountiful utopia post-war. Included in this series are pictures of cans of spam, while a contemporary of Ed Ruscha, Robert Heinecken, depicted a Swanson's TV dinner tray as part of an artwork. This is no advertising: he presents the TV dinner in all its reality, from the picture of what the dinner tray is meant to look like (plump shrimp, juicy green peas and crisp fries) to the sad reality – a congealed sauce, burnt shrimp, and fries so anaemic-looking they appear to be blue.

TV dinners, in their original format, were kicked off in the early 1950s by Swanson and typically included everything you'd need for your dinner, including dessert, on one tray. In the US, the dishes tended to include a meaty main course, a side of vegetables, a gravy and, from the 1960s, a sweet course. This tended to be an apple cobbler or a brownie.

In Europe, TV dinners were also made on plastic or aluminium trays designed to be shoved into the oven quickly, and also contained curry with rice as a main meal. The dinner trays were similar to those used on airplanes, and by 1969 the US experienced its first TV-dinner breakfasts, which included pancakes and Canadian bacon . . . on a tray.

This was fast-packaged, ultra-processed convenience, and the dishes were also cheap, costing the consumer just 98 cents. While women had previously been expected to slave over creating the Thanksgiving meal, which included cornbread, turkey, cranberry sauce and sweet potato, now they could buy a tray for under a dollar.

TV dinners soon became microwavable, with plenty of added salt and sugar to make the brown goo taste like something. I remember the joy of getting my first microwavable ready meals. My parents, despite working full-time, would almost always cook from scratch. We'd have big pots of soup, soufflés, salads and – the worst – a cheese pie my mum made which was literally home-made pastry with a block of grated cheese in it. My parents were avid but terrible cooks, although in hindsight I appreciate them making cooking from scratch seem like the normal thing to do.

Once a week I was allowed something different, and I chose freezer food: veggie fingers, slathered in ketchup, peas and mashed potatoes. That was as bad as it got.

As I got older, I remember more ultra-processed foods arriving on the shelves. I remember how easy it was to get a pizza to take home and heat up in the oven: this was still a novelty. Although we'd always have a side of salad with it, it became an every-Friday-night treat. Do you remember when you first saw Pringles? And I begged my parents to buy me Pop-Tarts, this American speciality that was brand new and fresh on our shelves. Even today, biting into a Pop-Tart sends me right back to that era of teenage madness where we emerged from our cocooned childhood selves into a world that's white and bright with newness.

An ultra-processed piece of food, says food writer Bee Wilson, is one that is 'so altered that it can be hard to recognise the underlying ingredients. These are concoctions of concoctions, engineered from ingredients that are already highly refined, such as cheap vegetable oils, flours, whey proteins and sugars, which are then whipped up into something more appetising with the help of industrial additives such as emulsifiers.'[2]

They include white bread, with its soft and thick textured mush, and Diet Coke, which bears no resemblance to anything natural. Food writer Michael Pollan calls ultra-processed foods 'edible food-like substances'.

Food is another measure of perfection, and how well we're doing at life. It's another way for us to beat ourselves up, to fail at being perfect. Juice bars, places that serve macrobiotic meals or faddish, gluten-free, vegan options are marketed towards women. Adverts for foods bursting with antioxidants are rarely shown being enjoyed by men; instead, young, glowing, thin women enjoy these wholesome, low-cal, high-fibre healthy options. Despite TV dinners, despite micro-waveable food, despite drive-thrus and despite take-out, there's an expectation that women are still expert house-hold managers. Eve Simmons is the deputy health editor at the *Mail on Sunday*, a food activist and author of *Eat it Anyway*. She thinks a lot of food culture is due to living in a patriarchal society. 'In the seventies, women's liberation was happening and food culture cottoned on to that. These UPFs allowed women to be freer and not spend all day standing in front of the stove cooking meals for their families. It's also a class thing. Today middle-class women don't need to eat super-high-calorie foods because they're rarely working in physically demanding jobs like waitressing or stacking shelves. That's when salad became popular – during the industrial revolution it was a way for people to show they didn't have the sort of physical, working-class jobs that needed potatoes and meat. We're back to that.'

This can be seen in the sheer number of cooking shows on TV, which attract mostly female viewers (according to research conducted by Cornell University).[3] I wouldn't want to be accused of gendering, but I think it's fair to say that when you walk into a bookshop there's a pretty clear distinction between the books written by men and those by women. Books written by men, for men, seem to be about meat and barbecuing. If they're healthy (see Joe Wicks), then they're about cooking lean for post-gym muscle-building. The other genre included is books for university students on how to cook their first bowl of pasta.

If books for women aren't about weight loss and dieting, then they're about absolutely everything else. They're about making your own granola, creating smoothies and shakes, protein bars filled with matcha and hemp and honey. They're about desserts and dinner parties, family breakfasts and lovingly whipped-up weekend lunches.

Food continues to be a conduit of love, but cooking is also one of the biggest parts of unpaid domestic labour. After all, cooking is more than just cooking. It's about researching what to cook, going shopping, keeping the fridge and basics stocked up, and then, more often than not, cleaning up afterwards.

In many cases, this still falls to women. In addition, a societal expectation exists to host dinner parties, to feed friends and to bake cakes to take into the office. If you've ever worked in an office that's held a charity bake sale, you'll know there's always one man who says he's 'never baked a cake in his life' and, when he has to bring one in, gets his wife to make one. It's always incredible.

There's huge pressure to buy seasonally and locally,

but this is also expensive. I feel judged when I buy imported blueberries, but I'm also told they're vital for antioxidants and skin health by the same magazine and health expert. Recently, I've tried to reduce buying anything that's not in season.

My bank account is furious. In fact, since starting to eat seasonally and avoid processed foods, my weekly spend on food has increased by 125 per cent, an unsustainable amount. While trying to do the right thing, I'm bankrupting myself.

Eve Simmons says she thinks people are definitely judged for not eating healthily, especially if they're poor. 'Poor people have always been demonised for the food they eat. They're seen as unhealthy or undesirable.' When poor people ate brown, healthy bread, the middle classes wanted to eat white processed bread, thinking it was cleaner and better for you. Similarly, when the poor ate stews and potatoes, the middle classes strove towards eating a meat-heavy diet. It wasn't healthier by any stretch, but they thought it elevated them.

'Yes, diet–related diseases are prominent, especially among poorer people,' acknowledges Simmons, but that's also down to poor social housing, tough jobs and institutional racism and classism. 'The whole thing with food is that it's so individual to everyone's special needs. If I had a disability which meant I couldn't reach my oven, or I had no money and my kids were malnour-ished and all underweight and the only food I could afford was a ready meal, then the highest-calorie food is always best."

The thing to remember, she says, is that our body always knows what's best. 'There's enough pressure coming from all different angles. Having spoken to hundreds of dieticians at this point in my life, they say there are no good or bad foods; it's all about having a variety and not thinking too much about what you're eating. Nothing about sugar or no sugar, or ultra-processed, or processed. If you remember that, you can't go wrong. Try to trust your body: at the end of the day everyone's trying to make money out of you. If you've had cake three days in a row, then that's fine – you probably won't want it the next day. Eat what you want – your body would tell you not to eat donuts for four days in a row because you'll feel sick. We're taught not to trust what our body is telling us. We have a complete distrust of how our body will react.'

Michael Pollan chastises the American people for being both obsessed with healthy eating and addicted to processed food. 'The American paradox is we are a people who worry unreasonably about dietary health yet have the worst diet in the world,' says Pollan. In his book, *In Defense of Food*, he advises people to eat whatever they want, as long as they cook it them-selves. It's much harder to binge on ice cream and cookies if you have to make all the items from scratch every time you want something. Pollan's sagest, most sensible piece of advice is this: 'Eat food, not too much, mostly plants.'

It's this sliver of sense in a world crammed with powdered food, vitamins, nutrient replacements, blended fruit and substitute meals that I've been looking for. We too often conflate dieting with nutrition, and experience guilt for eating chocolate or a slice of cake. Everything in moderation seems to be the best way to eat. I'll continue to volunteer at my local food-waste centre; I'll continue to blend an entire cabbage into pulp with my Magimix, but I won't beat myself up if I put some potato waffles in the oven from frozen.

Trusting that we won't die if I eat some processed food is important if we allow ourselves to be good enough. It's good to treat our bodies well, but none of us are going to jail if we eat a Mars bar.

Innuit people have existed for centuries eating fish, seal and whale blubber with no green vegetables at all, while there are indigenous tribes in Africa, like the Maasai, who eat mostly tubers and cow blood. We don't necessarily need food replacements like Huel. We probably don't need extra-enriched protein bars. We just need balanced food, and if we need to miss a day of eating healthily then that's OK, and shouldn't devastate us.

We have enough pressures on ourselves to always do the right thing, and if eating the odd ready meal means you can see friends, stay after work to finish a project, go and learn a new hobby, or even spend more time in front of the TV watching your favourite show and it brings you joy, then really, what's the big deal?

A sense of home

It feels like we're focusing more on food and food preparation because it has a transient life that can be explored no matter where you live. You don't need to own a house to cook a nice dish. You can feel like a homemaker and create a semblance of what feels like a normal life even if you only have a microwave and share a mouldy terraced house with seven other people.

In some ways, I feel as though cooking gives us stability and a small sense of what previous generations had. It can't be a coincidence that as the number of TV shows about food has increased since 2010, the number of young people buying houses has fallen.

After all, take a look at this series of tweets which blew up on Twitter back in January 2020.

How to infantilize an entire generation:

1) declare all the markers of adulthood to be linked to financial independence (home ownership, big wedding, nuclear family with professional childcare)

2) price them out of those markets/underpay them so those things are unreachable

3) declare that they are 'destroying' those industries by not participating

4) make fun of them for adjusting their lives to this new financial reality (living with parents longer, having roommates well into adulthood, etc.)

And 5) keep them too overwhelmed with debt and just struggling for those 'real adulthood' prizes for them to actually run for office and replace the people who created these no-win conditions in the first place/organize against them

Home ownership, however much we rally against it, feels like it's still a key marker of success, as shown by this brilliant tweet by Louisa @Louisathelast on Twitter. That it was liked by 129k people shows just how much individuals resonate with this tweet neatly summarising the status quo.

Although not being a homeowner by thirty is the new normal, especially in London and other big cities where house prices are high, it can still feel like there's a stigma attached to renting. You can feel this is especially true if you're a) ambitious, and b) want your life to look perfect and are told that home ownership is really what everyone should be pushing for. But what if you, like most people under forty, just can't?

In the UK, home ownership decreased by 9.9 percentage points between 2007 and 2016, to 63.4 per cent, according to the Institute for Fiscal Studies. The study found that around twenty years ago, 64 per cent of 25–34-year-olds in London and the South East owned a home, a figure that has now halved to 32 per cent. If you were born in the 1970s, there's a 43 per cent chance that you owned your own home by the age of twenty-seven, something which feels impossible today.

The reason for decreasing home ownership is, of course, rocketing house prices, which rose by 33 per cent between 2010 and 2019, according to a report by the UK's Nationwide Building Society.[4] The house-price-to-earnings ratio is the biggest obstacle when it comes to buying a house – when the number is high it means house affordability is at its lowest. It's also impossible to save as we're shelling out so much on rent.

And even if ownership was affordable, homes on the affordable end of the scale are, to put it bluntly, often horrible. House-hunting is a cold wake-up call for most of us, and if there's anything that the plethora of nineties' TV shows about house-buying has shown us, it's that compromise is key. For many first-time buyers, especially in expensive cities, compromising can go as far as simply buying a home, despite the location, size and price being completely wrong.

When I was buying my first flat, I viewed the property with an Italian couple. They, well-heeled, in their thirties; us, young, scruffy, hopeful. We didn't know how the game worked, but as soon as I saw the flat, I liked it, despite its proximity to one of the most polluted crossroads in south London and its location above a betting shop. The local group of ne'er-do-wells also congregated by my front door, dealing drugs, being rowdy and occasionally peeing over my entrance. This was all fine, as I was desperate to stop renting. Not because there was anything wrong with renting (although a creeping black mould had appeared over the wall of my rented apartment), but because that was the 'right' thing to do, and that's what society had taught me was the natural next step.

Why all those home-improvement shows in the nineties? How would I install all those decks and water features that *Ground Force* convinced me were the right ones, without having a home? We have all been conditioned for too long to have our own place to 'do up'. Women and girls in particular.

Since the dawn of time, women have been instructed

in how to manage a home. We were the ones who literally kept the home fires burning while men were at war, while Mrs Beeton's 1861 book took it a step further by writing the first ever tome of household management. The guide was intended as a way to help newly middle-class people come to terms with how to treat maids or cooks or housekeepers. How to cook and prepare for dinner parties. What your silverware should look like. How to keep a thrifty home. It's an ingenious book because it teaches us so much about Victorian expectations.

And today, so few millenials own their own home, it feels like this information will never be relevant to us. Striving to keep a beautiful home, even when you only have a small one, is still important. After all, we need somewhere to live, and just because we don't all own our homes doesn't make this any less real.

Speaking to the *Financial Times*, Hansen Lu, a property economist at Capital Economics, said: 'The pace of adjustment [in the house-price-to-earnings ratio] has been very slow. We expect house prices to stay high relative to incomes for the foreseeable future . . . [which] will continue to constrain house price growth over the next few years.'

With this in mind, is there any point striving to own a house when it feels almost impossible? Should we instead be focusing on fighting to make rental rights fairer? Or pushing the government to increase inheritance tax so there's less disparity between wealthier families and poorer families from the get-go?

Owning a small home was a signifier of success of adulthood (as @Louisathelast points out) but it was still achievable by the 'average' person in the 1970s, 80s and 90s. Maybe you'd managed to buy your council property; maybe you'd managed to scrape together enough for a family home in the suburbs. The possibility to own your home, grow your family and create a space that was private and just for you was there.

In a recent podcast for the *Economist* on the global housing crisis, Colin Williams, senior economics writer, spoke about the massive economic consequences of the perceived importance of home ownership.[5] 'On the political side, there's evidence that when somebody sees something as a kind of right that everyone should have, it creates lots of dissatisfaction with the status quo and this is arguably one of the main reasons why there's been a surge towards populist parties across the rich world.'

The episode suggests that the original sin seems to have been pursuing the idea that home ownership was both an economic and personal virtue, an idea embodied in the UK by Margaret Thatcher, who spoke out strongly about the 'right' to buy. In a speech made in 1980, she said: 'If you've been a council tenant for at least three years, you'll have the right by law to buy your house and that's that.'

The problem, says Williams, is that there's a feeling in the West that home ownership is a 'self-evidently good thing and it's better than renting, and in fact, renting is a bad form of tenure. There's a general feeling that in order to succeed and be a good person you need to own your own home, and this idea has structured Western society for thirty to forty years.'

Many of us under the age of thirty-five are completely priced out of buying a house, at least if you want to buy in a big capital city. Move out of the capital and your options improve, one of the reasons why places like Cleveland, Ohio, are becoming magnets for young professionals fleeing the West Coast.

But it's not just a London-, New York- or Hong Kong-centred problem. In the UK, although property prices are significantly cheaper outside of large cities, they're still hugely out of reach for most people. They require savings which many people don't have. As inflation rises and savings rates drop, there is a moment when many younger people suddenly realise how impossible buying a house is.

This is when the 'avocado syndrome' hits. 'Why put £100 a month away when you now need a deposit of around £80,000 to buy a very small, one-bedroom flat in Hong Kong?' It would take sixty-five years to creep towards this savings goal; and by this point, unless you're a freak of nature, you'll literally be dead.

The right to a fixed abode is crucial. It's a drive shared by people from the poorest countries to the richest, because we need space to think, to study, to procreate and to bring our own families up. The right to privacy isn't a wild one, and yet anyone reading this will know that they, or a friend, or a child, are currently living with multiple people in a shared house because any other option is completely out of reach.

And we're not talking about creatives or people who are doing internships (although unless they're trust-fund kids they definitely will be too). Bankers, consultants, lawyers, tech bros: unless they struck lucky with family wealth, anyone wanting to buy a house today is screwed without a large deposit.

Home ownership, at least for me, is not a sign of success. It's a sign of luck, privilege and of being in the right era at the right time. It's also not a panacea. Buying my recent flat as a single person, after I sold my share of my old flat to my ex, has been hugely stressful. Buying a bed when there's two of you is fine. It's expensive, but far more cost-effective than when you have to stomach the cost alone.

At the risk of simply stating the obvious, owning (or in reality, paying your mortgage provider every penny you earn) as a single person is extremely expensive. I'd had no idea just how staggeringly expensive council tax was, even with a 25 per cent single-person discount. Somehow, every three months, I have to find £400 out of nowhere. Service charge is an extra £1,200 a year. If the boiler breaks, I can't afford to replace it.

In 2019, at the World Economic Forum in Davos, the worldwide trend for spending on experiences rather than objects was discussed.[6] 'In our overpopulated world, stuffed with an ever-growing stockpile of products, offline experiences have become key to personal fulfilment. While 78 per cent of millennials choose to spend money on a desirable experience over something material, the trend extends beyond just young people, to every age bracket and socioeconomic class.'[7]

The reason why is obvious: what's the point in buying a state-of-the-art oven if you don't have a house to put it in?

That's the reality.

And yet, home ownership, or a room of one's own, is still seen as so vital by many of us that it can seem problematic not to want to put all your effort into trying to get a house. A friend sat down with me once and said: 'The thing is, I can save around £1,000 a month – I'm lucky. But it's still not enough. I'd need to save for five years to get a house deposit and, you know, really, really scrimp on day-to-day things. It just feels like a really,

really long way away. So I might as well go on holiday and buy nice things because it feels like there's no point saving.'

There's a reason young people spend more money on fun experiences rather than material possessions, and that's because our definition of success has to change or we'll spend our entire lives completely disillusioned.

I did a quick Twitter poll to see whether people on my timeline still associated success with home ownership. My twitter followers are mostly creatives; mostly actors, writers and journalists – bluntly, the sort of people who, without a trust fund, are going to struggle to buy a house near their workplace.

The final poll came in: 42 per cent thought it was a marker of success, 39 per cent said it wasn't, while 11 per cent said it depended. It's true that it does depend on a number of factors. A few people messaged me and said they'd answered 'it depends' based on whether that person had managed to buy their house by themselves or not. If their parents had helped out, then it wasn't the person's success, but their family's.

Thea, who rents but is looking to buy in south London, said: 'Increasingly, being able to buy a house is a mark of wealth (whether that's family/inherited wealth or, of course, money you've made yourself). I think aspiring to traditional markers of success may sometimes be an indicator that they haven't really considered what would really make them happy, but not always.

'Class is a big factor in this as well. Earning an above-average salary and owning a home will be a far more impressive achievement for someone who started out poor or working class than someone middle or upper class.'

Stephen Russell feels lucky that he managed to get on the housing ladder at all. 'I do own a house, but bought late – a first-time buyer at thirty-six. I'm in a shared-ownership house that I bought with my partner. I'm happy not to be renting because it feels more secure. I worked mostly low-paid assistant jobs before a career break that led to me being self-employed.'

Russell acknowledges that he couldn't have made the deposit if it wasn't for his family inheritance. 'I'm happy to say I managed to buy, mostly for the benefit of my two kids, but I don't link it to being successful.

'A lot of my uni mates bought when they were twenty-one in Newcastle [UK], but I moved back to London so it wasn't really an option there. I was jealous for a while, so I'm lucky that my inheritance could even the scales. The system feels rigged against home ownership being a practical option now, at least; it's less feasible than it was for my parents.'

A recent infographic took a snapshot of central London and illustrated how much money you'd need to be earning before you could buy a property, based on 2020 data. In London Bridge, you'd need an average salary of £115,000; in Southwark, £137,000. Westminster you'd need an average of over £150,000. It's easy to see how easily people in normal jobs – not hedge-fund managers or oil brokers, for example – are priced out of the market. An extremely senior job in the civil service as head of department earns around £90,000. They wouldn't be able to live even in spitting distance of their workplace.

More crucially, where do nurses, cleaners and care workers live? Those aged thirty-five and under (or, those who came of age in the financial recession post-2007), unless they're living in subsidised housing, are facing long commutes from either London commuter towns or zones which require expensive travel cards.

This is nothing new. The generation gap is nothing new.

But the frustration is that those who were able to buy centrally twenty years ago may one day be able to pay off their mortgage. There is huge disparity between people who have parents living in London (who bought their property) and those who don't.

It can feel frustrating to try to put aside money every month when the goal feels so far away. The average UK salary is £27,000, while the average London salary is £34,000. How does one rocket up to £155,000 without making sacrifices that might not sit well either morally or ethically? The stats are bleak. One in three of us will never own a home.[8] And, if you're around thirty today, you're just half as likely to own a house as your parents were at the same age.[9]

As we saw in the chapter on careers, very few of us start out in life aspiring to become a banker or a lawyer. We want to be firemen, writers, storytellers, acrobats, scientists, bus drivers. Unless you're the head of the fire department, J. K. Rowling, an established TV presenter, the chief acrobat of the Cirque de Soleil, a programmer or the head of the Department for Transport, these jobs are unlikely to translate into careers that can help you secure a central London apartment or townhouse.

To achieve home ownership, we have to manage our expectations, whether that's about choosing to have less fun in our careers or more fun and shifting our priorities.

Home ownership is about more than just what success looks like. It's about safety and security; it's about having a place to call your own and to decorate and to live in and to protect you from the outside world.

An all-party parliamentary study looking into housing among the elderly found that we could be facing a homelessness crisis. They used the term 'inevitable catastrophe' to describe what will happen to millennials in the UK who aren't able to climb onto the housing ladder throughout their lifetimes.[10]

Their reasoning was that people's incomes tend to halve upon retirement. Currently, those of us who live in private rented accommodation pay around 40 per cent of our earnings on rent. This means that in retirement, when our income halves, 80 per cent of our earnings could go on rent. This is also assuming that the cost of rent stays static.

In any case, those who continue to rent could be declared homeless or be forced into government temporary accommodation which would spell an enormous crisis for the health service and welfare system.

Striving for the opportunity to buy can feel overwhelming, especially for those of us used to setting goals and achieving them. Among my friends, all of whom are pragmatic and sensible people, I've heard the words: 'I feel like I'm suffocating because I can't see a way out' and 'I don't care any more. Right now, it's fine. I'm OK living in a single room at thirty-two, I guess. I have to be because if I think too hard about it, I get very upset.'

The final example, and for me most poignant, is my friend who recently got married. The couple share a rented two-bedroom apartment with another couple and would like to have children. Both work for the government and earn around £37,000 each. 'We need to be close to London because this is where our very London-centric job[s are]. But we'd also like to start a family soon. We're both thirty-two.'

His husband chimes in. 'We won't be able to adopt because you need more space. And even if we did have a child, what are they going to do? Are we meant to all live in one room and we get kicked out every six months by a landlord looking to make more profit?'

We meet to talk in a pub in Clapham which is full of young parents who have managed to get on the housing ladder. Servers deliver bowls of chips to tables and the room on this Sunday afternoon smells of vinegar and roast meat. Looking around, we realise they're not actually young parents. They're older parents, many around their late thirties or even early forties.

The housing crisis has changed the way young people live. As a generation, we procreate less because many of us don't have our own spaces. We're also hunting for cheaper places to flee to.

Studies show that more people are leaving London than ever before, but in turn this pushes house prices up in other cities. Manchester, Leeds and Cambridge are seeing booms, so the pattern repeats and repeats until young people across the whole country struggle.

So what can we do about it?

The thing that's mostly to blame for the UK's housing crisis is the lack of houses. Building regulation is overseen by a culture of Nimbyism – 'not in my back yard': generations who were once able to clamber onto the housing ladder but now don't want their view despoiled by new developments or new roads that might change the surrounding landscape but would also improve the next generation's chances of not being stuck in a crisis of homelessness.

After all, other countries have managed to counteract this. Between 2013 and 2017, Tokyo put up 728,000 new houses. There was little pushback and the number of rough sleepers fell by 80 per cent. In other countries, like Switzerland, local authorities are given subsidies to build new houses, and even in the UK the government has tried to get more people on the housing ladder by offering help-to-buy ISAs and alternative buying options like shared ownership.

The problem in the UK, and America at least, is the initial cost in cities where people want to live is too high: San Francisco, New York and London have experienced enormous growth in demand. In 1990, baby boomers aged around thirty-five owned a third of American real estate. Today, almost the same age group, at thirty-one, owns just 4 per cent.

One thing is to improve the UK's very unfair rental system and look to countries like Germany, which has more equitable living conditions. In Germany, just 50 per cent of people own homes, and according to the *Economist*, which recently published a report called 'The Horrible Housing Blunder', Germany's real house prices are no higher than they were in 1980.

Although the situation is bad, there is growing recognition that this is the case, and some elements of society are trying to do things to encourage alternative solutions to the crisis. YIMBYism – 'Yes, In My Back Yard' – is, according to the same *Economist* report, a fledgling movement which promotes construction and housing initiatives.[11]

The question, when it comes to success and our desire to be happy and to achieve, is can we do that without owning a home, or without having home ownership as our ultimate goal?

Shelter is a human right. Those who rent have shelter, but they do not have, particularly in Britain, particularly good rights. It's all very well saying, 'Hey, take a step back, simply renting is good enough, no need to buy a house,' but the reality is renting can suck.

If, like in Germany, the alternative can be good too – strong rental agreements which gives renters more rights and landlords fewer rights – then there are clearly options.

Something that irks older millennials (over the age of thirty-two) are the rules and regulations that Louisa described in her infantilising-an-entire-generation tweet earlier on. 'I might want a pet, but I can't get a pet. I'm thirty-four,' says Gabbi. 'I'm not going to get a boyfriend, because I work too-long hours to go on dates. I'm priced out of getting a house – just let me get a cat, for fuck's sake!

'Also, my landlord has a huge problem with me putting up pictures in my house. Hello! Wake-up call! I'm not there hammering posters of Slipknot or whatever on his walls. I'm putting up a Japanese linocut which I spent ages researching, tracking down, and then I was told I couldn't put it up. But I was offered a helpful solution to "lean it" on my shelf.'

What irritates Gabbi is the reason why she doesn't want to share her surname – her landlord is the best she's had. 'He hasn't raised rent once for two years, which in my experience is unusual. He lives in Nigeria and his parents bought him some flats, so I'm just hoping he doesn't know the rent goes up every so often. Maybe he's from a kind, decent, renting background, who knows? But I do want a cat. Gives me something when I'm still sharing with students in my nineties.'

Vicky Spratt is a housing journalist and a campaigner for Generation Rent. In 2016, she launched a campaign called Make Renting Fair with magazine *The Debrief*, which, among other things, campaigned to ban letting-agents fees. These fees can be extraordinarily high; as the campaign argued, they were sometimes so high (around £500 each time someone rented a new property), that it was pushing people into debt.

Perpetual moving is just what young people are used to. For the lucky minority it can be possible to stay in one place for several years, but what tends to happen is rent creeps up year after year. 'To account for inflation,' landlords say. 'For more repairs,' they say. But when salaries don't creep up at the same rate, or when after a few years you suddenly find yourself paying hundreds of pounds more for the same crappy studio flat, something is clearly broken with the system.

According to Spratt, London tenants spend 72 per cent of their income on rent. The average New Yorker would need to earn $115,000 each year to afford to rent a one-bedroom apartment. In Hong Kong, young people give up and just live at home until they get married. The average apartment there costs 19.4 times the average income, putting properties way out of reach.

The thing is, in the UK capital, one in five of us rent from a private landlord. It can be hard to feel good about that when they can ask you to leave on a whim. According to Generation Rent's website, in 2019, five million people rented from a private landlord, which is more than double the number doing so in the year 2000.

There are three key issues with the private rental market – four if you count the inertia some young people have when they think, just because they've never been affected, that bad renting conditions couldn't happen to them. The first is insecure tenancies, when people can be kicked out with just two months' notice.

And before you think it's all students, 57 per cent of

people who rent from private landlords are over thirty-five. If you know anyone at all, chances are they've got some pretty terrible landlord stories. At university, some of the worst renting stories came from students who rented from private landlords. One was unable to get out of her room because the door handle fell off and the private landlord refused to come around and fix it or help her out because it was a Friday evening.

I lived in one flat-share where the wall was decorated with an intricate, black lacy mould. Not just a band or vertical strip, the entire wall was crawling with stains. After many weeks of my sending photographs in different lights, posing next to the wall so he could see the scale of the wall, and finally saying, 'I'm asthmatic, my breathing is bad,' he sent a man over to . . . paint the wall white.

'All done,' he said. Unfortunately, he'd used cheap white paint, so the mould was clearly still visible underneath. And how much was I paying for this gem? Around £900 a month for the room. At the time, significantly more than half my monthly take-home pay.

Delicious.

Not being able to have pets, live a mould-free life or sleep on a bed that doesn't give you backache are just some of the things renters gripe about. But much more serious is that many private renters in England are on 'assured shorthold' tenancies. This means that landlords can give just two months' notice to tenants to vacate and give no reason for it.

The process is called Section 21, invented in 1988 to make it easier for people who were not officially landlords to rent their homes out easily. It was for people who might want to easily take their house back with little fuss. The issue is that now so many of us are privately renting, some with kids enrolled at school, and many with jobs close by, that to be kicked out at short notice could be disastrous.

One of the biggest issues, Generation Rent says, is that Section 21 is being used to 'bully tenants'. If you ask your landlord to fix something and they don't want to, there's a chance they could suddenly issue you with a Section 21 notice which means you have to leave.

The campaign, along with Acorn, a fair-rent provider, is also fighting to provide a register of safe landlords. This would mean if a landlord has been involved in issues in the past, they might not be able to rent their property out again. It's the council's role to uncover and reveal information that could be important for future tenants. Not all councils do this, and as council cuts increase, the opportunity for more people to know what faults lie in their homes (which could be lethal if it involves poor wiring or cladding, for example) is crucial.

Finally, there's a goal to make deposits more affordable.

The average deposit for privately rented accommodation is £1,088, a sum most private renters have but which is usually tied up in the deposit for the previous house. Rent is too expensive; it eats up an enormous part of our monthly salaries.

According to Generation Rent's website, 10 per cent of those who faced homelessness in 2018–2019 were evicted by private landlords who wanted to sell their property, rent it out for a higher return, or didn't want to make requested repairs. The sad reality in cities like London is that demand for 'nice enough' places to live outstrips supply.

An article for the *Metro* newspaper in 2019 by Jessica Lindsay[12] eatured landlord horror stories by tenants. Many included the landlord not fixing things or blaming tenants for shoddy fittings. Several included female tenants being called up by landlords 'just to chat'. In the piece, Lindsay reminisces about a former landlord who had put the living room furniture in the garden so they could let out the living room as a bedroom. She also reports that the tenants' sink and washing machine were broken.

'He eventually told me to buy sulphuric acid and put it down the sink myself. I refused because it's extremely dangerous (and only sold in specialist shops because of this, with multiple news stories online about people literally burning their faces off) and decided to just leave because it was a hellhole. Once I left, he came round and did it himself, blowing the full kitchen to pieces – which I'm sure he'd have charged me for if I'd have followed his advice and done the home plumbing myself.'

Another woman had a landlord who refused to fix the lift even though she'd just given birth and had pregnancy complications.

If there's one thing stimulating (and widening) the generational gap, it's those who are renting and those who rent out. Although there are plenty of over-fifties (over a million) who don't have the luxury of owning their own homes and continue to rent, one in six boomers (over-sixties) now own a second home.

Most are probably extremely considerate landlords (if they rent out their properties). Others may remember their time living in rented accommodation in the seventies and eighties, when they squatted or lived in a much more carefree way than many young people do now. After all, the millennial generation and Generation Z take the least number of drugs, are environmentally considerate and don't drink much. Boomers liked to go out; we like to stay in.

Our experiences clash and are directly mismatched. People under thirty-five enjoy nights at home, hosting friends and watching Netflix. This is partly because we're spending so much money on rent, we can't really afford to do anything else. Gone are the days of *The Young Ones'* crazy party-hard antics.

Perhaps this is the reason that every landlord who wants to make a quick buck throws together a hotch-potch of IKEA furniture and offcuts that they found in a skip. ('They'll only be trashed anyway.')

One landlord only bought a new bedframe after I lay on it for a month propped up in the middle with a stack of books. He was generally an excellent landlord, but I've had a bad back ever since. A friend's landlord had a new gas hob fitted, but they forgot to connect the gas and then went on vacation, leaving him with no way to cook food.

A final landlord complaint: when I didn't get my whole deposit back because I hadn't cleaned the inside of my kitchen drawers to a 'satisfactory level'.

These problems amount to more serious issues. Generation Rent has found that around 630,000 privately rented homes (14 per cent of the total) would fail safety standards. A further 25 per cent are considered 'non-decent', which means that fixtures and fittings could be described as safe, but may have bad-quality fittings or bad heating. A direct contrast? Four per cent of housing-association homes are unsafe while just 11 per cent are 'non-decent'.

But perhaps just as importantly, the current situation can stop us from progressing in our lives. The rental system causes us to stagnate and, as Louisa said at the start of this chapter, it infantilises us. Even if we want to leap to the next stage of our lives and learn how to do some tiling or paint a wall, chances are we won't be allowed to.

Removing the signifier that buying a flat is an achievement and an unmissable life goal is crucial. Moving the goalposts so we no longer feel as though we aren't good enough because of market forces is vital.

I'll never forget an article I read on the BBC's website a couple of years ago about a very young couple and how they'd managed to buy a house aged around twenty-two. One of the questions was whether the couple had had to make any sacrifices, and the man said he made his girlfriend buy cheaper make-up so they could save. I also seem to recall that they had spent their entire lives at home, or living in their parents' homes, saving. This is admirable, but at twenty-two this whole-life sacrifice feels like panic. There's no need to buy; there's no need to sacrifice the most carefree decade of your life to achieve a goal that another generation has set.

There are plenty of horror stories about renting from unscrupulous private landlords. But there are also the same number (if not more) horror stories from people who have been totally hoodwinked by estate agents when they've bought their first property.

What if we just improved our private rental system?

Could we all just stop trying to buy? What if we slammed on the breaks and just said: 'Nuh-uh. I'm just not gonna do that'?

Let us stay in rented houses for five years. Let us decorate. Let us own dogs. Let us cook spicy food if we want to. And if it means you have to replace some furniture every decade, or need to repaint more frequently than once every lifetime, then maybe that's a good thing. Let us chip away one per cent into your already enormous profit because it'll improve the lives of millions of private renters, and maybe make you sleep better at night too.

Although I love my flat, I felt that there was a lot of pressure on me to buy. I would have been quite happy to keep renting if I'd known I could have stayed in one place for a few years, painted the walls an appealing colour and made it feel like I was at home, rather than squatting in someone else's flat. I'm working two jobs to pay my mortgage, and there are thousands, millions more out there who are denying themselves fun and a life, in order to keep saving, to one day buy a house because that's the goal someone else has set us.

Make renting fairer, and society can become more equitable. Let's reduce the stress, pressure and expectation that everyone wants and needs to buy, and see what happens. Making renting fairer will create a big shift towards happiness while also reducing the pressure on us to 'achieve' and buy a house when the costs are so prohibitive it's out of our hands.

There are things you can do. Sign petitions at Generation Rent, at Make Renting Fair on Change.org or use your local council's website to demand changes and fixes to communal problems.[13] We, the young, do have a voice; renters, as Vicky Spratt has shown, just need to learn how to use it again.

Gym

If you've ever had any sort of breakdown, or mental health issue, you'll know that doctors are really keen to get you into the gym.

'Just go for a walk, just to get your legs moving and your mind working again,' they say.

I'm starting to think the gym is not a positive place for me. Telling me to go as part of a medical opinion is probably less beneficial than they think. Sometimes, I go twice a day. The day I don't go to the gym (Thursday) I compensate by not eating anything, walking everywhere and going for a swim.

I tell my doctor, who is now a young Irish man, that I go to the gym a lot. And he positively beams. He tells me, like I'm a child, that that is the very best thing I could be doing, and I try not to roll my eyes because I've been doing this for fifteen years and I still tried to end my life, so clearly it's not as great as he thinks.

He needs to go to the gym, I think, staring at him. I'm being a bitch inside, so I shut my brain up and turn it off.

'Will you keep going for me?'

'Yes.'

'That's very good.'

'Yes.'

'Good, good.'

The gym I go to is called Third Space, which is a very calm, zen place with lots of glass and exposed beams. I should hate it, but I like the way it makes me feel and the other people who go seem friendly. There's a view over the River Thames, which means when you come out after class you can just stand and look at the sunlit rippling water and take a deep breath. It's a good way to start the day.

Sometimes, like a smoker, I consider what the money I spend on gym membership each year could give me. A really nice sofa. A miniature schnauzer. A holiday. I wonder this all the way from my apartment to the door of the gym.

Inside the class, the lights are so dim I can't see anyone. Bass music pumps out and the instructor takes us round each station, describing the way we'll beast our bodies. What works at this gym is how everyone is toned, but not too toned. There are a few ultra-serious people who look like they could do with a square meal or five, but there are – including myself – normal people here, because going to the gym is just what you're kind of meant to do.

Going to the gym is meant to do a lot of things. It's

meant to stop us from getting fat, from losing bone density as we age, and it's meant to make us more rounded, entertaining people (say the adverts). We look to the gym to solve a lot of our problems, and now improved mental health has been added to that list.

In 2018, the UK fitness industry announced that it was as healthy and buoyant as its clients. In fact, it's not just buoyant, it's booming. Ten million people pay for gym membership in the UK, which is about one in seven of us. For the first time, the number of gyms has topped 7,000 across the UK. That's a 4.6 per cent increase from 2017, an increase other industries would kill for.

Reasons for its boom are manifold, but there's no getting away from the mental health benefits a good workout can bring. The Primary Care Companion to the Journal of Clinical Psychiatry found that:

Exercise improves mental health by reducing anxiety, depression, and negative mood and by improving self-esteem and cognitive function. Exercise has also been found to alleviate symptoms such as low self-esteem and social withdrawal.[1]

But working out maniacally, as though the world is going to end unless you do a minimum of seventy burpees, might be more unhealthy than good for you.

Take these stats. Just 21 per cent of gym-goers work out

because they want to improve fitness, and 2.96 per cent go to train for an event. The vast majority head to the gym because they want to lose weight rather than gain fitness. The gym can feed into a negative cycle: a place that's tied up in feelings of self-hatred and lack of self-worth.

So why do we keep on going? The same survey reported that around 5 per cent of us go to the gym to compensate for unhealthy eating and drinking. This is me, hands down. I will never give up chocolate, so I must go to the gym.[2]

There's going to a regular gym a few times a week to burn calories, keep your health in check, and beat stress – that's positive. It slots wonderfully into a healthy, balanced life. And then there's the brutal training offered by a growing breed of so-called ultra-gyms.

Yet, do we need them?

We don't *need* to lift 40kg weights or sprint for one minute, because there are very few life situations we would find ourselves in where that sort of physical exertion is necessary. If the bus was a one-minute sprint away, I'm certain I'd just wait for the next bus. Likewise, if my shopping basket weighed 20kg, I'd get a trolley. There's no genuine reason for us to work out at intense HIIT classes, but more of us are doing it. Why?

Sometimes when I stand in the gym and look at the dumbbells and kettlebells neatly lined up, and the instructor starts to shout motivational slogans into her mic, I wonder what I'm doing there. I'm the sort of person who, if asked to high-five someone else, would leave. And yet every morning, between 7 a.m. – 8 a.m., I'm here, in the gym, preparing to 'smash it' and 'beast it out'.

I get down on my knees and do commandos. I do an intense version of downward-facing dog. I slam 15kg rubber balls and box-jump with weights on my back. And why?

I like to think it's because I care about my health. I want to be at peak fitness and not have dangerous levels of fat around my core. Maybe it's about just wanting to lose some extra weight, but, if I'm honest with myself, I don't really carry any.

'I like the vibe. I love working out here,' says one woman, queuing for her protein shake after class. 'Don't use my name though – I don't want everyone to think I'm like one of those fitness-crazy people.'

When the rest of your life can feel like it's scooting out of grasp, exercise is something you can control. When I can't make that early-morning gym slot because life gets in the way, I can feel myself panicking. Does this mean I'm not good enough any more? I beat myself up because I'm not at the gym pumping iron, doing burpees, or being high-fived by personal trainers. The task I am doing – usually something mundane like having an early meeting with a colleague – does not make me successful. It does not fist-bump me and tell me I'm winning.

This brings with it its own elements of anxiety. There's been a noted rise in cases of exercise addiction; where people are over-exercising to the point of injury, yet continue because they cannot fathom a life routine which doesn't include it. Not exercising causes anxiety attacks and low moods, and I've felt these when I haven't been able to do a class.

Typing it out, I realise I sound crazy. If my workout has been lax, I'll chastise myself for taking the Tube and make myself walk or cycle to a meeting instead. There's a gnawing feeling of panic that eats away at me. Hearing about other people's workouts has the same effect, and when I see people out running, I immediately wonder whether I've done enough that day.

Is a need for perfection causing addiction?

Perhaps it's about more than just weight gain. Perhaps it's a last-ditch attempt not to be average. I'm never going be a lawyer or a banker, so maybe I need to feel successful in other aspects, and perhaps that's how this weird exercise-addiction manifests.

Zoe (not her real name) is addicted to exercise, and for her it's completely about being better than everyone else. 'That's why I'd prefer to stay anonymous,' she says. She's petite and brunette. 'Growing up, my dad would feed me and tell me to put on weight, while my mum made me anxious about it. I was a fat kid.'

Zoe works out at a high-end gym, and she likes it because no one's asked her to leave yet. She is noticeably underweight. 'I don't have a good relationship with food, but I'm healthy. I do the right things. My last gym told me to leave because they said I was working out too much, but the way I feel is that I'm paying them.'

She checks again that this interview will be anonymous.

'[My gym] have never mentioned it. They want my money and I want to pay them, so it works for me. The gym's about getting strong, and learning how to manage my anxiety through fitness, and that was all there was to it. At least at the start.'

How does she think it began?

Until her mental health deteriorated, Zoe was a successful management consultant. 'I couldn't cope with the long hours. I was feeling like I couldn't keep on top of my work and I didn't have time to work out. I began to set my alarm increasingly early – 6 a.m., 5 a.m., then 4 a.m. – as I needed more and more time for workouts.'

'A run, then a strength workout, then I might run to work on top of that. I got this thrill turning up at work with my running stuff on when everyone else looked lazy, like they'd been on the Tube. I was going to be better than them, make more money . . . but in the end I guess I was the one who left, so that was ironic.'

An article in *Vice* by Kimberly Zapata,[3] which went viral, begins to chart the rise of her exercise addiction. She talks about pulling her trainers on and feeling panicked and irritable when she couldn't get out. Miles turned into multiple miles, and she'd run through injuries.

'Today, I ran to the point of blacking out, and passing out. The bile in my stomach rose in tandem with the sun, and tears streamed down my face. The salty blend of sweat and sadness combatted the bitterness which flowed up (and through) my throat,' she says in the piece.[4]

In the article she wrote: 'I struggle to sleep because, when I am not running, I am lost and empty. I struggle with pain. My legs tremble constantly. I feel like I am in motion even when I am still, and I can tell you what it's like to measure life not in moments, but in miles.'

Anyone who has felt the need to go to the gym or run may understand this. There is a desire to keep moving, because if you don't stop then you feel like you're doing something. You feel like you're achieving, and it might not be the sanest way to manage your feelings of inadequacy, but it helps.

For some people, it can really help. I thought I was one of the people exercise was helping. And although, after decades of being obsessed by what I could get from working out, I realised that it took control of me. A tool

I was using to manage my anxiety and stress was now causing it.

But is there a way we can try to manage our expectations, and reduce the hold the gym has on us? One way we could start is to think about marketing budgets, and how the gym is essentially marketed at us so we part with lots of money. The gym has us wrapped around its little finger. It is at once the place to mend all ills and a place that generates guilt. When I go to my gym and work out, the instructors high-five me and tell me that I'm going to be successful because I'm working out in the morning. 'That's what successful people do.'

Think about the gym too much and you begin to realise what a bizarre concept it is. Here in your city, village or town, which is criss-crossed by roads and has paths and pavements, is a box. Inside, there's a place that pumps loud music – home to lots of people who like to sweat indoors and build muscle.

Gym owners are marketing gods. They have convinced us, a population in need of stimulation and entertainment, that we need them. But in reality, they need us. They need us to feel rubbish about our bodies to meet their sales targets. They need us to be having a fat day so they can open another gym across town. And they do this by playing with our most motivating emotion: guilt. Our fear of being average. Koinophobia.

Is gym-going partly fuelled by guilt?

Fear is about the threat of punishment. We feel it, and then it disappears. We can manage fear with logic. But guilt niggles.

If you think too hard about that extra pint you drank last night, or the cake you ate for breakfast, you feel guilt. It sits in our stomachs like too much sambuca after a night out – oily and slippery. It spreads easily too. Sometimes guilt can weigh us down and make us unable to remedy our own situation because we feel so affected by it.

Guilt is ever-present, says Naked Communications partner Will Collin in an article for *Marketing Week*.[5] 'While fear may come and go, guilt is always on consumers' minds.'

Gyms play to this. After all, we've all seen the billboard adverts that play on our pre- and post-holiday body shape fears.

You're not imagining that the world wants you to feel bad so you work out harder. It really does. Because all marketeers know that shame sells. The fear of being average sells, because it's a rare person who wakes up in the morning and says: 'Being average, of moderate strength and relatively obesity-free, is great.'

The downside to this is guilt has side effects. So, as you panic about not going to the gym, you're more prone to muscle tension, sleep disturbances and headaches. Emotional side effects of guilt are more nuanced. They include feeling sad, not being able to sleep, overthinking and being more irritable.

Feeling guilty because you're not working out, feeling guilty because you're not ticking the correct marketing box, is frustrating. But it's all part of the curse of being average. *Hey, you can do better*, marketing says. And the easiest way is by going to the gym.

The UK average dress size for women is size 14, with a 31.3 inch waist. Average in Britain is not toned and sporty, so gyms are able to successfully play on our fears and our drive to be better.

And the average waist size is expanding. In 2018, the *American Journal of Fashion Design, Technology, and Education* announced that the average clothes size in the US had jumped to a 16–18. The West's waists are getting bigger, despite a huge surge in gym membership.[6]

Some gyms describe themselves as 'extreme' or 'life changing', and these are often clustered in areas near shiny offices. One such gym, F45, is booming. It claims it's the world's fastest-growing franchise, which has 'cutting edge' techniques and 'high-grade equipment.' It is the 'ultimate gym experience', according to the website.

It's difficult to walk past an F45 (my local branch offers big, clear windows so you can see the people inside sweating) and not look down at your flab and feel a twinge of guilt. The people inside are pushing hard. They look exhausted. But it's also lunchtime on a Tuesday. Their suits hang in the cloakrooms. Rows of high-heeled shoes line up next to the wooden benches. In forty-five minutes their owners will return to working in real estate, or to coding at Microsoft next door. But for now, they are true athletes. Pushing the limits of man in a see-through box just off the North Circular.

The gym offers classes called things like Firestorm, and Romans: Resistance. Angry Bird. Renegade. Gladiators. It's about making fitness fun. It makes sense in a world where our waistlines are bulging and more people are dying from obesity than car crashes. But at what cost does this sort of high-intensity, success-driven ultimate workout really have on our minds and bodies?

Let's start with the bottom line.

The cost of membership at F45 is as brutal as the workouts. Rates start at £20 a class. Desk-bound people across the world are coughing up for the 'ultimate session'. And why? Because the average person spends around nine hours of their waking day sitting down and we know, deep in our hearts, that's bad for us.

Other popular joints, like 1Rebel, marketed mostly at women who want more from their workouts, describe their offerings as 'ultimate'. The 1Rebel website is full of pithy statements about how what they offer is better than everywhere else. They spit on the traditional spin-class concept. 'We don't spin, we Ride. Banging playlists, amazing lighting and sick sound systems.' When I sampled a class, it felt very much like a spin class. But if it helps to pretend you're doing something unique when you work out, then you do you.

This is an elite experience, targeted at only the most well-paid executives living and working along London's Southbank. An unlimited session-pass costs £249 per month, while four sessions would cost £69. To put this into context, the local council-run Better centre offers memberships for £19.99 a month, which includes classes like aerobics and 'cycle'.

At my own gym, classes are described in the sort of way that would leave the kid picked last for PE screaming and jumping out of the window. 'Welcome to The WOD's evil twin. This class replicates Third Space's toughest class, but always comes at you in one format – a Chipper session. A high volume of exercises in a series that you must 'chip' away at until you're finished or the clock hits zero.'[7] I'm obsessed with my sessions at Third Space and am there at 6.15 every single morning. Some days I do double sessions, which can become two HIIT classes back to back or maybe a run class and a HIIT class.

During a recent work trip to New York, I decided that I'd eaten too much gnocchi and bao, so I checked myself into a class at F45. They charged me $36 and threw in a free bottle of water. Thanks to the exchange rate, my decision to work out on a rainy Friday morning in Lower East Side cost me around £32 for a forty-five-minute session. We jumped and skipped our way to a sweat. Like in London, the class was packed with extremely toned young professionals. The instructor, Lils, pitched her class to those who were, as in London, time poor and keen to maximise the session. No one smiled. Fitness here was extremely serious and I finished the workout absolutely pumped with endorphins and having smashed my jet lag.

I popped into a coffee shop on the way back to my hotel and bought a soy flat white, completing the cycle of millenial nightmare in just forty-seven minutes.

Across the pond, the average American spends $155 on their health and fitness each month, which equates to $122,000 in a lifetime.[8] This isn't just gym fees, which actually only equates to about $33 a month, but includes other expenses like lycra and health supplements.

In the UK, gyms such as Equinox can cost more than £200 a month, while other luxe propositions, like Core Collective (which provides Chesterfield sofas to relax on post-session as part of their offering), don't even publish their membership rates online. Gyms and working out are a privilege that few people can afford financially, or time-wise.

You can't plan a gym class when you don't know when

your zero-hours contract wants you to work. In households that receive benefits, gyms are a luxury cost. Despite a range of gyms spreading across London, like The Gym and Pure Gym, that offer no-frills services at cut-price costs, £19.99 a month, £240 a year, is still a massive chunk out of the budget.

Ultimately, luxury gyms promise something else. They offer reassurance that we're on the right track. They offer compliments. They tell us that we'll feel better about ourselves afterwards. And because none of us really – unless we're driven by religion – are quite certain about what we're doing or why, they become a place of reverence, where it feels as though we're in control.

We may use our hobbies to claw back control when it feels like the world is running away from us, which is one of the reasons why we all know people who turned to marathons when they hit a mid-life crisis, says psychologist Elim Fetter.

It's hard to become a rock star, or become a doctor, she says. She explains that the gym is one way for people to thrive and to drive and to sweat their way to the top.

If you're striving to be a super-successful person, the chances are you want to be fit and healthy too. You want to have a challenging day at work and box your way through the stress. You wake up early and think a 10km run sounds like a smart idea.

But at what other cost? When does fitness become too much fitness?

Aisha, a twenty-seven-year-old who works out in an 'elite London gym', realised her workouts were becoming too much when she fainted. 'Then I had a nose bleed. And then I collapsed.'

We meet in a coffee shop in Shoreditch. I'd not met Aisha before, but it was easy to find her. Collar-bones-jutting-out thin, she's stylish, with a tautly pulled ponytail. A cup of fresh mint tea steams in front of her, and she flicks through her phone with a nervous energy.

'Look,' she says, as soon as I've sat down with my coffee. 'It's easy to compare yourself when everyone looks like this.'

She shows me her phone.

Gym junkies may follow fitness influencers on Instagram, who they call their #fitfam. This isn't as cringe as it sounds: it can be extremely motivating to feel like you belong to a wider fitness community. The community can feel inspirational, at first. It can feel like a welcoming, caring group of people who make exercise seem simple; like a no-brainer. They post nifty little videos showing themselves working out, doing incredible push-ups, occasionally on one finger. #Fitfam is made up of bloggers who have trained as personal trainers, and people who are perhaps just looking to get back into fitness after years away.

The fitness community often share motivational comments and tricks they've picked up while at the gym, discussing new techniques or the benefits of LISS (low intensity steady state). That's running, walking or slow cycling to you or me.

Can fitness trigger eating disorders?

But the community has shades of the pro-ana community (a group that encourages anorexia) too. There's also ongoing criticism that #fitfam can encourage dangerous or reckless behaviour. Overworking is a given, and, in an article for Business Insider, David Barton, who ran his own chain of gyms, points out that it's impossible to know whether the people on Instagram advertising their techniques would be naturally thin anyway. You don't know anything about the people on social media, so following their Instagram accounts and copying the way they do a certain type of exercise or push-up can result in injury.

'Our obsession with social media is dangerous, especially when it comes to bodybuilding,' says personal trainer and fitness journalist Sabi Phagura. 'I've noticed people sharing information about big bodybuilding competitions from people who maybe used to do a fun run for example. It's a huge issue, especially with the

Instagram shots people share. Most of these people have trained for years, and it's easy to see them on Instagram and think that what they've achieved is possible in a week.'

But you have to do this slowly, she says. 'This is where I see the most injuries happen: when people have unrealistic expectations. You wouldn't just diet for three days and expect a bikini body, would you?'

David Barton agrees that it's 'great to get people inspired' by using social media but says there's a 'lot of misinformation' around working out. 'I think seeing somebody who looks great and looks great because of a million factors – one of which [may be] they may just have looked great before they ever stepped into a gym because of their genetics.'[9]

One such Instagram account, run by Australian fitness leader Kayla Itsines, has developed a worldwide following. In 2014, the self-professed guru developed a twelve-week programme called the Bikini Body Guide, which promised to tone and hone abs, arms, legs and bums. She even released an app that is full of sensible advice built around the HIIT model.

But like all fitness programmes that promise results, people can take them too far. Kayla is a likeable personality: she's tanned and has white teeth and a perfect ponytail. Her mantra is about doing your best and subscribing to a positive fitness movement. Her followers are obsessed with her, tagging themselves as members of 'Kayla's Army', creating an exclusive club. Toned, predominantly white bodies and faces stare from the phone screen. They pull poses and post videos of themselves completing Kayla's newest workout.

Although the captions and messages sound positive – 'You just got to do what's right. Today I only managed to run three miles and I promised I'd run four' – they feel like humble brags. To anyone not deeply embedded in the community already, these statements can seem unrealistic.

'This morning I just had a slice of lemon in some hot water before my workout and honestly it feels SOOOOOO good,' says another.

The people I know who subscribed have gone from posting pictures of dogs and brunches to evangelising Itsines. Kayla doesn't encourage this behaviour. In fact, she's all about body-positivity. But it's clear that some of her followers have taken it a step in the other direction.

You only need to flick through Instagram for a few seconds to see pictures of men and women and their abs with hashtags where they thank Kayla and unironically use the term 'blessed'.

The friend who began posting about Kayla the most, thanked her for helping her get over her eating disorder (#ED). She joined the army of fanatical Kayla worshippers. They followed her advice to the letter. Although she worked out, it seemed as though this particular friend had replaced her eating disorder with an obsessive addiction to fitness. I realised the idea of a #fitfam could be dangerous.

Phagura says she has seen people develop eating disorders because they just constantly compare themselves to others. 'They flick through social media and look at bits of their bodies they like or don't like. Looking at others.'

Aisha is a former Kayla follower, and her story goes to show what the pursuit of success meant for her.

'I ask myself what I was doing. Checking my phone first thing when I woke up, last thing before I went to bed. Everything I did felt like I was testing myself and trying to beat who I'd been the week before.

'I was constantly comparing myself to other people on Kayla's platform. I hashtagged that I was part of her army, and honestly this was fun at first, and sort of ironic, but then it got serious. I'd look at everyone else, look at their before and after pictures, and think: "I will never, ever look like this."'

She was wrong. Her own body was changing and developing. Because she was eating less, she was becoming skeletal. 'Then my body changed into something that wasn't even strong. I couldn't make it to the gym and I felt like I was letting myself and the rest of the "army" down.'

Looking back, she realises how challenging this period

was. She was exhausted and even found going to work difficult. 'I'd fall asleep at my desk, but I'd also live for the next workout. I'd be terrified if a meeting ran over so I couldn't make my session. I was just so tired all the time, but I couldn't see the problem right in front of my face. Eventually, I had a breakthrough when I got a serious injury, so I deleted social media and stopped.'

Devinder Bains is a personal trainer and nutrition coach who is also co-founder of personal training company Fit Squad DXB. She lives and works in Dubai, where, she says, the drive to look good is higher than anywhere she's lived before. She understands exactly where Aisha is coming from.

After spending fifteen years in the UK working as a journalist, she moved to Dubai to head up *Stylist* magazine. She quickly saw how obsessed everyone was with training. 'There's looking-great-in-clothes fit, like in the UK, and there's looking-good-in-a-bikini fit, like in Dubai. It's hot year-round, and you spend all your time by pools wearing bikinis. You have to look amazing. CEOs know that and that's why they hire me.'

She's not immune to the pressures of always pushing. 'As a kid, always I wanted to be the best, sports-wise and everything, really. When I didn't get a good time running the London Marathon, I signed up to the Marathon des Sables [described as one of the toughest on Earth, across the Sahara desert]. I wanted to prove to myself and to everyone I was super-fit, and I blogged about the run as I did it.'

Since moving to Dubai, Bains acknowledges it's been tough, especially since turning forty. 'The pressure to look good is just huge. The pressure on "normal" women is bad enough, but for PTs, you know everyone's staring at you. It really matters here.'

She says that she'd had enough. 'It's been a constant battle my whole life to stay fit and beast myself in the gym, but I just had a realisation of "What is it for?" Don't get me wrong, I still workout, but it's definitely been less structured since I turned forty, especially since I finally have an excuse to chill. I'll do whatever I feel like, rather than a regimented workout.'

The reason people push themselves so hard in the gym is because they never reach their goals. Ever. The posts just keep changing, says Bains. 'People say, I just want to get to this size, and then once they're there, it's on to the next goal; I just want to lose that little bit more. They want to be thinner, a bit lighter, desire more shape in some cases. We never really finish.

'You're always trying to attain perfection, which is impossible, because what even is perfection?'

To some degree we are never satisfied as people. Many great philosophers and psychologists have debated whether it's possible for humans to ever really be happy. In Jennifer Hecht's book *The Happiness Myth*, she says we all experience different types of happiness, but attaining these varieties of happiness will impact the way we feel about other types.

Working hard at the gym and looking physically fit means sacrificing other things that would also, in their own way, lead to happiness – eating indulgent meals with friends, for example, sitting slurping carbs during long lazy summers under the garden's olive trees. Lie-ins in winter, where the comforting warmth of bed lulls you to stay swaddled in the soft cotton bedsheets. Successful people who work out may put the effort in, but at some point the happiness stops.

The gym ruined my holidays

Family dinners become arduous affairs as separate carb-free dinners must be cooked. Holidays become fraught with tension as gyms are located and good places to run are found on the map weeks in advance. 'What if I can't work out?' is whispered into the sky during take-off. If this sounds unrealistic and ridiculous, it's not to Aisha or, to be candid, me.

'I used to google pictures of the hotel-room floors to see if they were hard enough to work out on. Concrete was great. Wooden floorboards were the worst. I refused to stay in hotels like that.'

She says she used to get frustrated with everyone sunbathing too. 'I hated holidays. I needed to move, I needed action. When I was in the pool, I'd do thirty lengths and have to drive my way through couples snogging and stuff. I cringe looking back, but being fit and being beautiful was so important to me. That was three years ago, and I know that I ruined everything.'

She remembers a holiday she went on with friends. They'd been planning it for a year and her friends were really excited. But every time she thought about it, Aisha would feel nausea in her stomach. She lay awake at night wondering how she could cancel. Her WhatsApp group messages were full of texts about what alcohol they'd be buying for the pool and how they were going to eat pizza every night. They were in Italy after all.

Aisha cancelled the holiday the night before, but she didn't change the time of the alarm set for an early flight. Rather than head to the airport, she got up, pulled her trainers on and went to the gym. 'I ran for about two minutes. I kept looking at the clock and realising that my flight was about to take off. I felt this huge, crushing guilt. And I got really desperate and panicky because I had to stop running, my time was bad, I didn't want to do weights, and I just went from machine to machine doing the most pointless stuff. I saw myself in the mirror and I just wanted to cry.'

It took a long time for her friends to forgive her for

cancelling the trip last-minute. 'I'd lied and that was that. I'd said I was sick, but they saw my Instagram uploads. I lost friendships because of this . . . gym obsession. I wish I'd never pushed myself so hard. Today it's different. I take it far, far easier. It doesn't rule my life.'

Trying to be the best is something people who drive to be successful want, so it's inevitable that whatever you choose to focus your energy on, you become good at it. It's not even about being better than everyone else, it's just crucial to be the best you can be, says Bains. 'One of the most important sessions is rest. At least twice a week, your session is rest day, and so many people forget that. Sometimes I'll have a complete day off every week, other times I have a stretching day. You can damage your muscles if you overwork.'

The clients that 'beast themselves in the gym the most', says Bains, tend to be the most successful people she trains. 'It's the one hour out they allow themselves to do something just for them. They look forward to the gym for this reason. They can come and chat, work out, and lose themselves in the workout a little.'

Getting up and going out for a run is extremely good for your brain. It gives you time out to think about other things, and for many busy people, exercise is the only time off they allow themselves.

Working out is not always great for the mind

But the risk of all downtime being fitness-based can be problematic for our mental health. When your body is overstretched physically, you're actually more prone to depression, irritability and tiredness than if you were doing nothing. Fitness isn't regulated enough, says Bains. It's assumed that being fit and physically healthy is all-round positive, but it's possible to fall off the cliff-edge too.

Adrenaline-filled workouts like HIIT are tough on our bodies, and not just in a fat-burning way. This kind of workout is like receiving a lot of stress in a very short amount of time. Our bodies react to that by raising our stress hormones, like cortisol, which can actually increase the amount of adipose tissue being stored.[10] In plain English – work out too hard and your body could store, rather than lose, fat.

I remember when I first started doing HIIT classes, all I wanted to do was sleep. I was exhausted and could barely motivate myself to move once I got home.

I began to spend more time lying asleep on my sofa in the afternoon and I felt totally lifeless. The magic exercise pill that was meant to be dragging me out of my slump didn't appear to be helping.

After a month of working out in high-intensity classes, I began to cancel on friends.

Despite this, the draw is addictive. The music, sweat and positive vibes makes you want to come back. First thing in the morning you're on top of the world, and then it's a slow, low crash, like the first line of the night, the lifeline, and then the downer.

According to national government health guidelines, the average adult should be exercising for thirty minutes a day. That includes walking, swimming or slow cycling. Exercise is anything that causes our heartbeat to rise, yet according to #fitfam, you'd think the only way it's possible to exercise is by doing an epic number of push-ups or smashing a HIIT workout.

In 2018, researchers from the University of Yale[11] monitored more than 1.2 million people's exercise patterns. They discovered that team-oriented sports like football, baseball and basketball were best for people's overall mental health. Other sports, like cycling and running outside, also contributed to better mental health. The paper, published in *The Lancet Psychiatry*, also found that people who had a college education experienced a 17.8 per cent reduction in bad mental-health days, compared to those with no college education, during the period in which exercise was increased, while the researchers found that those who benefited most were those who spent between thirty and sixty minutes exercising for around three to five times a week.

The study, led by Dr Adam Chekroud, found that

participants who worked out for more than three hours a day actually experienced worse mental health than those who did no exercise. It's been taken for granted that working out is an elixir that will smooth down all rough edges, but this clearly isn't the case.

'Doing exercise more than twenty-three times a month, or exercising for longer than ninety-minute sessions, is associated with worse mental health,' he explains in an article for Medical News Today.[12] This could be down to participants displaying excessive behaviours, he says.

Devinder Bains, unusually, does not think that excessive working out makes you successful. It's not even aspirational. 'For me, success is someone who feels like they have it all, regardless of whatever that is. It's somebody who is mentally strong enough to have their body weight, whatever that is, and to be happy with it. And be successful at their career level and be happy. Someone who is so comfortable with their own achievements, and their own body – and you know what? That is having it all. Few of the women I train have that. It's all about chasing and chasing and moving the goalposts. For me, that's not success.'

Pushing our bodies excessively and to the brink does more than just break us slowly over time: it normalises the spending of excessive sums on working out.

Aisha says that she started cutting the gym down

gradually. 'I gave up a day at a time,' she says. At first, she found it really hard, and then when she quit the gym, she suddenly had £120 extra in her bank account each month. 'It felt amazing. I had to keep checking my bank balance because usually my account would run down by the end of the second week, and now I was able to manage my finances better.'

Aisha weaned herself off the gym initially by buying a bike. 'I cycle to work now, and at home I have apps for whenever I want to give myself a tougher, sweatier workout. I walk everywhere, I've taken up running and I've started playing in the local netball league, which costs £18 a month. It's also a lot more sociable. I feel competitive as part of a team rather than as an individual.

'I was addicted, simply. I felt panic and relief when I walked out of my high-end gym for the final time, but I knew that I needed to give myself motivation and set goals, rather than relying on someone else to do it for me.

'I never thought I could be the person who turned their back on the gym, but I've done it.'

For me, it's a slower road to recovery. The gym is somewhere I go when I feel anxiety building. If I have a difficult talk with a friend or receive some bad news, I'll head to a class where the music will be pumping loudly and the only focus is on getting through the difficult exercises.

There's no doubt in either my mind or in the mind of

the psychologist who sat there interviewing me in the cramped hospital room last August, that over-exercise contributed to my broken mental state. I was constantly exhausted by exercising all the time, and I didn't give my brain time to recover. I remember being so tired I'd feel like I needed to sleep by 11 a.m., which wasn't a look that went down well in early-morning meetings. Exercising so much was grinding me down and I began to lose my interest in the day. The exhaustion made it hard for me to get my brain in gear and to start mending. And for what? Is ironing out every inch of fat really worth it?

I've started to introduce small acts of rebellion into my routine to disrupt the way I approach working out. So, in the morning, for example, I'll snooze the alarm and take a thirty-minute-later class. Or once a week I'll skip the class and go for a swim instead. Reminding myself that not everyone can work out first thing in the morning, or that one day off won't make me balloon into a mammoth, is important. Small things can help us shake off our feeling that we're not doing enough. We're giving our bodies a bit of a break.

To some people reading this, they might think this sounds insane. And I suppose seeing it in black and white makes me question again what I'm doing and why. Is it because I want to be the best? The fittest? No. It's because in my slightly mad world, working out gives me a tiny sliver of control, and, when I'm cycling to the gym in the rain at 6 a.m., I cling on to that. I want this, and I actually enjoy this. Perhaps it's obsessive and perhaps it's just raising my endorphin levels, but actually, I cling on to that post-gym buzz and it helps me navigate the rest of the day.

Until I break my leg, it's one thing I probably won't be changing.

Staying Put

'He who is tired of London, is tired of life.'

The same has never been said of Sheffield.

For me, leaving Sheffield had always felt like the right thing to do. When I was a kid, I wondered why grown-ups would want to live there. But as I get older, craving normality and stability, I'm wondering if that feeling will ever change.

Every so often I get a phone call from my mother, who tells me about a friend's son or daughter who has moved back to the Steel City. 'It's so nice now. It's so green, and it's so close to the hills and there's loads of hip and trendy things.'

The thing is, Sheffield is a really lovely city, with its big tree-lined avenues, large Victorian stone houses, fifteen-minute drive to the Peak District, lots of excellent coffee, a multicultural community, fantastic theatres, great sports teams and an actual strip of city known affectionately as 'the lentil belt'.

I'd (and if my mother is reading, she should look away now) move back in a heartbeat.

Every time I go back, it feels like home. It's full of memories and familiar faces of old PE teachers you bump into when you're buying muesli. Former classmates you didn't get on with walking arm in arm down Ecclesall Road, still in tight-knit friendship groups that have barely changed since school.

But before I go on Rightmove and rent the first flat that comes up, I wonder why it is that now, at thirty, I'm getting an urge to move back. There's no getting away from it: life is beautiful and tough. It gives you days where you wake up feeling ready to conquer the world and on some days you do. But on some days, you just want to revisit the crisp woods of childhood, where you'd walk with your mother in silence, throwing the ball for the dog, listening to woodpeckers and feeling safe.

For me, returning to my childhood hometown is about grasping the safety net of being at home, of feeling secure. But it also comes with the unnerving slant that everything has changed. I don't really know anyone *properly* back in Sheffield. A few wonderful people I know still live there, but they have families, jobs. It's unlikely I would move back and we'd still go to Corp nightclub on a Wednesday night.

Myth versus reality

And it wasn't all perfect. When I lived in Sheffield, I strongly felt there was more world to see. That I needed to understand life beyond the city, which would help me to, in turn, understand Sheffield. Why some streets were boarded up and unemployment was high. Why there was some casual racism. Why so many people voted Leave in the referendum. It's all there, and now I've seen the bigger picture I feel as though I can understand it better.

I think I saw a fridge magnet slogan once which said, 'You have to leave places in order to come back to them,' and although I probably threw-up in my mouth when I read that, it's actually right.

According to a study, the average British person lives just 100 miles from where they were born[1] and a huge 72 per cent of Americans live in or close to the city they grew up in. And it's hardly surprising: staying close to family creates a sense of familiarity and comfort, which is something many of us crave as we get older and experience adult challenges.

There's something that draws me back to Sheffield constantly. Something that means, whenever anyone says, 'Where are you from?' the answer is immediately 'the North'. I don't sound it. But there's a northern attitude that's much more matter of fact, and (I'm biased) much friendlier and blunter than the south.

Without alcohol involved, women have sat down next to me on trains and told me about their sons being bullied at school; a man who worked as a judge chatted about the criminal justice system; and another man – a lawyer – rifled through a bag of books I'd just bought from Waterstones and commented on each of them politely and thoughtfully.

Anywhere else this would have annoyed me. In London, my privacy would have felt violated, but up North, there's an easy-goingness to human interaction. There's a quick 'May I?' nod of the head, and a sort of universal language that if you make eye-contact and smile quickly you're open and ripe for conversation.

I haven't gone back to Sheffield as much as I'd like. It's a city tied up with bittersweet childhood memories – friends, being bullied, happy family time, first gigs, trying to find my identity by shopping for Punkyfish tops yet looking awful, dinner with friends at noodle bars where we all tried green tea drunk out of ceramic pots and thought we were wild, getting drunk, sleeping with the wrong people, my innocence, my step into adulthood.

It's for this reason that I don't know how people can stay in the same cities they were born in. Each time I step off the train in Sheffield, there's a deep longing for a simpler time, and these memories come back as I walk down the steps into the main station and remember seeing my dad or mum there waiting to pick me up. I remember I'm a grown-up now, and this city I lived in has different textures. I lived here when none of us had phones or social media – now I need to find somewhere to charge my phone and the city's purpose shifts to suit my adult needs.

As I step into the sun, I'm met by a sea of familiar faces. Faces that all bear a passing resemblance to people I once went to school with, or played sport with or ate sand out of the sandpit with. It's a weird feeling, coming home.

I meet my dad, who also no longer lives here, but in a village an hour's drive away, and we go to the Waitrose I used to shop at for special occasions. It used to be a Safeway, and I wonder if anyone else here knows that. If anyone else even knows what Safeway was.

Friends who have stayed in their hometown all seem to have a tight-knit group of friends they can lean on in times of crisis. Those of us who left do our best to stay in touch, but friend after friend has child after child and new puppy after new house, and then suddenly our lives are so different that conversations just stop. I envy their permanent community and their 'drinks with the girls' after work. Drinks that I don't have in London because one friend has a headache, another is staying late at work and another lives in Walthamstow so has to leave at 8 p.m.

'My parents are here to help me look after the kid,'

says an old friend. She does sometimes feel pangs of envy when she sees her old friends jetting off around the world, but she's spent time and money investing in supporting her family. 'The grass is always greener, isn't it? Sometimes I wonder if this is it; other times I feel great about staying in a city I can afford a house with a garden.'

Should I stay or should I go?

One of the ways researchers explore the psychological impact of staying home or moving away is by studying high-school reunions.

In the late 2000s, a group of researchers decided to crash a number of high-school reunions in the United States.[2] They wanted to interview around 300 people or so about why they chose to stay or leave their place of birth.

The three researchers, John Cromartie, Christiane von Reichert and Ryan O. Arthun, would ask people attending why they hadn't left their hometown – if they showed up, that is. Initial studies showed that the people who had stayed in their hometown were less likely to even turn up to their high-school reunions.

Cromartie said even asking those who had stayed why they had chosen not to leave was a 'difficult question to broach'. In an article for Vox, Cromartie spoke to Alvin Chang. 'There's perhaps a stigma associated with not leaving. And high-school reunions tend to be places where the people who come are relatively more successful.'

The study found that those who stayed in their hometowns tended to be less well-educated and, on average, earned less than their friends who had moved.

There are greater nuances to this, however. In the UK, people who move to London, for example, often do earn more, but that's because there's a London weighting on salaries. Companies know that the cost of living is significantly higher in the capital so have to attract workers.

In addition, places like Sheffield traditionally had jobs and skills that didn't need a master's degree and a PhD, so why would most of the older generation (who may have been very successful in their own careers and jobs) initially require so much education?

The researchers from the study Chang refers to in his article found that people who stayed home were 'less hopeful' and 'less open to immigrants', tending to support people like Donald Trump. In the UK, those in smaller, more remote communities also tended to vote Leave or Conservative.

Another group of American researchers, from the Public Religion Research Institute, who interviewed people during the 2016 presidential election, found that those who had stayed in their hometown were more likely to support Trump, and those that lived 'significantly further' away from their hometown would be giving their vote to Clinton. Finally, their research explored how afraid so many Americans were of 'otherness'. White, working-class Americans who had not left their hometowns were most likely to fear change and want to 'make America great again'.

After Finland and Denmark, the United States and the United Kingdom are the countries where people are most likely to have moved house within the past two years.

But in the US, there is a concept of 'manifest destiny', where to make it big and make it successful you need to head West to strike your fortune. This concept is rooted in the American dream – the idea that we need to migrate to make money to send back to our relatives, who can invest and build and grow.

Even in the UK, the idea that it is the most successful people, the risk takers, who leave, persists. Look at Dick Whittington, Mayor of London in the thirteenth century, who allegedly left home with all his belongings tied to a stick and became mayor of London not once, but three times. Rightly or wrongly, there is a notion that those who stay are worse off, but I wonder if the opposite is actually true.

Are people who stay in their hometowns, surrounded by old friends and family, actually better off?

Is this potentially another situation where people tell us we'll be happier and more successful if we leave, but actually the reverse is true? Consider, also, the rise in freelancing and remote work, where people can earn the same regardless of where they live.

And actually, numerous studies have shown that living in the city can have a detrimental impact on our lives. Whether that's air pollution stunting the size of babies' lungs, or evidence that rates of anxiety are higher across cities, there are plenty of reasons to celebrate staying home (if that home is a small town or village, that is).

Urban inhabitants have 21 per cent more anxiety disorders and 30 per cent more mood disorders than their rural counterparts,[3] the University of Heidelberg found.

In the UK, according to the Office for National Statistics, the number of people migrating internally has been slowly increasing since 2002, and there has also been a steady increase in the number of people choosing to leave London.

In the US, on the other hand, internal migration is at its lowest rate since the statistics started being collected, in the 1940s. There's less of a large migratory pattern in the UK than the US because there are fewer large, world-level cities in the UK than the US. London, Manchester,

Birmingham and Edinburgh have a slew of international firms, while in the US the same could be said of Boston, New York, Washington, Miami, Seattle, San Francisco, Houston, Los Angeles, and the list goes on.

For corporate go-getters, there are few places to migrate internally in the UK. The biggest trend for movement remains young families leaving the capital in search of more affordable housing, but many remain within commuting distance of London. Covid-19 and the sudden spike in home working might change this, but for now, an exhausting way of life remains.

There are a number of people in my office who have commutes of more than an hour each way, in addition to a young family. They either spend a fortune on childcare or have a lovely partner who has opted out of the rat race.

One former colleague says he only sees his kids for ten minutes before bed each evening, and he feels enormous guilt that he is essentially an 'absent father, which is exactly what I had when I grew up and something I swore I'd never be. I feel intense guilt when I go to work and leave my partner with the children. We're a very equal family and always have been. I consider myself a feminist. But she earned a lot less than me and it didn't make sense for us to try to survive on her income, so she is at home being a wonderful mother and I'm at work being a terrible father.

'It doesn't feel like a good position to be in,' he says. 'I hope it won't be like this forever, but my job is in London and my family are in Kent and I feel totally torn.'

Staying put and not leaving the city you grew up in needn't be so detrimental to a good quality of life. Instead, the web of support and familiarity is a good thing. Putting down roots, whether that's knowing how and where to volunteer, or supporting local cafes and businesses run by friends, is a lovely way of living.

I moved away younger than most. When I was fifteen, I decided I wanted to see the world. So I moved myself to South Wales, to a beautiful, wild windswept castle on a hill. The school, which is sixth form only, is unique. It was founded in the 1960s by educationalist and Outward Bound founder Kurt Hahn, who believed children should participate in service by giving back to their community.

The school is part of the United World Colleges network, founded in 1962 to bridge differences during the Cold War. It was the inaugural school.

There were around two people from every country in the world attending – a few were a little more widely represented. A number of Norwegians, a bunch of people from Nigeria, a good handful of Americans and Canadians. But there were also people like my first roommate, Zeina, from Jordan, who went on to get full marks in her International Baccalaureate and ended up at Harvard. Tenzin, my other roomie, was from Tibet. Lala, from Western Sahara. People and faces who now scatter the whole world.

I went there almost on full scholarship because I wanted to see more than Sheffield. My childhood had been full of books with stories of school and adventure. My Sheffield comprehensive was multicultural, and I wanted to understand more and see more.

The UWC movement, when I went in 2006, had around nine schools across the world. Today there are eighteen. Each has a particular focus on service, so Atlantic College focuses on working an RNLI boat and lifeguarding the local shore, Mahindra College in India focuses on offering a wildfire service, and in Norway there's the Red Cross youth group working in tandem with a local rehabilitation centre. The schools have popped up across the world, offering adventure for those who've wanted to leave their hometown.

Not everyone was rich. Students were chosen based on their 'UWC ideals' and those who could paid higher fees, which in turn helped to fund refugees and those with less financial means. After all, the aim of a UWC is 'to use education as a force to unite peoples, nations and cultures for peace and a sustainable future'. How can you do that with just the financial 'elite'?

There were many great things about the school, which

continues to thrive today. There was the roar of winds in off the sea which buffeted the thick stone castle walls. There were the ways the yellow glow of the light from the Great Hall shone on to the flat grass outside that tumbled down to the seafront. The desks in the eaves of the castle that we were assigned and studied at late at night, eating biscuits with friends and highlighting lines of information in our thick biology textbooks. The library, with its vaulted timbered ceiling, crammed with bookshelves full of books in different languages. The scream on birthday evenings when at midnight you were thrown into the shower or the outside pool and covered with baked beans or shower gel. The jousting field which unfurled into the woods that turned into the cliffs, and a coastal path that stretched down to a pub at the local village of Marcross where we sat, freshly eighteen, and had cold beers on warm summer nights.

The conversations and debates that spilled out of the dayrooms, with their distinctive, dirty smell and beaten up and battered old red sofas.

I was homesick and sad, but also pinching myself that I was in such an amazing place. It was a contradiction that would run with me all the way to today, where I have felt guilty for not enjoying my success. Where I wished that I hadn't left and pulled up the roots I'd spent my childhood putting down in Sheffield. On long walks along the cliffs, staring at gorse bushes and unfamiliar plants and trees, while I'd grown up with ferns and moor-land moss, I missed my elderly piano teacher, Michael Routh, and his hot living room. I missed my friends who had all chosen to leave their schools and join together at King Edward's. They were picking universities now while I was being wooed by American liberal arts colleges and Ivy Leagues, as other friends at Atlantic College prepared for the Cambridge and Oxford interviews.

What I was probably missing was the safety and comfort of my childhood.

But what I realised quickly was just how much more momentous it was for friends who had left their homes at fifteen and flown all the way from South Africa or Hong Kong. My roommates who had left their homes in Nigeria or Canada or Norway or even Ireland and had had to navigate a whole new world with a whole new language.

What incredible power.

What incredible force, and what incredible character.

Coming from the north of England, my cross-country journey to Llantwit Major in Wales was just over five hours, but it felt like a lifetime away. It wasn't exactly crossing continents, but it gave me the power to not think twice about travelling by myself during my gap year, and it gave me the confidence to move to London in a heartbeat when it took others longer.

I know now that I was probably too young to leave

and to appreciate what I was being given. Like all stroppy teenagers, I'd kicked gravel around Sheffield thinking how boring it was, but the psychological repercussions that the need to create a home has had on me since have been huge.

Leaving home young has meant, for me at least, that I want to settle down. For a raging, angry feminist, I'm also an ardent homemaker. Even when I was at university, friends commented that my little flat felt like a slice of home. It still does. Having your closest family living many hours away means that home has to be wherever you live, rather than wherever they live.

We will always try to make our own communities for sanity's sake, whether that's by attending a religious institution or simply linking up with the nearest yoga community.

Being able to leave home is a privilege

I don't regret leaving the city where I was born. To me, it's an important rite of passage and one that enabled me to quickly stand on my own two feet. Of course life is trickier – for example, taking taxis with kitchen tables and mattresses rather than asking my dad to come and do a quick drop-off (although he has driven down to help when I've moved house). London can be isolating at times, I love knowing that there are loads of people who are also open to chat and make friends, whether that's at the gym or a book club.

Not everyone has the luxury to just move cities either. It requires financial capital to put down a deposit on a new room or flat; it costs money to transport furniture to a new city. One friend decided to go to university close to his hometown. He tells me his story in the sort of matter-of-fact way you do when you're trying not to let emotion seep into your voice. Joel chose a course close by because of his family reasons.

'Family issues meant I wanted to be close to home, which is a small village in the countryside. I'd also started seeing a new girlfriend, so I wanted to be able to go back to her at the weekends.

'The moment I knew I needed to stay close to home was when I was about seventeen and I'd gone to pick my mum up from work and she was unwell. I thought I'd be abandoning my family if I left, and I didn't want to leave my sister or father with her. They couldn't just get up and leave.'

The problem was that Joel was a bright kid – he got a first for his undergraduate degree and a distinction in his master's. He talked to his English teacher at school, Mrs Gertle, who gave him a lot of support that he remains grateful for. 'She made me feel like I had choices. Despite that, I feel like I made a mistake. I was going home every weekend to see a new girlfriend too. I was missing out on that university bonding experience with friends.'

The other thing he realised was that he'd put too much effort into his degree. 'Getting firsts wasn't important. I quickly realised that I'd spent too long working and not enough time building connections or having a holistic university experience. This meant going back to living at home while I applied for jobs.

'It made me feel like a failure. I had a good degree but there I was working in a call centre rather than the government or the Fast Stream. I was envious of my friends in London. Not having my own space was the worst, and I found it emotionally difficult going back into a family place that only three years ago I'd basically tried to run away from. My mum's health had improved, but I was always worried about what I'd come home to.'

A few years ago, I mentored a lovely, straight-A girl who was from a Muslim Pakistani background. She (let's call her Leila) was searingly smart and she could have gone to any university. Leila had been put forward for the mentoring scheme I was volunteering for by a teacher at school who was worried she might throw away her opportunity.

After several months of remote tutoring, the time had come for her to choose her university options. 'Bradford,' she said. 'It's where my family would prefer me to go.'

This was a girl who could have gone to Cambridge. After some negotiation and discussion, she came back with another option.

'I may also be allowed to go to Huddersfield, because my aunt and uncle live there.'

Here was a person also putting family needs before her own, and although at the time it felt frustrating, now, after trying to work out why people move and why people stay, I understand why she made her choice. I'm also certain that she's the sort of person where, if there was a will, there would be a way, and I had no doubt she'd succeed in becoming a doctor.

Going abroad

Internal migration is one thing, but what about international migration? What about the drive that forces you to choose to migrate to not just a different region or a different city, but a different country?

We may choose to move for many reasons, but for the purpose of this book I'm focusing on the financial drive. The focus on why people in the UK or the US or Western Europe, for example, choose to move to the Gulf or Hong Kong, and whether they're further rewarded by moving.

No matter where you are in the Gulf, it's hot. It's not

just hot, it's like a furnace. My plane landed at 5.30 a.m. and as soon as I stepped off it I was in a dark oven of heat. Men in white dishdashas stood around talking, while a burned orange orb was already visible on the cusp of the dawn sky. Doha, with its crescent city clasped around a warm inlet of water, is an attractive proposition for young grads and millenials trying to make a bit more money. People I know who have moved out to the Gulf – whether that's Dubai, Abu Dhabi or Doha – tend to make a lot of money tax-free doing similar jobs to those they were doing back in the UK. Working in the Gulf means they can save enough money to live a more stable life back home, whether that means buying a house or putting money aside for a pension. Or . . . not.

'That was the plan,' said Laura, who returned from two years working in Dubai for an American company. 'But actually, the cost of living is so high; not the houses or cars, but doing things. Everything revolved around drinking, around brunches, around doing things like quad biking for a stag do or spas for hen parties. We travelled a lot because, really, no one likes Dubai, so we all wanted to leave and you have great airline connections.'

A 2018 study by Hoxton Capital Management found that 85 per cent of expats were not putting anything aside for their pension, while another 47 per cent weren't saving 'appropriately', with many expats worse off when they returned. A statement by Chris Ball, who works as a managing partner for Hoxton Capital Management, confirmed Laura's findings that although expats are getting paid well, people are not saving well.[4]

'Around two thirds of individuals who relocate return to their country of origin less wealthy than when they arrived. 'Many expats find themselves in an awkward position after a number of years abroad where they have essentially outspent what they have earned. This could be down to inadvisable investments or leading a more extravagant lifestyle than they would at home. Individuals who find themselves in this position might be forced to repatriate, and in most cases such an upheaval isn't desirable.'

Laura and I met up in a cafe on London's Southbank and she still has the faint hint of a tan from her time in the desert, despite being in London for the past four months. Would she go back?

'No. No way. I became a different person out there. It's odd. Let me try to explain it. You're homesick, so you look for people like you. Friendships are based on realising you had the same favourite bar back in London – at least that's what it felt like to me. Everyone just wanted to have a connection, so you'd end up in these big groups of people and you all felt something, like you were sharing something, but actually I've spoken to maybe one or two people since I've been back.'

She mentions the few hardcore people who stay out. The longer you stay out, the more money you make, she says. 'But the few people I knew who had been out for ten years or so were quite different. They might be in their late forties and were still going out and having boozy brunches and clubbing and then working really long hours. And I'm not saying there's anything wrong with that at all, there isn't, but I didn't want that to be my future, I guess. You talk all the time about when you get home, and I don't think, for most people anyway, the Gulf is ever really home. You're made to feel about as welcome as how much money you have.'

Since coming back, Laura has changed jobs and now works for a charity. 'I'm not a saint. I really did go out there because they offered me cash I couldn't say no to. But when I hear about bad human rights treatments, it doesn't feel good. I maybe regret going out.'

So should we keep moving or is there a 'grass is always greener' mentality when it comes to migration? Adrian Favell wrote, in his book *Eurostars and Eurocities*, that 'beyond European mobility, there is a pure expat world, one with no continuity at all'.

It leads on to the deeper question of whether a place creates our identity or whether we arrive in a place fully formed.

I know one day I'll leave London. I'll probably go further afield before going back North. I know, for similar reasons to how I felt aged fifteen, that I need to see more. I've travelled the world but I've not lived anywhere for longer than a month, and although I don't expect the place to change me fundamentally as a person, the fact that I still feel envy when I hear how a friend is moving abroad for work suggests that I'm not quite ready to thread my roots down in London just yet. My school was full of people born to parents with restless-expat syndrome, where they'd moved from school to school to school.

I guess, in the future, I'd like to settle down in my London or Sheffield home, and think, God, I really made the most of the world, and sadly, no amount of telling myself to be grateful for having a safe and secure home in a fantastic city is going to stop that niggle.

Conclusion: Should we all just ... give up?

When I started writing this book, I had one hope. That somebody would read it who needed to hear that it was OK to take a step back, skip the gym one morning, or say yes to a job that pays £10,000 less.

If this book has helped you with anything, I hope it's that you now feel entitled to take a break. To say, 'Today, actually, I don't think I am going to make that deadline,' and call your boss or your editor and explain why.

Why?

Because we only have one life. We have one stab at this planet. And we should try to be satisfied and content at the most basic level. For some of us that means having a family. For others, it might mean having a successful (on our own terms, whether that means lucrative or flexible) career. It could mean having a low-paid job but working in theatre, surrounded by creativity and passion. Maybe you love kids, so you spend your weekends childminding.

Maybe you love working out; love swimming outdoors; love cooking.

These are all valuable, individual choices and desires, and the purpose of this book was never to suggest only one way is the right way.

But hell, if you wake up on Saturday morning, stretch out your sorry, gym-work legs and think 'I don't deserve a lie-in, I need to get to class', that is a sure-fire indicator that you do.

Similarly, if your boss tells you that you can't leave until you've finished this piece of work, and it's 10 p.m. already, stand your ground. Ask if she is certain it couldn't wait until tomorrow. Try. And if the feedback is bad, is that job really worth throwing every minute of your life at? At the very least, say you're going to go outside and take a quick breather. The world will continue as it is, with its scathing competitiveness and pushing ourselves until we die, unless sometimes we push back and say enough is enough.

This isn't about being fragile or being weak. It's about being strong enough to recognise that your body and your mind can break, and to know you're doing everything in your power to prevent that.

Enough with overachieving, enough with judging somebody because they went to a lower-tier university, enough with feeling superior because you can lift 10kg more than the girl next to you. You want that biscuit? Eat that biscuit!

Life can be a tough, cruel merry-go-round without making it harder for ourselves. If anyone knows that, I do.

I am the queen of taking the long road. The emperor of Hey, I know there's a direct road through the mountain but why don't we go over the top to see what we can see?

Take the direct road sometimes. It's taken me a really, really long time to learn this, but sometimes pushing hard, doing two gym classes rather than one, pulling an all-nighter, cooking a three-course meal to impress a new boyfriend? It's not worth it. Just order pizza.

Back in August 2019, my head fizzed in pain and unrelenting sadness. Depression followed me around, usually to the heat-baked fields of Hampstead Heath, where I went to escape it, lying on the ground and watching white clouds scud across the sky, feeling the dry scratchy grass tickle my sweaty neck.

When I was too hot, I would walk into the beech woods, listening to the sound of my sandalled feet on the dry leaves, trying to create a sense of permanence. One day I climbed a tree. Twenty-nine years old and I pulled myself up into the tree and lay back on the bark, scuffing my white top with brown tree sap.

I didn't think, I just felt. I felt so heavy that the thought of climbing a tree was beyond me, but then I did it.

And I'd thought that I was so heavy in my legs and my mind that I'd sink if I swam, too, but after sitting in the tree for a while I made my way to the Ladies' Pond.

In August, on a Tuesday, the pond was quieter than normal. A hushed humidity surrounded the pool and I itched to sink into the silky water and wash off the fug of the day, the week – hell, my whole goddamn life.

I slipped down the mossy ladder and kept climbing down, forcing myself below the waterline so my lips and eyebrows and forehead were submerged, feeling strands of my hair float to the surface like plant stems searching for sun.

Kicking away from the ladder, the pond opened up. Coots, ducks, an old lady: all bobbed about as they have done for decades and would continue to do whether I was there or not.

Instead of trying to make my mark that August day, kicking brown water among the fowl and the silver birch trees, the topless sunbathers, the ice-cream van serving cones and the scorched yellow grass that ran down to meet the city of London shimmering silver in the heat, I'd accidentally found my state of impermanence.

And, for some reason, I began to feel better. I started to swim.

Afterword: In the Wake of of the Covid-19 Pandemic

Viewing the planet as a kind of perpetual growth machine is churning the earth in successive waves of creative destruction.

There's an agricultural concept called lying fallow. In Judaism, the Torah commands it: it orders a *'shmita'* year, where the land must be left to breathe and no farmer can dig or farm the crops. Farmers can prune. Some gentle watering is allowed. But every seventh year, Jewish farmers walk away from their land.

Lying fallow is a tradition that has been followed in farming communities since the beginning of time. In the medieval period, one strip of land always lay bare, allowing nutrients to return to the soil to ensure it was as fertile as possible for the next agricultural year. And yet, in some cases, land is given more opportunities to re-nourish than we are. In an essay by Julia Smachylo in *Architectural Digest*, she discusses the 'ecological imperative of idleness'.[1]

And yet this same affordance isn't given to humans.

We are seen as a 'kind of perpetual growth machine', expected to churn out more and more and more, whether that's physical labour or replying to emails. Humans are not expected to need to lie fallow. We are not the land. We're not built that way.

And yet, during the Covid-19 pandemic, many of us endured an enforced period of lying fallow. Even those of us who found our hours creeping up each week, hunched in front of Zoom calls, were gently watering and pruning rather than making big changes. We were putting out fires rather than, I imagine, networking heavily or winning new clients. And putting out fires on video calls was the best-case scenario.

I put this to a friend who had been furloughed during the pandemic. She liked the idea of lying fallow and acknowledged what a privileged position she was in to be able to do that. 'I've spent the last year worried about job security and finances, yes. But I've also been able to read the list of books I'd never allowed myself to read before. I did Duolingo and got pretty good at French. I gave myself a recharge. It was really nice, actually. But I tried not to say that to anyone struggling, and just felt good that I had this space to be an adult and grow, without needing to clock in and out every single day. How lucky.'

Luckier than NHS workers and frontline staff, working tens of hours each week, wearing masks and safety equipment, battling an increasingly tragic situation. Teachers struggled with the yo-yoing between class-room teaching and virtual teaching, managing the thank-less task of trying to keep an army of five-year-olds captivated over video calls. Between March and April 2020, 813,000 payroll jobs disappeared; 355,000 from hotels and restaurants, and 171,000 in shops. Half of all employees made redundant from these jobs have been under twenty-five.

The UK's furlough scheme helped. 4.7m workers were on furlough at the end of February 2021, but econ-omists predict a rise in unemployment. How can bars and restaurants clustered around offices survive when so many office workers have regained some control over their working location?

All of us, regardless of whether we're a retail worker or a paramedic, have been affected by the pandemic. Job progression, skill development, life enhancement, became secondary to just surviving. Get through Covid first, survive this disease, and then if I'm still here in a year, we'll get to it.

For many of us, for the majority of the pandemic we've been confined to our rooms. We've existed in the same four walls we wake up in each day. At times, we've been allowed to the park – to sit on a bench and have a socially-distanced coffee with a friend. And while the period has been exhausting – mentally and physically

– for so many of us, there is a danger of feeling guilty for not having achieved more. Those of us who had to leave the house to do an essential job lived with fear that they were just a breath away from catching a debilitating and, in a lot of cases, deadly virus.

2020 and 2021 have not been years to smash personal bests or achieve great things, unless you're Uğur Şahin and Özlem Türeci, the two scientists who have dedicated almost all of their time to infectious diseases and created the Pfizer vaccine, or Captain Tom Moore (RIP), who raised £33 million for the NHS by walking around his garden.

Other, smaller stories of insane achievements filtered through: from Elisha Nochomovitz running a marathon on his seven-metre balcony, to parents heroically balancing work calls with childcare for a year. We may not have got a big promotion or ticked off every resolution we'd set for ourselves, but the resilience so many of us have shown is an achievement in itself.

For the first few weeks I tried to use my time productively: I made myself discover other countries' museums, spending hours on virtual tours and trying to force myself to read small font next to pictures of Andean vases. I signed my friends up to watch online theatre shows.

But after a while, it just didn't feel right. Nothing felt enriching, and it felt as though I was simply trying to replicate the life I'd had pre-lockdown, but via my laptop. It wasn't long until my body forced me to stop. My eyes hurt, I got headaches, and like so many of us, I got into the routine and rhythm of work Zoom-calls followed by eating chocolate and more Zoom calls with friends. I completed deadlines but they were just another marker of the year. What would have been exciting opportunities in the past just became distractions – things to do until we were released again.

Lying fallow works. It's an agricultural practice that has continued for the last 12,000 years, since our hunter-gatherer ancestors discovered farming. Leaving the land to rest was undoubtedly frustrating for ambitious farmers, who wanted to leach every possible ounce of potential from the soil. But they knew that that would be a short-term solution, and it would lead to soil burnout. When the next year rolled around, and they could touch the soil again, farmers had no doubt spent the year concocting plans for their plots, buying seeds, hatching ideas on how to maximise their yield. They were raring to go.

'I'm thirty and meant to be in the prime of my life. I've lost a year to the pandemic, and although I'm grateful to have lived through it, I feel that I've got even less chance to find someone to marry, have kids, and progress in my career. I wake up at night so anxious about that because I feel like I've got a lot of time to make up,' says Jen, who lives in London and works in product marketing. 'Like, I understand that we're all in the same boat, but I've been furloughed for six months. What am I meant to do? I've just existed that whole time, while so many people I know have been promoted or are learning musical instruments, or furthered themselves in some way. I've just been "being".'

I think more of us are like Jen than we are like the friends learning musical instruments. But for people who push hard and are ambitious, there's underlying guilt that they haven't done enough, or achieved as much as they wanted. 'Before the pandemic, every minute of every day was structured,' says Livia, who lives in Leeds and was made redundant several months into the Covid-19 pandemic. 'Before, I'd wake up early, do a workout, go and see friends, hike, go to theatres, and all before twelve on a weekend. My mind was always full, and what's been hardest is being alone with my thoughts over the past year. I'm more tired. I no longer really want to do any of these things. And I'm scared to admit that the pandemic has just given me apathy.'

During the pandemic, the words 'be kind' have come up a lot. 'Be kind – you don't know what the other person is dealing with.' And that must go for ourselves too. At the start of the pandemic, I felt, like so many others, that I'd never be able to stay inside and only venture out for an hour each day. The thought pressed down on me and made me hugely anxious and depressed. I increased my antidepressant dosage and followed relentless morning gym workouts, hoping I'd be exhausted enough to want to take an after-work nap.

The multiple lockdowns we experienced began to merge our public and private lives. We took our fears out into the world, and brought them home, scrubbing them with Dettol and panicking about making payments. But it also made some of us angry, and like we weren't deserving, or good enough.

'I became hugely resentful during lockdown,' says Melissa (not her real name). She spent almost eighty hours a week on her computer during the pandemic, organising calls for partners at the law firm where she works. 'I have worked off an ironing board, sitting on the side of my bed, my back just like, breaking, and I log on and over-hear partners saying things like, "Oh, I booked out the entire golf course so I could work on my swing during lockdown." It's made me really resentful, and really made me understand the huge disparities. Of course they can afford to rise to the top when they have wives doing things for them. I live with three other people – all of us have MBAs by the way – but we're stuck in this shared house, and I just feel so jealous.'

She tells me she began screenshotting their Zoom-call backgrounds to show her parents, who couldn't believe how different their lives were. 'One partner took calls during summer by his swimming pool. I was still in my shitty hot room with no breeze.'

My former colleague, Stephen, relates. 'During one meeting with a client, they interrupted the call to mention that the designer for her new "professional kitchen" had just arrived because she'd really got into cooking during lockdown. I've just had a baby and my partner and I live in a one-bedroom flat with two gas rings. I smiled, but inside, I have to say, it felt like a kick that I'd let my family down so much. At that point I definitely didn't feel good enough. I felt really subpar.'

Over the past few months, I've received emails from gyms urging me to recapture that 'pre-pandemic body'; 'Here's a training regime you might like to beat the lockdown bulge.' The guilt niggles. I feel my extra inches, put on during a static year of slow, cold walks around parks and sitting on hard benches, and I think: this is disgusting, this is hideous, but it, this body, also survived. I survived the pandemic with this body, eating comfort food when I needed, refusing to deny myself a line (or four) of Dairy Milk pleasure, because I knew it would help. It did help. And now I know I have to beat myself into submission again, lifting weights, jumping on small boxes, doing things to destroy the physical imprint of a year spent at home.

The gym messaging works, so I sign up for some online classes to try to regain my strength. I'm no longer as obsessive. Lockdown has made us invisible as we live behind closed doors, and who I am or what I do doesn't really matter. We're all more invisible now. I listen to new podcasts started by public speakers who have nobody to speak to. I listen to a

Line of Duty podcast as I go on my walk around the park, thinking that I'd never have had the opportunity to do this pre-pandemic. I'd have been racing to meet friends. I developed an odd new interest – Formula 1 races pre-1997 – despite not being able to drive. And I filled up the old time spent 'rushing' to do things, with reading, moderately panicking about the state of the world, and going on increasingly long and dull walks.

Over lockdown, I could relate to Melissa and Stephen. On social media I scrolled past people clinking ice in their backyard negronis. Yet in real life I walked past tower blocks in West London at the height of summer, their windows pushed wide open, wondering how people living so high coped with being stuck inside. I had no balcony or garden, but could sit on my communal walkway, legs swinging into the car park below.

Inequality exists, and that starkness has been laid bare during the pandemic. Those who have a financial cushion to support themselves, and those who do not. Those with gardens, who talked about investing in their outside furniture, and those who did not, but relied on governments to greenlight the return to parks.

'We have things called "SEEs" that happen in life, or Significant Emotional Events. These can cause us to change our perspective on things and create a shift in values. When this happens, we'll find ourselves taking stock of where we are in life and perhaps either feel unfulfilled and not do anything about it, leaving ourselves feeling anxious or down, or take some action and set new goals to make a change,' explains Rebecca Lockwood, a neurolinguistic programming and hypnotherapy coach. She adds that usually-significant life events are changing jobs, getting married or having children. The interesting thing, she says, is normally these happen at different times for everyone. 'Yet here we are where everyone has gone through it all at the same time.'

Stress is likely, she says. 'The increased pressure of needing to have things done by a certain time could leave people feeling more stressed about taking action than normal.'

It's easy to be inspired by envy. To be driven by a yearning for more. To be angry at the disparity. I stopped being angry and just became exhausted by the inequality, the unfairness of it all. For a moment, during the pandemic, I stopped feeling like I needed to be good enough. I thought: *Good enough isn't enough*. I was hot and bored and tired, and I wanted a house by a lake that ran down to the water and I didn't want to work on Zoom any more. I read *Nomadland* and toyed with the idea of living in a van.

I thought for a long time about acceptance, questioning whether good enough was enough. The pandemic made me ask whether it was about being subservient in the face of inequality: being meek, accepting, knowing that you would never achieve as much as others, and accepting that. But then the fire spoke: being good enough isn't accepting the status quo. It's about acknowledging the inequality, acknowledging the gaps that exist, and that we all start from different starting blocks, and making allowances for that. It's about cutting ourselves some slack, and after the pandemic this is more necessary than ever before.

'There's a huge sense of having missed out during the pandemic,' says Dr Nilufar Ahmed, Lecturer in Social Sciences at Bristol University, who is also a psychotherapist at the Harbourside Practice. 'We've seen it in young people especially, who are coming up to life milestones with a sense of loss. Undergraduates coming into university hadn't taken their exams – they had serious imposter syndrome and were questioning whether they should have been there at all. Children didn't have their last day at their schools; employees left their jobs and moved to new ones without saying good-bye to colleagues. There was no closure, and that has brought a sense of loss with it.'

She mentions this because she agrees that the pandemic has halted human beings' desire to be the best we can. 'Our innate need is to do our best, but due to the furlough scheme or not being able to be in the office in person, it's affected our ability to progress. And it affects women and minority groups much more. Back in the first lockdown, in many countries, governments didn't know how to control it. So many of us were discouraged from leaving our houses and we just stayed within the same four walls for weeks on end. Psychologically, moving on from the pandemic is a bit like leaving prison: we need to gradually readjust, pace ourselves, and see what feels right.'

Dr Ahmed touches on something that affected me, as a woman in my early thirties. The fear that I had to achieve everything in my life before having children, because after having kids, if I chose to have them, life would be over. Although that's clearly not true, it's a common fear among women: 'I need a promotion and I need it now because if I have children, I'll miss out on five years of my working life and be stuck in a bad role for life.' We've seen the stats and read the testimonies.

During the pandemic, many of us had an enforced year off from doing all those things that denote success: marriage, career enhancement, meeting somebody who we would one day, perhaps, like to start a family with. And that's quite stressful.

'First, it's important to remember that it's not about you or how good you are,' says Dr Ahmed. 'Plenty of places had a hiring freeze during Covid, so there's a good chance there could be a downturn for several years. This doesn't reflect your ability and everyone is in the same boat. It can cause a negative mental health spiral as people's wellbeing decreases as they try to find a new or better job. But try reframing the situation and looking at the horizontal positives, rather than the vertical ones. Maybe it's time to move to the seaside, and, if you're lucky enough to, work remotely, or consider how blended working really suits your style.'

Dr Ahmed's words reassure me. I'm sure I'm not the only one looking at life mentally calculating just how much extra work I need to do, how many more gym reps I need to complete, how many friend-dates I need to book in, to make up for all the lost time.

Having a fallow year where we don't hit every single new cinematic release, where we don't get promoted twice, where we don't get a pay rise because the economy is tanking, where we don't make new friends because we're not allowed to see anyone, where we don't finally write that fiction book we dreamed of because, frankly, who the hell is inspired by their own four walls, where we don't do anything productive because the world has pressed pause – all that is fine. That's absolutely fine.

The risk is that we come back too hard. That we've lain fallow for a year and now we need to prove we're still here, still alive and raring to go. That's hard to do when you're coated with a layer of exhaustion and apathy.

We're never going to be ripped after a year of lockdown, unless you have the privilege of a home gym. But plenty of incredible people took up running when they never thought they could do it. And yet, the flipside to 'a little extra time' was the jolt-increase in poor mental health. A survey across fifty American states found that there was a 27 per cent spike in mental health problems among young people, while in the UK, anxiety and depression increased by 13 per cent among those whose pay dropped during the pandemic.[2]

Embracing the mantra of Good Enough is not about flying a white flag. It's not surrendering. It's about giving ourselves space and accepting that we can't always operate our lives on full throttle. It's not staying in your lane. It's not stepping back and letting those who have always got ahead get further. It's about knowing that you can't be everything to everyone all of the time, especially during a period of trauma.

By all means till the field. Water it. But the one, tiny sliver of positivity that the pandemic taught us is that, if you can, if you are able, and if you have the privilege to, lying fallow – enforced idleness – isn't always a terrible thing.

Acknowledgements

I suppose I should acknowledge all the people who gave me a hard time over the years, without whom I wouldn't have any content for this book. So, thanks to them.

But the people I really want to thank are my friends who stood by me and who supported me over my lifetime. I'm there for you whenever you need me too. There are too many people to name who I owe my life and survival to, but know that I love you. To Autumn, Ana, Bobbie, Adam, Stella, Helen, Laura, Sasha, Jon. Thanks to my parents, to Dr Priscilla Ross and (soon to be) Dr Andrew Middleton. You are the most wonderful MOF and MOM. Thanks to Dave Abbott and Clare Mulgan, who have supported me and always been there no matter what. To Patricia Dugdale (Nana) who inspired a love of literature. To my Auntie Claire. To my teachers at school who told me I could be a writer – to Mrs Harrison at Hunters Bar, to Mrs Baldwin who encouraged me all the way, to the Better Than Being Fisted Whatsapp group – Harriet, Thea, Abby, Frankie, for all the advice and general laughs, and to all the amazing journalists I've had the privilege to know through the years, and who have made it work despite the obstacles. Thank you to Jim Connor and Andrew Hubbard for giving me work support while writing the book. To LJS. To my theatre friends, to my dog-walking pals – thanks for keeping me sane. To Hannah and Rob, for the odd cup of neighbourly sugar. To Noel for the support and being there no matter what. Thank you for everyone who agreed to be featured in the book, whose stories lift and inspire. And huge thanks to my stoic and patient agent Anna Pallai, whose sage comments and easy-going attitude made it a lot easier to write. Equal thanks to Briony Gowlett and Cameron Myers at Hodder for being great supports and for taking a punt on me. And to Myrto Kalavrezou and the rest of the Hodder marketing team, ta!

Anti-acknowledgements

My dog, Mabel, without whom I would have written this twenty times faster and with significantly fewer interruptions.

Notes

Introduction

1 Mark Townsend, 'Cold, alone and scared: teenage refugee tells of Channel crossing', *Guardian* (9 June 2019), https://www.theguardian.com/uk-news/2019/jun/09/teenage-refugee-tells-of-channel-crossing

2 Thomas Curran and Andrew P. Hill, 'Perfectionism is Increasing, and That's Not Good News', *Harvard Business Review* (26 Jan. 2018), https://hbr.org/2018/01/perfectionism-is-increasing-and-thats-not-good-news

3 Kerrie Thompson Mohr, 'Perfectionism's Dark Side: Lessons from Japan', Pysched (n.d.), http://www.psychedinsanfrancisco.com/perfectionisms-dark-side-lessons-japan/

4 Thomas Curran and Andrew P. Hill, 'Perfectionism is Increasing, and That's Not Good News', *Harvard Business Review* (26 Jan. 2018), https://hbr.org/2018/01/perfectionism-is-increasing-and-thats-not-good-news

5 Report, 'People in employment on a zero-hours contract', Office for National Statistics (last updated 15 March 2017), https://www.ons.gov.uk/employmentandlabourmarket/peopleinwork/earningsandworkinghours/articles/contractsthatdonotguaranteeaminimumnumberofhours/mar2017

The 1%: Hitting the glass ceiling

1 Song Jung-a, 'South Korea struggles to root out nepotism in work-place', *Financial Times* (2018), https://www.ft.com/content/bf954bd0-3191-11e8-b5bf-23cb17fd1498

2 https://www.gov.uk/government/publications/elitist-britain-2019

3 Natalie Robehmed, 'At 21, Kylie Jenner Becomes The Youngest Self-Made Billionaire Ever', Forbes (5 March 2019), https://www.forbes.com/sites/natalierobehmed/2019/03/05/at-21-kylie-jenner-becomes-the-youngest-self-made-billionaire-ever/

4 Cydney Henderson, 'Kylie Jenner admits that she's not "technically" a self-made billionaire after all', *USA Today* (18 Dec. 2019), https://eu.usatoday.com/story/life/people/2019/04/01/kylie-jenner-admits-shes-not-technically-self-made-billionaire/3336076002/

5 Cathryn Newbery, 'What is blind recruitment – and does it work?', CIPHR (14 Aug. 2018), https://www.ciphr.com/features/what-is-blind-recruitment/

6 https://www.london.gov.uk/sites/default/files/mayors_good_work_standard_-_employer_guidance.pdf

7 Kerry Alexandra, 'Muslim women at "disadvantage" in workplace' BBC (11 Aug. 2016), https://www.bbc.co.uk/news/uk-37042942

8 Richard Adams, 'Social mobility in the UK "virtually stagnant" since 2014', *Guardian* (31 April 2019), https://www.theguardian.com/society/2019/apr/30/social-mobility-in-uk-virtually-stagnant-since-2014

Social Media

1 Aja Romano, 'YouTube's most popular user amplified anti-Semitic rhetoric. Again.', Vox (13 Dec. 2018), https://www.vox.com/2018/12/13/18136253/pewdiepie-vs-tseries-links-to-white-supremacist-alt-right-redpill

2 Will Sommer, 'Joey Salads, YouTube Star Famous for Racist Pranks, Launches Congressional Bid', The Daily Beast (last updated 8 May 2019), https://www.thedailybeast.com/joey-salads-youtube-star-famous-for-racist-pranks-launches-congressional-bid

3 Susan Greenfield, *The Private Life of the Brain*, London: Penguin, 2002

4 https://www.amazon.co.uk/Generation-Notification-lucrative-smartphone-addiction-ebook/dp/B07Z2CHYQK

5 Trevor Haynes, 'Dopamine, Smart Phones & You: A battle for your time', SITN, Harvard University (1 May 2018), http://sitn.hms. harvard.edu/flash/2018/dopamine-smartphones-battle-time/

6 Simon Parkin, 'The YouTube stars heading for burnout: "The most fun job imaginable became deeply bleak"', *Guardian* (8 Sept. 2018), https://www.theguardian.com/technology/2018/sep/08/youtube-stars-burnout-fun-bleak-stressed

7 Olivia Rudgard, 'Why are Silicon Valley execs banning their kids from using social media?' MSN (1 Nov. 2011), https://www.msn. com/en-ie/news/other/why-are-silicon-valley-execs-banning-their -kids-from-using-social-media/ar-BBPcNZP

8 Robert Booth, 'Anxiety on the rise among the young in social media age', *Guardian* (5 Feb. 2020), https://www.theguardian.com/society/ 2019/feb/05/youth-unhappiness-uk-doubles-in-past-10-years

Career

1 https://www.motherjones.com/media/2014/03/ newsweek-ibt-olivet-david-jang/

2 https://www.gallup.com/analytics/248906/gallup-global-emotions-report-2019.aspx?g_source=link_NEWSV9&g_ medium=SIDETOP&g_campaign=item_249098&g_content=Gallu p%25202019%2520Global%2520Emotions%2520Report

3 'Case Study: *Karoshi*: Death from overwork', International Labour Organization (23 April 2013), https://www.ilo.org/global/topics/ safety-and-health-at-work/resources-library/publications/WCMS_ 211571/lang–en/index.htm

4 'The 2018 UK Workplace Stress Survey', Perkbox (Jan. 2018), https: //www.perkbox.com/uk/resources/library/interactive-the-2018-uk -workplace-stress-survey

5 http://www.ourchemist.com/2019/05/ how-stockholm-became-the-city-of-work-life-balance/

6 Richard Orange, 'How Stockholm became the city of work-life balance', *Guardian* (22 May 2019), https://www.theguardian.com/cities/2019/ may/22/how-stockholm-became-the-city-of-work-life-balance

7 https://link.springer.com/article/10.1007/s11116-019-09983-9

8 'Maximum weekly working hours', gov.uk (n.d.), https://www.gov. uk/maximum-weekly-working-hours/weekly-maximum-working-hours-and-opting-out

9 Sam Francis, 'Londoners work "three weeks a year more than the rest of the UK"', BBC (18 April 2017), https://www.bbc.com/news/uk-england-london-39516134

10 Jan-Emmanuel De Neve and George Ward, 'Does Work Make You Happy? Evidence from the World Happiness Report', *Harvard Business Review* (20 March 2017), https://hbr.org/2017/03/does-work-make-you-happy-evidence-from-the-world-happiness-report

11 BBC News, 'Why hard work makes people happy', BBC (last updated 3 Jan. 2006), http://news.bbc.co.uk/2/hi/health/4577392.stm

12 Argyro Avgoustaki and Hans Frankort, 'Hard work probably doesn't pay off. Here's why', World Economic Forum (7 Sept. 2018), https://www.weforum.org/agenda/2018/09/working-long-and-hard-it-may-do-more-harm-than-good

13 Sarah O'Brien, 'Consumers cough up $5,400 a year on impulse purchases', CNBC (last update 23 Feb. 2018), https://www.cnbc.com/2018/02/23/consumers-cough-up-5400-a-year-on-impulse-purchases.html

14 Miles Brignall, 'Average UK household debt now stands at record £15,400', *Guardian* (7 Jan. 2019), https://www.theguardian.com/business/2019/jan/07/average-uk-household-debt-now-stands-at-record-15400

Mental Health

1 'Mental health facts and statistics', Mind (June 2020), https://www.mind.org.uk/information-support/types-of-mental-health-problems/statistics-and-facts-about-mental-health/how-common-are-mental-health-problems/

2 Carl Baker, 'Mental health statistics: prevalence, services and funding in England', House of Commons Library (8 Feb. 2020), https://commonslibrary.parliament.uk/research-briefings/sn06988/

3 'Mental health facts and statistics', Mind (June 2020), https://www.mind.org.uk/information-support/types-of-mental-health-problems/statistics-and-facts-about-mental-health/introduction-to-statistics/?gclid=jwKCAjw4KD0BRBUEiwA7MFNTS5mG0EWjRqVgiPB7qiZ-vEXBYEoBMsgqHgieq2QElu_9yxWtAdwd4RoCwSkQAvD_BwE

4 'Mental Health Care in Prisons', Prison Reform Trust (n.d.), http://www.prisonreformtrust.org.uk/WhatWeDo/Projectsresearch/Mentalhealth

5 Lori Holleran and Gabrielle Poon, 'Dying in the Shadows: Suicide

Among the Homeless', *Harvard Public Health Review*, 20, Autumn 2018, Harvard Public Health Review, http://harvardpublichealthreview.org/lori/

6 Julie Beck, 'Diagnosing Mental Illness in Ancient Greece and Rome', the *Atlantic* (23 Jan. 2014), https://www.theatlantic.com/health/archive/2014/01/diagnosing-mental-illness-in-ancient-greece-and-rome/282856/

7 Renee Fabian, 'Why Successful People Still Struggle with Mental Illness', Talkspace (8 Aug. 2018), https://www.talkspace.com/blog/why-successful-people-struggle-with-mental-illness/

8 Joe Pinsker, 'Why So Many Smart People Aren't Happy', the *Atlantic* (26 April 2016), https://www.theatlantic.com/business/archive/2016/04/why-so-many-smart-people-arent-happy/479832/

9 Ibid.

10 David Z. Hambrick and Madeleine Marquardt, 'Bad News for the Highly Intelligent', *Scientific American* (5 Dec. 2017), https://www.scientificamerican.com/article/bad-news-for-the-highly-intelligent/

11 Annie Ferguson, ' "The lowest of the stack": why black women are struggling with mental health', *Guardian* (8 Feb. 2016), https://www.theguardian.com/lifeandstyle/2016/feb/08/black-women-mental-health-high-rates-depression-anxiety

12 'Black/African American', NAMI (n.d.), https://nami.org/Your-Journey/Identity-and-Cultural-Dimensions/Black-African-American

13 'Black and African American Communities and Mental Health' Mental Health America (n.d.), https://www.mhanational.org/issues/black-african-american-communities-and-mental-health

14 Greg Lukianoff and Jonathan Haidt, *The Coddling of the American Mind*, London: Penguin, 2018

Sleep

1 https://www.webmd.com/women/features/martha-stewart-best-and-worst-health-habits#1

2 Megan Willett, 'This man's morning starts at 3 a.m. but he doesn't go to bed early – here's how he does it', Business Insider (10 Feb. 2016), https://www.businessinsider.com/early-morning-routine-2016-2?r=US&IR=T

3 'The Most Powerful Woman in Finance Breaks Down Her Early Morning Routine', *The Newsette* (15 July 2019), https://thenewsette.

com/2019/07/15/the-ceo-and-co-founder-of-ellevest-tells-us-about-her-early-morning-routine/

4 Steven J. Frenda, Shari R. Berkowitz, Elizabeth F. Lotus and Kimberley M. Fenn, 'Sleep deprivation and false confessions', *PNAS* (23 Feb. 2016), https://www.pnas.org/content/113/8/2047

5 Matt Apuzzo, Sheri Fink and James Risen, 'How U.S. Torture Left a Legacy of Damaged Minds', *New York Times* (8 Oct. 2016), https://www.nytimes.com/2016/10/09/world/cia-torture-guantanamo-bay.html

6 Brian Palmer. 'Can you Die From Lack Of Sleep?', *Slate* (11 May 2009), https://slate.com/news-and-politics/2009/05/can-you-die-from-lack-of-sleep.html

Leisure Time

1 'The Side Hustle Economy', Henley Business School (4 July 2018), https://www.henley.ac.uk/sidehustle

2 Benjamin Myers, ' "I was half-insane with anxiety": how I wrote myself into breakdown', *Guardian* (3 Jan. 2020), https://www.theguardian.com/books/2020/jan/03/i-was-half-insane-with-anxiety-how-i-wrote-myself-into-a-breakdown

3 James Manyika, Susan Lund, Michael Chui, Jacques Bughin, Jonathan Woetzel, Parul Batra, Ryan Ko and Saurabh Sanghvi, 'Jobs lost, jobs gained: What the future of work will mean for jobs, skills, and wages', McKinsey Global Institute (28 Nov. 2007), https://www.mckinsey.com/featured-insights/future-of-work/jobs-lost-jobs-gained-what-the-future-of-work-will-mean-for-jobs-skills-and-wages

4 Katie Bishop, 'Why Glamorising Side-Hustles Is Bad For All Of Us', Refinery29 (19 Aug. 2018), https://www.refinery29.com/en-gb/side-hustle-extra-money

5 Ibid.

6 Ferris Jabr, 'Why Your Brain Needs More Downtime', *Scientific American* (15 Oct. 2013), https://www.scientificamerican.com/article/mental-downtime/

7 Chris Maxwell, 'The rise of learning holidays', *Director* (17 July 2015), https://www.director.co.uk/9052-expert-learning-holidays/

8 Ibid.

Education

1 Rachel Schraer, 'Is young people's mental health getting worse?', BBC (11 Feb. 2019), https://www.bbc.co.uk/news/health-47133338

2 Susan Greenfield, *The Private Life of the Brain*, London: Penguin, 2002

3 Hannah Richardson, 'Sharp rise under-11s referred for mental health help', BBC (14 May 2018), https://www.bbc.com/news/education-44083625

4 Haroon Siddique, 'Mental health disorders on rise among children', *Guardian* (22 Nov. 2018), https://www.theguardian.com/society/2018/nov/22/mental-health-disorders-on-rise-among-children-nhs-figures

5 Ibid.

6 Sally Weale, ''An education arms race': inside the ultra-competitive world of private tutoring', *Guardian* (5 December 2018), https://www.theguardian.com/education/2018/dec/05/an-education-arms-race-inside-the-ultra-competitive-world-of-private-tutoring

7 Marisa Lascala, 'What Is Tiger Mom Parenting? Experts Say This Parenting Style Can Be Harsh, But Warm', *Good Housekeeping* (23 April 2019), https://www.goodhousekeeping.com/life/parenting/a27197790/tiger-mom-parenting/

8 Esther Duflo and Abhijit Banerjee, *Poor Economics: A Radical Rethinking of the Way to Fight Global Poverty*, PublicAffairs: New York, 2011

9 Ibid.

10 Nicole Lyn Pesce, 'Parents are going into debt over their kids' extra-curricular activities', MarketWatch (5 June 2019), https://www.marketwatch.com/story/parents-are-going-into-debt-over-their-kids-extracurricular-activities-2019-04-26

11 Perri Klass, 'Language Lessons Start In The Womb', *New York Times* (21 Feb. 2017), https://www.nytimes.com/2017/02/21/well/family/language-lessons-start-in-the-womb.html

12 Dr Holly Ruhl, 'It's science: 5 ways to awaken baby's senses in the womb', Motherly (n.d.), https://www.mother.ly/child/awaken-babys-senses-in-the-womb-5-ways-your-little-one-is-learning

Friendship

1 Maria Konnikova, 'The Limits of Friendship', *New Yorker* (7 Oct. 2014),https://www.newyorker.com/science/maria-konnikova/social-media-affect-math-dunbar-number-friendships

2 Joe Smith, 'Loneliness On Its Way To Becoming Britain's Most Lethal Condition', *Independent* (30 April 2018), https://www.independent.co.uk/life-style/health-and-families/loneliness-lethal-condition-therapy-psychology-cox-commission-ons-health-a8311781.html

3 https://www.amazon.co.uk/Loneliness-Human-Nature-Social-Connection/dp/0393335283

4 Harriet Sherwood, 'Attendance at Church of England's Sunday services falls again', *Guardian* (14 Nov. 2018), https://www.theguardian.com/world/2018/nov/14/attendance-church-of-england-sunday-services-falls-again

5 John T. Cacioppo and William Patrick, *Loneliness: Human Nature and the Need for Social Connection*, W. W. Norton & Company: New York, 2008

6 Olga Khazan, 'How Loneliness Begets Loneliness', *The Atlantic* (6 April 2017), https://www.theatlantic.com/health/archive/2017/04/how-loneliness-begets-loneliness/521841/

7 Coco Khan, ' "Friendship out-of-office" messages are all very well – until you find yourself in need', *Guardian* (20 Nov. 2019), https://www.theguardian.com/commentisfree/2019/nov/25/friendship-out-of-office-messages-compassion-emotional-labour

Homemaking/Food

1 http://www.fao.org/fileadmin/templates/nr/sustainability_pathways/docs/Factsheet_FOOD-WASTAGE.pdf

2 Bee Wilson, 'How ultra-processed food took over your shopping basket', *Guardian* (13 Feb. 2020), https://www.theguardian.com/food/2020/feb/13/how-ultra-processed-food-took-over-your-shopping-basket-brazil-carlos-monteiro

3 Roberto A. Ferdman, 'The problem with watching too many cooking shows', *Washington Post* (18 March 2015), https://www.washingtonpost.com/gdpr-consent/?next_url=https%3a%2f%2fwww.washingtonpost.com%2fnews%2fwonk%2fwp%2f2015%2f03%2f18

%2fthe-unfortunate-side-effect-of-watching-too-many-cooking-shows%2f

4 Valentina Romei, 'UK house price affordability worsens over past decade', *Financial Times* (7 Jan. 2020), https://www.ft.com/content/afead1e2-3143-11ea-9703-eea0cae3f0de

5 https://www.economist.com/podcasts/2020/01/17/expensive-housing-has-massive-economic-social-and-political-consequences-some-home-truths

6 https://www.weforum.org/agenda/2019/01/the-experience-economy-is-booming-but-it-must-benefit-everyone/

7 Kate Hughes, 'Half of millennials would rather save for holidays than a house', *Independent* (3 March 2019), https://www.independent.co.uk/money/spend-save/millennials-house-deposit-saving-holiday-experience-budget-finances-a8802736.html

8 https://www.resolutionfoundation.org/media/press-releases/up-to-a-third-of-millennials-face-renting-from-cradle-to-grave/

9 Matthew Whittaker, 'Time for some housing honesty', Resolution Foundation (2 Jan. 2018), https://www.resolutionfoundation.org/comment/time-for-some-housing-honesty/

10 https://www.ageuk.org.uk/our-impact/politics-and-government/all-party-parliamentary-group/

11 'The Democratic coalition is split over housing costs in cities', *Economist* (17 April 2019), https://www.economist.com/united-states/2019/04/17/the-democratic-coalition-is-split-over-housing-costs-in-cities

12 Jessica Lindsay, 'People's worst landlord stories show just how bad the situation is for tenants', Metro (18 April 2019), https://metro.co.uk/2019/04/18/peoples-worst-landlord-stories-show-just-bad-situation-tenants-9223801/

13 https://www.generationrent.org/

Gym

1 Ashish Sharma, Vishal Madaan, M.D., and Frederick D. Petty, M.D., Ph.D, 'Exercise for Mental Health', *Primary Care Companion to the Journal of Clinical Psychiatry*, 8(2), 106, 2006, NCBI, https://www.ncbi.nlm.nih.gov/pmc/articles/PMC1470658/

2 Andy Tee, 'Gym Motivation Survey 2014', Simply Social (2 Jan. 2014), https://simplygym.co.uk/gym-motivation-survey-2014/

3 Kimberly Zapata, 'Exercise Addiction Is an Underdiagnosed

Epidemic', *Vice* (28 Aug. 2019), https://www.vice.com/en_us/article/mbmv53/i-thought-running-was-a-release-it-was-really-an-addiction

4 Ibid.

5 'The guilt appeal', *Marketing Week* (8 Dec. 2009), https://www.marketingweek.com/2009/12/08/the-guilt-appeal/

6 Tod Perry, 'Turns out, size 14 is no longer the average size for an American woman, (14 Aug. 2018), https://www.someecards.com/news/news-story/size-14-is-no-longer-the-average-size-for-an-american-woman/

7 'Classes', Third Space (n.d.), https://www.thirdspace.london/classes/

8 Jeanette Settembre, 'This is the insane amount millennials are spending on fitness', MarketWatch (21 Jan. 2018), https://www.marketwatch.com/story/this-is-the-insane-amount-millennials-are-spending-on-fitness-2018-01-21

9 Mallory Schlossberg, 'Instagram fitness stars are creating a new problem', Business Insider (24 July 2016), https://www.businessinsider.com/the-dangers-of-instagram-fitness-2016-7?r=US&IR=T

10 Chelsea Bush, '10 Signs You're Exercising Too Much', *US News* (5 Nov. 2010), https://health.usnews.com/health-news/blogs/on-fitness/2010/11/05/10-signs-youre-exercising-too-much

11 Maria Cohut, 'Exercise for mental health: How much is too much?', Medical News Today (10 Aug. 2018), https://www.medicalnewstoday.com/articles/322734.php

Staying Put

1 Giles Sheldrick, 'Britons live 100 miles from birthplace on average, says family history site', *Daily Express* (7 April 2017), https://www.express.co.uk/life-style/life/788745/British-people-birthplace-miles-average

2 Alvin Chang, 'Those who leave home, and those who stay', Vox (updated 25 July 2018), https://www.vox.com/policy-and-politics/2017/6/15/15757708/hometown-stay-leave

3 Sarah Sloat, 'What Never Leaving Your Hometown Does To Your Brain', Inverse (28 Sept. 2015), https://www.Inverse.Com/Article/6517-What-Never-Leaving-Your-Hometown-Does-To-Your-Brain

4 https://www.internationalinvestment.net/news/4000825/-thirds-expats-middle-east-return-home-poorer-arrived

Afterword: In the Wake of the
Covid-19 Pandemic

1 Michael Chieffalo and Julia Smachylo, 'Lying fallow: the value of idleness', *Architectural Review*, 11 September 2019, https://www.architectural-review.com/essays/lying-fallow-the-value-of-idleness
2 Patrick Butler, 'Sharp rise in mental illness among those whose income fell away during Covid', *The Guardian*, 28 April 2021, https://www.theguardian.com/world/2021/apr/28/sharp-rise-in-mental-illness-among-those-whose-income-fell-away-during-covid